Social Groups
And Religious Ideas
In The Sixteenth Century

Edited by
Miriam Usher Chrisman
and Otto Gründler

Studies in Medieval Culture, XIII

The Medieval Institute
Western Michigan University
Kalamazoo, Michigan
1978

Copyright 1978 by
The Board of the Medieval Institute

ISBN 0-918720-02-8

CONTENTS

PART THREE: THE UNIVERSITIES

PART FOUR: EXILES

PART FIVE: THE INTELLECTUAL MILIEU OF THE
             IBERIAN PENINSULA

FOREWORD

With the publication of this volume the Medieval Institute journal *Studies in Medieval Culture* appears under a new format.

The papers published in this journal in the past have reflected the vast range of interests, both chronologically and topically, represented at each of the annual Conferences on Medieval Studies sponsored by the Medieval Institute. Both the very gratifying growth of medieval studies and the often discouraging economics of publishing have caused us to reevaluate our editorial policy. Beginning with this issue, *Studies in Medieval Culture* will publish the results of significant research presented at the conferences by focusing on a single topic or on interdisciplinary approaches to a specific subject. We hope that this will increase the usefulness of the series to scholars and their students both by aiding instruction in the various disciplines and by encouraging further research.

The change to typescript facsimile was made in order to reduce printing costs as well as the sale price.

The papers contained in this volume were presented at the Twelfth Conference on Medieval Studies, May 5-8, 1977, in six special sessions sponsored by the American Society for Reformation Research. We are especially indebted to Miriam U. Chrisman, who planned and organized the conference sessions, arranged for the publication of the papers, did the initial editing and provided the introduction for this volume. Compositor and editorial assistant Linda Fortino worked tirelessly to produce the camera-ready copy before the final deadline. Finally, I wish to thank my colleague, Professor Clifford Davidson, who spent many hours in copy-editing the manuscript and whose editorial expertise and practical advice were most helpful in preparing this book for publication.

Otto Gründler

INTRODUCTION

The men and women of sixteenth-century Europe faced the
dissolution of the traditional society and the religious and intellectual formulations which had given their lives meaning.
New forms were developed to replace the old. The American Society of Reformation Research in its Spring meeting at the Medieval Institute in Kalamazoo in May 1977 focused on the question
of social change, the development of new social groups, and the
new religious interpretations of man's relation to his society.
The papers covered a broad spectrum: the nobility, the
patriciate, the poor, the universities, refugees, and exiles.
They are an indication of the scope of work in progress.

Although the participants were unable to correspond before
the meeting, certain general themes emerged. Evidence of
the power and the authority of the nobility was found not only
among the traditional, landed nobility, but also among the new
men who moved to New Spain and among the urban patricians in the
Old World who began to assume noble status. There was an increasing self-consciousness and self-awareness within each
group, a sense of differentiation from other elements of society, an identification with a particular function or *calling*--a
word used as much by laymen as by the clergy.

Finally, there was a new sense of *professionalism*--a word
used in its modern sense for the first time in the sixteenth
century. A profession originally meant the promise given when
entering a religious order or a declaration of religious belief.
By the middle of the sixteenth century, it had come to mean an
occupation in which one was skilled or a vocation in which one
had a professed knowledge. As society became more complex, each
group justified its position by claiming exclusive competency or
aptitudes. These claims were further supported by the theological doctrine of calling. While the unity of society was still
assumed, in actual fact men were increasingly divided in terms
of wealth, status, education, training, and occupation. The
Reformation added to this by creating religious divisions. Society of the sixteenth century was distinguished by its diversity.

The first set of papers is devoted to the nobility. Elizabeth Teall's research, based on close analysis of the Journals
of the Sire de Gouberville, reflects the continuity of the traditional nobility in the sixteenth century. The conflict so
often cited between the local nobility and the monarchy did not
exist in the Norman Cotentin. Rather as the monarchy fully recognized, the seigneur acted as its unpaid administrator. The

loyalty of the Sire de Gouberville to his sovereign was unques-
tioned. He continued to fulfill his local functions of leadership; he was the source of justice, of economic aid, of military
action within his neighborhood. The problems inherent in combi-
nation of public authority and private responsibility cannot be
traced to a conscious sense of conflict between the two.

The German Lutheran pastor, Cyriacus Spangenberg, whose
treatise on nobility is discussed by Robert Kolb, perceived the
role of the nobleman in much the same terms. While he drew on
the ancients and the historians as sources, his ideal nobleman,
like the Sire de Gouberville, was responsible for the secular
welfare of his subjects, for civil administration, and for the
dispensation of justice. Spangenberg, who had suffered persecution for his own religious views, believed that the nobility
should take an active role in supporting the true faith, protecting the teaching and preaching from the Bible, defending
pure doctrine (the Confession of Augsburg), and purifying the
religious practices in their lands. At the same time they were
to leave matters of ecclesiastical doctrine and polity in the
hands of the clergy. These first two papers provide clear evidence that the nobility in the sixteenth century were by no
means facing a systematic or deliberate diminution of their powers. They remained the dominant political and judicial figures
at the local level and acquired new responsibilities due to the
religious upheavals and the crises which followed.

Schalk's extensive survey of the literature written on and
by the French nobility in the latter half of the sixteenth century reveals that the strength of the group was reflected in a
conscious change in the concept of nobility. *Noblesse* was no
longer a matter of birth or virtue, for it had become a profession with its own particular requirements with regard to education and preparation, encompassing its own functions and obligations. Traditionally nobility had been regarded as a status
or a condition. It now involved specific action within the
community which justified its prestige. Stuart Schwartz's study
supports this thesis, although he describes very different conditions in New Spain. The accepted hypothesis has been that the
younger sons of the Spanish nobility were among the first to
emigrate and that the New World created ideal conditions for the
expansion of the nobility. Schwartz' research indicates instead
that the nobility which developed in New Spain represented the
formation of a new class, based on their activity as military
leaders and administrators rather than on the transfer of the
peninsular nobility to the New World. While both the Spanish
and Portuguese nobility were given major positions as viceroys,

governors, and ambassadors, they then returned to the home country. Recent research shows that true *hidalgos* formed only a
tiny minority of the emigrants, although many who arrived in the
New World behaved like *hidalgos* or claimed high birth. The
Spanish crown, for its part, was opposed to creating a new nobility in the Indies. Very few titles were granted to any of
the *conquistadores*, nor was membership in important religious
orders, another sign of nobility, extended to settlers in the
New World. Faced by this unwillingness of the crown to legitimatize their demonstrated leadership by granting the customary
titles and privileges of nobility, the military elite and the
encomenderos created their own system, a *de facto* nobility based
on the pragmatic reality of the economic and social control
which they wielded. Not until the seventeenth century was this
formalized by the granting of titles, military orders, and the
other trappings of noble status. This development in the New
World reflected the conditions described by Schalk. Nobility
was based on what a man did rather than on a title or a particular legal status. Taken together, the four papers show that
the nobility were by no means an obsolescent remnant of the
past. They adapted themselves rapidly to changing conditions
and emerged as the dynamic leaders at all levels of the society.

Thomas Brady's paper, like the two preceding studies,
points to the accumulation of power in the hands of the elite.
In this case, however, the elite were urban dwellers--nobility
who had moved into the cities to live, to invest in commerce, to
do business while retaining their ancient lands, and great merchants who were using their wealth to acquire land and power in
the countryside. Rather than being consciously separated, Brady
finds, the nobility and the burghers were combining their
wealth, their economic interests, and their families. As part
of this process the nobility acquired new political power since
they assumed positions formerly occupied exclusively by the middle class. This was accomplished without conflict because, at
the same time they infiltrated the political positions, the nobility opened its ranks to the upper merchant class. Thus class
divisions became less evident and less important among the
wealthy. The interests of the urban nobility and the great merchants merged, creating a new and stronger urban aristocracy
based on the economic and social interpenetration of city and
land.

Friedrichs' work boldly places the Reformation in a broader
perspective by carrying the analysis of the relationships between competing social groups to the end of the Holy Roman Em-

pire in 1806. This extension of the bounds of the early modern period was subjected to rigorous criticism when the paper was presented, yet Friedrichs' data forces Reformation historians to reexamine some accepted assumptions on the nature of urban unrest in the sixteenth century. As Friedrichs points out, we have tended to see the urban conflicts of the period as a manifestation of the dying communalism of the medieval past. The Reformation was formerly interpreted as the last gasp of the autonomous city. Friedrichs' research shows that urban unrest did not end with the Reformation. He describes continuing conflicts in German cities through the eighteenth century. There were conflicts between Catholics and Protestants, Lutherans and Calvinists, Lutherans and Lutherans in the cities of Aachen, Dinkelsbühl, Brunswick, and Hamburg from 1555 to 1712, indicating that religious concerns did not die back after the initial wave of the Reform. Political and economic unrest was even more pronounced. There were intense constitutional conflicts in which the citizens challenged the authority of the magistrates. Friedrichs sees this persistent and dogged defense of their rights as an indication that the burghers continued to adhere to the ancient ideal of communal self-government. He also shows that the middle classes who lost their powers to the new urban elite, as described by Professor Brady, did not do so willingly. The artisans, guildsmen, tradesmen, and professionals, who were being displaced by the new alliance of the nobility and the wealthy merchants, fought to maintain their traditional positions and their right to participate in municipal affairs. Communal government remained as an effective ideal.

While the important groups in sixteenth-century urban society were the patriciate and the burgher citizens, as much as a third of a city's population fell outside these groups, enjoying neither political rights nor economic security. This group, "the inhabitants," the journeymen, the apprentices, together with the attempts of the magistrates to meet their needs, are described in my paper. Examination of the documentary sources indicates that the magistrates understood the interlocking problems of inflation, population pressure, and unemployment. Powerless to provide basic solutions, they developed many of the standard mechanisms of modern welfare assistance: public works, employment, sheltered workshops, in-house relief.

Universities are examined as special communities within sixteenth-century society by the next two papers. James Farge provides a new look at the Faculty of Theology at the University of Paris, usually depicted as obstinately upholding Scholasticism against the reforms of the humanists and the Protestants.

He shows that the Faculty had a clear view of their function in the church as consultants on matters of faith and morals, as inquisitors and censors. Like the nobility, the theologians regarded themselves as professionals with a particular role, in this case the duty to explain the faith and defend it against error. Far from accepting the doctrine of the primacy of the pope as supreme head of the church, the Paris theologians were still strongly conciliarist and opposed major papal decisions, including the decrees of the Council of Trent. They supported the authority of bishops against the pope, with one exception, and challenged the authority of the king himself on a matter of heresy. When the Faculty took a strong position against Lefèvre d'Étaples, Erasmus, and Roussel, these men were popular and enjoyed royal favor. Not until 1543 did Francis I accept the Articles of Faith drawn up by the Faculty as the established doctrine of the French church. The theologians of Paris were neither obsolescent nor tradition bound; they acted as a group of trained professionals in a period of religious and political conflict, maintaining their independence against pope and monarch.

Richard Harrison's paper provides detailed documentation of the problems encountered in training professional theologians in the sixteenth century, in this case in the University of Tübingen, a Catholic bastion turned Protestant. An initial difficulty stemmed from the transfer of authority. There was a protracted struggle over the granting of degrees—a power which the former Roman Catholic chancellor refused to surrender. Despite the question of the legality of their degrees, the Protestant faculty established a new curriculum based on the study of the Biblical sources. Very quickly the Deacon of the Theological Faculty was given the functions, similar to those of the Theological Faculty of Paris, of maintaining and assuring the orthodoxy of faculty and students. The establishment of a well-endowed *Stift* provided adequate funds for theological students, created close relations between students and faculty and strengthened the general position of the theologians in the university. During the Schmalkaldic war and the Interim, when the Protestant theologians were forced to flee, advanced students and refugee pastors registered as students were able to maintain teaching and training through the *Stift*. Students trained in these crisis years became the nucleus of a strong center of Lutheran orthodoxy at Tübingen. As was the case in Paris, ideological orthodoxy, loyalty to a particular Confession of Faith, provided a rallying point for the development of a professional group. Religion played a dominant role in the development of a conscious group awareness or in determining special group behavior.

This was even more clear in the case of exiles. Since exile was one of the significant common experiences in sixteenth-century life, three scholars were asked to provide a comparative look at these experiences and to relate them to the theological formulations of exiled groups. Professor Gottfried Locher, of the University of Bern, places the experience of sixteenth-century exile within the whole tradition of Judaeo-Christian exile. The Exodus motif, together with the preaching of the prophets, was used in Jewish society to justify fundamental changes and to revitalize the faith at different times. The same themes were then developed by Jesus and the fathers of the early church, particularly in the period of Christian persecution when the experience of isolation was seen as a reaffirmation of faith. In the sixteenth century the Reformers recognized that a refugee congregation could stand as an example to the whole Christian community. Locher traces the development of a theology of exile from Bullinger through to Calvin and the Marian exiles, noting that the refugees were, at one and the same time, extremely progressive and extremely conservative. The conservatism surfaced theologically in the demand by Luther, Melanchthon, and Bucer that all Christians, including refugees, accept the will of the state. The progressive element lay in the overwhelming belief, common to many groups in exile, in the coming of the Kingdom of God, a transcendence over earthly life. Calvin and John à Lasco, both refugees themselves, created a theology and a polity which could be adapted by any refugee group anywhere. The essential elements were the belief in divine election, sanctification, pneumatology, and the provisions of a strong church constitution which established a political framework as well as religious and social discipline. In the period of the Reformation itself, exiles and refugees were a major factor in revitalizing the rest of the Christian community.

Danner's paper on the Marian exiles shows that exile was not necessarily a disruptive experience, that the uprooting could lead to continuity of development. He defined the basis of the English Reformed tradition as Christian humanism—the return to the Bible as the source of values, and the hermeneutic and theological dynamic represented in Luther's *sola gratia, sola fide* and *sola Scriptura*. The experience of exile then forced the English refugees to create their own church order. They chose as their model the church of the New Testament as they saw it established in Calvin's Geneva, incorporating stronger articles with regard to discipline. Yet their theology

and their concept of the church still reflected their continuing
search for renewal through antiquity, their anti-papal feelings,
and their strong restitutionalism. Exile made it possible for
them to maintain their former values. It crystallized their
differences and permitted them to continue to develop their particular English tradition.

Friedman's paper adds an important dimension to the study
of exile since it places the Jewish diaspora of the sixteenth
century in the context of Christian exile. Unlike the Marian
exiles, the Jewish refugees, both the *Marranos* who stayed in
Spain and those who left, developed theologies of crisis to help
explain their position and to assuage their suffering. Messianism and cabbalistic mysticism assumed a new importance as the
Jewish form of transcendence. The cabbalists projected the
coming of the Messiah within the span of the sixteenth century
and numerous false Messiahs arose, all but one of them *Marranos*
or Sephardic Jews. When the messiah failed to appear, the Jews
turned to a redefinition of the purpose of suffering and exile.
The most important was Isaac Luria's doctrine of the scattering
of the divine emanations of God at the time of the creation
throughout the universe. Only when these sparks were again uni-
fied could righteousness be achieved and the Messiah arrive.
The Jews, according to Luria, were the agents chosen by God to
collect these divine sparks and thus were sent into wandering
and exile. Thus exile became a part of God's final plan for redemption, a cause for rejoicing rather than sorrow. This was
the same progressive element noted by Locher. A belief in
transmigration of the soul further justified the suffering of
individual Jews since suffering was necessary to achieve
righteousness.

The *Marranos*, for their part, picked up elements of these
same ideas to justify their own apostasy. Lurianism was extended to mean that there must be men of Jewish descent in all
areas of the world to retrieve the divine emanations, thus giving them a religious purpose for staying within Spain. Conversion was made the highest form of religious expression, essential to save the people of Israel. Clearly the Jewish experience of exile was far more shattering than that of the English
Marian exiles. The Englishmen in Geneva knew they would eventually return to their homeland. The Jews knew the gates were
shut forever to their return.

The final papers were devoted to the intellectual movements
of the Iberian peninsula. Since Spain and Portugal were the
dominant political forces in sixteenth-century Europe, the intellectual milieu takes on particular significance. Professor

Hirsch's paper makes evident the different focus of Portuguese humanism. For the Portuguese humanists there was a direct connection between the men of their own time and the heroes of antiquity. The exploits of the discoverers could be compared with the great deeds of the ancients, and the value of the new geographic and scientific knowledge was fully appreciated by the humanists. Portuguese humanism also developed an important strand of social and religious criticism. Gil Vicente was willing to admonish the monarch himself not to bend to popular pressure to persecute the *conversos*. João de Barros, for his part, spoke out against the priestly control of the church and in favor of a simple, lay Christianity, going so far as to deny the concept of original sin. Men, by implication, were capable of creating a decent society through the use of reason. Further Erasmian influence came into Portugal through Damião de Gois and André de Resende, both favored by King John III who bent every effort to establish a College of Arts at Coimbra staffed by Portuguese humanists trained at Paris. These French-trained scholars carried the religious debates from the North with them to Portugal, arguing the virtues of the *via activa* as against the *via contempletiva,* as well as the question of the Real Presence in the Eurcharist. Far from being removed from the mainstream of European intellectual life, Portugal until 1568 developed a vigorous humanism which combined the heroic tradition with a belief in religious toleration and the unity of mankind. They failed to realize, however, that the colonial expansion which they praised effectively denied these very ideals.

Professor Morón-Arroyo provides an all-embracing view of Spanish humanism. More than any of the Northern humanists (with the exception of Erasmus) the Spanish were able to comprehend the full implications of the linguistic methods of Lorenzo Valla, involving new forms of criticism and stylistic analysis as well as an understanding of the historical development of words and meaning. The introduction of Valla's method to Spain by Antonio de Nebrija resulted in an immediate conflict with the Dominicans who defended traditional scholastic analogical methods. This conflict foreshadowed the intellectual struggle of sixteenth-century Spain--the confrontation between orthodox Catholicism and the Erasmians, the *alumbrados,* and the mystics. In the early decades, the humanist philologists maintained their important positions in the church without conflict. Cisneros, as archbishop of Toledo, inaugurated the work on the polyglot Bible, certainly one of the major achievements of European humanism.

Gradually, however, the threat of the new philological

methods not only to academic scholasticism but to the whole traditional authority of the church became clear, and the orthodox
church could defend itself most effectively in Spain. Morón-
Arroyo quotes a series of sources which indicate that the Spanish conceived of the struggle between Protestantism and Catholicism, between mysticism and orthodoxy as secondary to the basic
conflict between scholasticism and philology. By 1559, with the
quadruple repression, the philological movement was dead.

Morón-Arroyo gives the scholastics their due in his review
of the work of Melchior Cano. Cano was able to deal with the
philosophical implications of theological reasoning and attempted to create a rational foundation for faith. At the same
time he held out firmly against the philologists and regarded
the Vulgate as the authoritative text of the Bible. If there
were differences from the original text, the Vulgate should be
preferred.

Mysticism was the third important element in sixteenth century Spanish religious life although it sprang from an entirely
different source. Indeed as a humanist Valla had questioned the
very source of Christian mysticism--pseudo-Dionysus--while the
scholastics continued to accept its validity. The scholastics
and the mystics clashed for different reasons, essentially because the latter attempted to achieve their union with God outside the established rituals of the church. Despite the total
disparity of their spiritual aims, the mystics were, nevertheless, equated with Luther and Erasmus and thus were regarded as
heretical. As the campaign against them accelerated, the mystics' use of the vernacular language created yet another element
of conflict, and the movement was finally crushed by the promulgation of the *Index of Prohibited Books*. The Spanish experience demonstrates the strength and weakness of humanism as an
element of change. The humanist scholars of the sixteenth century founded the field of linguistics and recognized the sym-
biotic relationship between human thought, behavior, and language. Yet no one in the intellectual establishment was able
to accept the full implications of this insight.

The papers emphasize the plural nature of the sixteenth-
century historical experience. Changes occurring within one
sector were not assimilated within the other sectors. Economic
and religious forces fostered the development of group differen-

tiation and greater group consciousness, while social and political forces led to the concentration of power in the hands of one group—the urban and rural nobility. Religious institutions, even those created by the Reformation, were unable to accept dissent. Their answer to diversity was orthodoxy.

Miriam Usher Chrisman

I.
THE MYTH OF ROYAL CENTRALIZATION AND THE REALITY OF THE NEIGHBORHOOD: THE JOURNALS OF THE SIRE DE GOUBERVILLE, 1549-62

In 1913, Roger Doucet came upon the final injunction of Francis I to his heir, the future Henry II. What message did the prince of chivalry deliver? "Guard the kingdom, preserve the church, uphold the nobility, and cherish the people." We do not know how this parental admonition was received by the "somber child of the joyous Francis," but we do know that it made Doucet quite cross. Here was the ruler whose reign had inaugurated real royal centralization, whose years of power had set the stamp of nationalization upon France, and here was the conservative, not to say old-fashioned, charge to his successor. Was that all he had to say?[1] A close look, however, at the private record of a seigneur in a rather restricted area of the kingdom--the Cotentin--in the last years of Henry II and in the few troubled years of his successors, gives the impression that, despite the disappointment of Third Republic historians, Francis knew his France. The journals of Gilles de Gouberville, which have come down to us for the years 1549 to 1562, reveal a world in which much of the responsibility for the preservation of life and limb devolved not upon a single-minded royal official, but upon a seigneur whose occasional royal commissions were far less important to this authority than was his familiarity with the ingrained habits of the countryside.[2] The Valois government rested upon what was essentially a juxtaposition of private and public authority. Arrangements of this nature are singularly dependent upon cooperation and goodwill. There are risks in such governmental dependence upon goodwill, chief among them the unsteady nature of feudal loyalty. The edicts of the Valois monarchy recognized the necessity of cooperation and the methods of local law enforcement bore out the necessity of such cooperation. But the course of the year 1562 in the Cotentin--the first year of civil war--as recorded by the sire de Gouberville, suggests the tragic limitations of a shaky amalgam of royal authority and feudal relict.

Roger Doucet did have reason to think he was right. Royal officials appeared in profusion in the mid-sixteenth century.

Lettres patentes of 1565, forbidding the export of grain,
were addressed, for example, to "lieutenants généraux, gouuer-
neurs, admiraulx, visadmiraux, baillifs, seneschaux, preuosts,
cappitaines, gouuereneurs des villes, citez, chasteaux & forte-
resses, maistres & gardes de Ports, ponts, peages, passages,
iurisdiction and destroicts," to all other "justiciars, offi-
ciers, lieutenants," and to any one else to whom the problem
might be of interest.[3] This battery of some twenty or more
grades of officials was presumably responsible for the defense
of the countryside, the supervision of the forests, the administration of justice and police--that complex of regulations by
which the monarchy attempted to improve the quality of life, and
to which Nicolas de La Mare was to devote four massive volumes
one hundred years later. And as the sixteenth century wore on
in misery, increasingly officials faced the problems of the enforcement of royal policies on grain control, the disarmament
of the private citizen, and religious pacification.[4]

These duties were spelled out with an attention to minu-
tiae that might well have stood as a model for the Jacobin authors of the *maximum* of 1793.[5] The inspection of pigs' tongues
for tell-tale postules, the adulteration of butter, the fraudu-
lent display of meat, the transport of fish from the coast to
Paris, the specification of wagon construction for the removal
of refuse--nothing was to escape the gimlet eye of the royal official.[6] Yet, when all is said and done, the private citizen
and the community were to bear the responsibility for the enforcement of law and the maintenance of peace and order. Heads
of households were to be responsible for wayward children and
errant domestics;[7] innkeepers were to check the credentials of
guests and monitor their behavior;[8] neighbors were to separate
combattants,[9] and baillifs were to deal with undisciplined sol-
diery in Normandy by calling up the countryside, "pour leur
courir sus et les tailler et mectre en pieces, comme ennemys de
moy et de mon royaulme," reads the grim command of Francis I.[10]
Community responsibility is always emphasized in the royal efforts at arms control, an age-old problem exacerbated when the
introduction of gunpowder gave a new means of expression to the
normally murderous proclivities of the countryside. As *lettres
patentes* of 1559 laid down procedure, "tous noz subjectz,"
whether officials or private persons, were to effect arrests,
whatever the protests of the armed.

> Et lá ou il aduiendroit que les susdictes personnes
> ne les peussent saisir & apprehender, seront tenus
> crier à haulte voix aux trahistres, aux boutefeux:

& auec iceluy cry les suyure de lieu à autre; Auquel
cry tous ceulx qui l'orront seront semblablement
tenuz (sur peine d'estre puniz de mesme peine que
ceulx qui porterŏt lesdictz pistoletz) de se mettre
à la suyte pour prendre & apprehĕder ceulx sur lesquelz
lon criera, & ceulx qui orront ledict cry iront
soudain sonner le tocsin à la plus prochaine eglise:
Et à ce son seront tenuz les paroissiens de toutes
les paroisses prochaines de faire le semblable, & les
paysans & autres estãs ausdictz champs, si tost
qu'ilz auront ouy ledict son, de sortir & se mettre
à la poursuyte & recherche de ceulx lá de lieu à autre,
iusques à ce qu'ilz ayĕt esté prins, consignez &
deliurez à nostre iustice, comme dessus est dict.[11]

Who were these "paroissiens" and "paysans" who were to
carry out the edicts of the Valois monarch? How were they effectively organized? Thanks to the fourteen year record left
us by Gilles de Gouberville, royal official, landlord, neighborhood patriarch, and old friend, we know something of the
temor of life in the Cotentin in the middle years of the sixteenth century. In the area bounded by Cherbourg, Valognes,
Bayeux, and the coast, the sire de Gouberville was a large
fish--in a small pond.[12] He held the seigneuries of Mesnil-au-
Val and Gouberville, and after the death in 1560 of his uncle,
the curé Jean Picot, the seigneurie of Russy.[13] The lands had
been in the family's hands since the fourteenth century, and at
least from the fifteenth century the holders had been recognized
as noble.[14] Gilles de Gouberville regularly answered the sum-
mons to the *arrière-ban*, always, be it said, to renew his exemption;[15] the family was declared "sans mestier" in 1555 in the
court at Rouen;[16] one ancestor, Guillaume Picot III, had died
at Agincourt.[17] In 1549, when we meet Gilles de Gouberville, he
held the post of *lieutenant des eaux et forêts*, as his father
had; he lost it--the circumstances are not entirely clear--in
1555, but held it again by 1561.[18] He was also a bourgeois of
Cherbourg, and held the living of Gouberville.[19] His connections with the neighborhood were many. His brother François,
the Anthony Quinn of the area (he maintained two families in
anything but amicable circumstances), was seigneur of Sorteval,
one sister married the sire de La Bigne, another the sire de St.
Nazair; a third sister lived in sin with the sire des Essarts.
Gouberville presided over a large household: Thomas Langloys,
sire de Cantepye, and Charles Brucan were his regular atten-
dants; his illegitimate brother, Symonnet, and illegitimate

sister, Guillemette, lived with him at Mesnil, as did apparently the other four illegitimate brothers whose status seems to
have been considerably less favored than the other two. A multitude of male and female servants completed the immediate entourage. Beyond this circle there were the tenants and neighbors, the parishioners. The families recur in the journal:
Drouet, Auvrey, Mesnage, Cabart, Berger, Vaultier, Liot, Mar-
geneste, Groult.[20] *Corvées* were regularly organized; seigneurial dues were received in money and in kind.[21]

It was a small world, geographically limited, self-con-
tained, agriculturally and commercially conservative, but in no
real sense isolated. Gouberville's perambulations took him
ordinarily to Cherbourg, Valognes, or Sorteval, trips that could
be made if necessary on foot. Occasionally he went to Bayeux or
Caen, infrequently to Rouen, and once he journeyed to Blois,
where, in the midst of unsuccessful attempts to renew his royal
office, he did some sight-seeing.[22] Gouberville's more elegant
relatives went to court and brought back news of the death of
Henry II, for example, or of the massacre of Vassy. The abbot
at Cherbourg regaled him with a synopsis of the fourth book of
Pantagruel.[23] An occasional child went to Paris to be appren-
ticed. An occasional salted pig was sold in the Paris market.
An occasional visitor arrived from England, as did sheep--
Gouberville found them scrawny.[24] On July 15, 1554, he saw an
elephant's tooth; on August 17, 1556, some blacks arrived at
Barfleur.[25] But for the most part the trips were errands and
the news was gossip: of the priest who knifed a man in a street
fight; of the priest who had suffocated his illegitimate children; of the woman burned at the stake for infanticide.[26] It
was an ordinary existence.

The ordinary tasks were in fact demanding. The routine of
agricultural work in three seigneuries called for constant surveillance and considerable knowledge, no matter how much habit
might alleviate the strain of initiation and innovation. There
were *fermiers* at Mesnil and Gouberville, and at Russy, but har-
vests were always supervised by Gouberville himself, meals were
fetched to the fields, and dancing and cider provided.[27] The
accounts were kept. In the years which are recorded, there were
no *emeutes*, and the ties between Gouberville and his work force
were close. If special efforts were made at Mesnil for the occasional visit of the great, there was no attempt made to exclude the small. Thomas Drouet, *fermier* at Mesnil, was not only
a faithful retainer, but a great good friend, and the tenants
dropped in, always at dinner time, with an informal frequency
that says much for the resilience of the seigneurial kitchen.[28]

Invariably the visitor was burdened with care. Life in the
Cotentin under the best of circumstances was fraught with haz-
ard. Falling trees, misplaced millstones, enraged stags, bolt-
ing horses, mad dogs, lightning, wolves, colic, colds, gout,
rash, poverty, overindulgence, premature death: the litany of
disaster is endless.[29] Faced with crises of illness, destitu-
tion, and catastrophe, the neighbors repaired to Gouberville,
who responded with advice, legal aid, medical care, and short
term loans.[30] He applied poultices, he examined urine (his own,
of course, and that of his immediate family, was dispatched to
specialists), and pronounced the diagnosis; he sheltered the
woman "troubled in her understanding"; he interceded for tax
relief for the blind widow; he sent Symonnet and Cantepye out
into the night to look in on the woman whose drunken husband had
beaten her to a pulp.[31] He made it possible for the orphan
child of Yvon Mesnage to enter the church; he loaned horses and
money and seed.[32] He distributed trinkets on his saint's day,
went to weddings, and named babies.[33] Much of life's distress
was alleviated in this informal and personal way.

Seigneurial immersion in the neighborhood also made possible real contributions to public order. A good deal of potential litigation went no further than the kitchen table at Mesnil. Norman contentiousness was a sixteenth century stereotype,[34] a stereotype given validity in the journal, through the
pages of which tenants and seigneurs battled, among themselves
and with each other, over inheritances, dowries, land-rights,
and personal affronts ranging from insult to open attack.
Gouberville adjudicated cases involving property simply by
bringing the contending parties together and presiding over the
settlement.[35] He also dealt with cases of theft and personal
injury, before those cases came to the attention of the courts,
and intervened at the behest of relatives for those whom royal
justice had incarcerated.[36] The guilty were apprehended--*they
were always known*, witnesses were examined, property was recovered (often it had already been cooked), apologies were
forced, agreements were reached as to damages.[37] If necessary,
recourse could always be had to the law, but familiarity and
trust made possible a system of informal justice.[38]

Such a system of informal justice--and the familiarity upon
which it was based--worked often to effect the re-absorption of
the congenital lawbreaker into society. The neighborhood
scourge Nicolas Quentin disrupted the Mass, hid from witnesses,
fought the assessors of the *taille*, insulted the servants at
Mesnil, and violated grazing rights. He bore false witness, he
refused to "listen to reason" when settlements were made; he

was hauled off to prison on December 5, 1551, accused of larceny and perjury. Eight days later he was enjoying dinner at Mesnil, and throughout the entire period he was a regular visitor at the manor, assisted the curé in the singing of the Mass, and invited the neighborhood to christening parties.[39]

Familiarity and informal justice served also to ease the lot of the victims of crime. The tragedy that befell the Chandeleur family, prey to the deprecations of the neighborhood terror, Rouland LeParmentier, is a case in point. Rouland Le-Parmentier was a bourgeois of Cherbourg, brother-in-law of Gouberville's old enemy, the vicomte de Valognes, and a murderer. In 1553, thanks to the intervention of Gouberville, summoned in the middle of the night, the curé of Cosqueville was released from captivity in his presbitery, where LeParmentier and his sons had held him under siege, and a settlement was reached; not, to Gouberville's mind, a very equitable one, for the LeParmentiers had inflicted grievous wounds upon the curé.[40] In August, 1558, the LeParmentiers ransacked the house of the Sire de Cosqueville, who then sent the sergeant Guillaume Chandeleur with a warrant for their arrest. On the morning of August 18, Guillaume Chandeleur was dead, and his widow, who had spent the awful night huddled beside the body, was alone. The neighbors had been too terrified even to come to her aid.[41] It was to Gouberville at Mesnil that Anne Chandeleur brought her burden of misery four days later, and it was through Gouberville and his cousin, the sire de Bretteville, Anne's seigneur, that the inventory was taken of Chandeleur's belongings, long-standing disputes over debts were settled, and an effort made to force the LeParmentiers to make some recompense to the be-reaved family.[42] The LeParmentiers were judged guilty in the courts at Rouen in 1560; the sons mounted the scaffold and their father did public penance.[43] And to the end of our record, Anne Chandeleur and the sire de Gouberville reciprocated kindnesses: soup, cider, company, and legal assistance.[44]

Royal justices sent Thomas LeParmentier and his brother to their reward;[45] the seigneurs Gouberville and Bretteville made more endurable the suffering that their carnage had caused. Neither in this instance nor in the cases of private adjudication of disputes is there any suggestion of rivalry between a royal and a seigneurial authority. Rather there appears to have been a tacit, if not organized or articulated, collaboration. Gouberville did not challenge; he cooperated. During his tours of duty as a forest official, he obeyed royal orders with alacrity and carried out his duties with an attention to the king's interest that prevailed even against the blandishments of his

own more powerful neighbors.[46] He made sure that the neighborhood obeyed the law. Nicolas Quentin was divested of his arque-
busque because he carried it in contravention of the *ordonnance;*
Nicolas DuBosc lost his arbalette because its size violated regulations; Symonnet was forcibly reminded of the fate of three
gentlemen then behind bars for the illegal possession of weapons. Nicolas Quentin twice tried to settle his accounts with
coins that fell short of official regulation; on both occasions
he failed.[47] The royal edicts--posted on church doors, delivered by travellers, announced at Mass, borrowed from other
officials--were carried out whenever their contents could be
ascertained.[48]

Gouberville was a conscientious public servant. He brought
other great assets, however, to the exercise of his public
duties. He had a guerrilla's knowledge of his territory and the
habit of command. He organized the transport of timber for the
fortifications of Ommonville in the summer of 1549; he allocated
responsibility for the provisioning of the garrison at Cherbourg
through the whole time of the journal; he checked lodgings com-
mandeered for the quartering of troops.[49] He granted a troop of
gypsies permission to stay in the parish of Mesnil in April of
1555.[50]

He also organized the community to avert disaster. On July
16, 1556, in the midst of a summer remarkable for heat and lack
of rain,[51] Gouberville recorded the outbreak of forest fire.
With five servants he did his best to extinguish the worst of
the fire, but by July 19, he had sent a messenger round to all
of the houses of the parish, and had himself sounded the tocsin,
to insist that at least one person from each house come armed
with pots and pans to help. In this case neighboring parishes
were also summoned, but the extreme heat, the distance from
available water, and the fact that many of the parishioners did
not have the necessary pots made the task very difficult. God
came to the rescue on July 23 with a thunderstorm.[52]

God and the community. Collective action and communal responsibility are always assumed. The married and unmarried men
of the Mesnil and the neighboring parishes lacerated each other
with regularity at the *choule;*[53] "les compagnons" conducted frequent round-ups of horses and cattle for whom the open stable
presented no particular boundary;[54] the same young men spent a
number of Sunday afternoons tracking wolves--an activity recognized as a community responsibility in an *ordonnance* of 1583.[55]
"Parishioners" as a body defended their liberties in the courts
with legal representation.[56] The assessors and collectors of
the *taille* were regularly elected in the parish churches at

Mesnil and Gouberville; they regularly reviewed their accounts, settled their differences, and came to blows with the taxpayers around the table at the manor.[57] *Montres du plat pays* supplemented the garrisons at Cherbourg and were called up by Gouberville himself in cases of emergency.[58]

The seigneur, then, and the countrymen with whom he had formed so close a bond, performed functions of a military, legal, and financial nature that essentially complemented the formal activities of the Valois monarchy--a participation, it need hardly be said, rendered the more necessary by the bad roads, the uncertain weather, and the accidents of demography which stood always to thwart the best efforts of the most determined bureaucrat.[59] As a royal official, Gouberville received compensation--that is, when money was available[60]--but his contribution to local stability really derived from his position as seigneur, from his multitudinous family connections, and from his familiarity and rapport with his neighbors. A royal appointment simply added another sort of authority.

This is a peculiarly ramshackle method of government, for the success of which the loyalty of the governed is crucial, and peace and quiet highly desirable. The mechanism did not easily weather the maelstrom of religious dissension and civil war unleashed in 1562. As that year wore on, the signs of disorder in the Cotentin became more numerous and more ominous.

On April 27, 1562, the abbé of Cherbourg fled the city and the commander of the garrison turned out "tous les juges, advocatz et plaideurs."[61] On May 16, there were stories of image breaking at Bayeux; on June 5, the advocate Pierre Collas found it impossible to send a messenger to Paris; on June 7, the tocsin sounded at Valognes.[62] On the 8th, six men, among them the sires de Hoesville and Cosqueville, were killed and more were wounded. The Cosqueville house was pillaged and the women of Valognes fell upon the bodies of the dead with stones and sticks. The forest jurisdiction could not be held.[63] Through the next week the tension mounted: the forest pasturage was deferred, strong boxes were hidden, the cautious fled.[64] On June 16, the Catholic commander, Jacques II de Matignon, the king's governor in Normandy, arrived at Cherbourg to marshal the countryside against the Protestant captain Ste. Marie.[65] He was preceded by three messengers, who informed Gouberville that the house at Mesnil was to be sacked. Baffled and frightened, Gouberville hid his valuables, sent his horses into the forest, and set out for the comparative sefety of the manor of Gouberville. News that all was calm in Valognes brought him back to Mesnil, but in a state of near exhaustion.[66]

The next few entries in the journal deal with the roundup of pigs, the cartage of wood, and the myriad errands that made up the usual fabric of a Gouberville day, and on June 30, Gouberville was once again at Valognes attending the forest jurisdiction.[67] Try as he might, however, he was not again easily to immerse himself in the comforting pattern of arbitration, adjudication, and paternal surveillance. These ordinary activities took place in an increasingly disturbing setting. Unitl the summer of 1562, the household at Mesnil seems to have been remarkably phlegmatic. Symonnet, coming home through the forest one dark wet night, did hear those palladins of Charles Martel for whom the coffin lids could never close; vagrants did see fairies and searched for buried treasure; St. Hubert did keep a weather eye on mad dogs.[68] But Gouberville's account is free of the bedeviled children, werewolves, and rains of blood that haunt other contemporary literature.[69] Rather it was the English spy and the English ship that the citizenry of the Cotentin were prone to see.[70] But through the first week of July, 1562, the countryside was plagued by the persistant sound of artillery fire--which was not then and has not since been identified. Rouen fell under siege, and the duc d'Aumale was alternately reported to have been wounded and to be on a rampage across Normandy. Flotillas appeared and disappeared off the coast near Russy and Sorteval.[71] Real trouble gave credence to rumor. The sire de Colombières held those unfortunate enough to cross his path for ransom. It became increasingly difficult to trade at local fairs, and the distress of the peasantry forced an early opening of the forest.[72]

The strains of the unhappy year took their toll of the patterns of allegiance and habit. Neighborhood tempers flared. The parish church at Mesnil was sacked, and its defenders were set upon by a known neighborhood marauder, the pig stealer Nicolas DuBosc.[73] Old scores were settled.[74] Quartered soldiers, noted without rancor in the early years of the journal, were now openly resented.[75] Relations within the family became more trying.[76]

Gouberville's own credibility came under question. In October he was summoned to Valognes to swear allegiance to the king and to the Catholic faith, an oath he was then asked to repeat.[77] His credentials as a *lieutenant des eaux et forêts* were challenged, and in August he agonizingly reviewed his application for exemption to the *arrière-ban* at Caen--ordinarily an unexceptional matter.[78] When he attempted, in the course of routine business, to intervene in a quarrel at Valognes, he was threatened in terms that have a peculiarly menacing undertone:

"Je appelle de vous et vous accuse," said his tormentor,
"d'avoyr esté au ravagement et saccagement des maisons et église
de ceste ville. Je demande l'ayde du peuple. Je le veux
prouver à l'encontre de vous." Worse, Gouberville could obtain
no redress.[79]

The tenants continued to apportion the levies for the ever
more urgent provisioning of Cherbourg and Valognes, and were
still to turn out in a body when a neighboring seigneur needed
extra help,[80] but Gouberville seems to have lost the easy rapport that once had been taken for granted. He did not distribute the usual little presents on St. Gilles's day in 1562; the
curé of Valognes took to the woods at the sight of him, and in
February, 1562 o.s., no one performed the customary courtesy of
escorting him to Mass.[81] After the harvest at Russy in September, when he came back to Mesnil over the dunes to bypass Valognes, the distress and discouragement were apparent.

> Il estoyt plus de quatre heures, et n'avoye de ce
> jour beu ne mangé, ny dempuis hier avant mydi pour
> ce que je me trouvoys fort mal à la teste et à ung
> costé, et estoye party de Russy bien malade;
> craignant qu'il ne m'empirast, je prins chemin à
> m'en venir, j'estoye le plus las et le plus
> doulant par les membres qu'il me souvienne.[82]

He does not sound a happy man. He was looked upon with
reservation, not to say suspicion, by his superiors; the neighbors were at each other's throats; religious controversy made
him nervous.[83] In a situation that demanded imagination and
courage, he reacted with bewilderment and panic. These are
straws in the wind, of course, and the journal comes to an
abrupt conclusion in March, 1562 o.s., but it may be suggested
that the wholesale disintegration of order mourned by the com-
mentators of the late century[84] was presaged in the Cotentin
in 1562.

Max Weber pointed out, some years ago, how hazardous it
is for governments to rely upon men who are not necessarily
trained, who have a thousand other problems at hand, and who
are not, consequently, single-mindedly dedicated to the task
at hand.[85] The dilemma was fully recognized in the edicts of
Catherine de Medici's guardianship. The full panoply of bureaucracy notwithstanding, the monarch fell back always upon
the seigneur and the neighborhood as the instruments of order
in the countryside--instruments effective only so long as the
neighborhood was cohesive and the seigneur loyal. Witness the

leit-motifs of love and devotion that underscore the edicts of pacification.[86] Witness also the weapons of control. The oath and the feudal levy: expedients which call up the ninth century. Public execution and the tocsin: violence and association to be met with violence and association.[87]

Could this have been otherwise? In addition to the problens presented by the heretic, the unpaid soldier, the over-mighty subject, the king of Spain, and her own wretched children,[88] Catherine was dependent upon a structure of seigneurial arrangements that had for centuries before her both infringed upon and made possible royal control in the countryside: a structure in which loyalty was of supreme importance. When the bonds of loyalty dissolved, peace and quiet became impossible goals. Francis I knew whereof he spoke when he ordered Henry II to preserve the church, uphold the nobility, and cherish the people.[89]

Elizabeth Teall

Westfield State College

II.
CYRIAKUS SPANGENBERG'S *ADELSPIEGEL:* A THEOLOGIAN'S VIEW OF A NOBLEMAN

Toward the end of the second volume of his *Mirror of the Nobility,* Cyriakus Spangenberg acknowledged with Pliny that reciting history wins disfavor more often than it gains gratitude. Nonetheless, Spangenberg persisted in his recitation of the circumstances of nobles of all times so that--as Tacitus had recommended--he might praise and encourage noble virtues and condemn the evils perpetrated by occasional members of the noble estate.[1]

The 953 folio leaves of the two volumes of Spangenberg's *Adelspiegel,* published in 1591 and 1594, contain citations from about 750 ancient, medieval, and contemporary authorities on the nobility of all lands and all times, compiled in commonplace fashion by one of the most brilliant graduates of Luther's and Melanchthon's university. It bears the marks of the Melanchthonian humanistic training which Spangenberg acquired as Philip's student, and illustrates the historical techniques and moral values which the Wittenberg humanists imparted to their students.[2] The *Adelspiegel* thus demonstrates the kind of intellectual influence which Melanchthon exercised even on those students, among them Spangenberg, who later rejected his ecclesiastical leadership and criticized his theological stance in the years after Luther's death.

Born in 1528, the eldest son of a prominent clerical convert to the Wittenberg Reformation, Cyriakus came to Wittenberg at age fourteen for four years of study. In 1550 he received his master's degree after another brief period of study in Melanchthon's lecture hall. He served as a pastor and ecclesiastical superintendent in the county of Mansfeld, where his father, Johann, had introduced the Reformation. In the turbulent years following Luther's death and the defeat of the Evangelical armies by Emperor Charles V at Mühlberg (1547), Cyriakus became a leading spokesman for the Gnesio-Lutheran party, the more radical party within Late Reformation Saxon Lutheranism. That party opposed the more conservative stance of Melanchthon and his band of disciples, the Philippists.[3] Other leaders of the Gnesio-Lutherans included a number of Spangenberg's fellow students from Wittenberg, among them Matthias Flacius Illyricus,

Nikolaus Gallus, and Johann Wigand. When in the late 1560's the party split over Flacius' view of original sin, Spangenberg continued to defend the Flacian position, that original sin is the substance of man.[4] Other Gnesio-Lutherans on the Mansfeld ministerium disagreed with Flacius on the definition of original sin, and after prolonged discussion and several attempts at reconciliation, Spangenberg's former friends and colleagues removed him from office in 1575. One of the counts of Mansfeld, Volrad, long a defender of the Gnesio-Lutheran party, provided a refuge for Spangenberg at Sangerhausen, but in 1578 Volrad's cousins and co-regents invited their Hohenzollern patron, Joachim Friedrich, administrator of the archbishopric of Magdeburg, to send troops into Mansfeld to evict Spangenberg and his patron, Count Valrod. Spangenberg spent the last three decades of his life--until his death in 1604--engaged in various intellectual pursuits, at times in the leisure of exile, at others in the routine of a pastorate. Throughout his career he published frequently on a wide range of topics. In addition to his polemical tracts on a number of theological issues, he produced works on music, Biblical commentaries, and, most importantly for the *Adelspiegel*, a series of historical chronicles.[5]

Out of his historical research came the collection of citations and observations which Spangenberg wove together into the *Adelspiegel*. His father had encouraged his interest in history at the time he studied in Wittenberg, in part out of a concern to counter the historical interpretation of Sebastian Franck's *Chronicle*.[6] Spangenberg had set aside his own work, but in the days of his exile he took history as a hobby (his *Lust von Kindheit*) and composed in addition to his Mansfeld, Saxon, and Henneberg chronicles this discussion of the nobility.[7]

Spangenberg knew a number of members of the noble class personally, and he had had mixed experiences with them.[8] One of his princes had lost his lands--at the hands of other princes--in the process of defending Spangenberg's theological position. As a pastor in Mansfeld Spangenberg had had close contacts with noble lords, as confessor and counselor. Even while enjoying a comfortable place in the Mansfeld establishment and serving these lords faithfully, however, he had published a rather sharply worded criticism of the hunting practices of the nobility.[9]

The *Adelspiegel*, on the other hand, was written with the stated purpose of honoring the noble estate and defending it against attacks by others, among them Sebastian Franck. Spangenberg wrote the two volumes not only to praise but also to cultivate noble virtues, virtues suitable for all people but especially important for nobles. He hoped to teach certain lessons regarding God's providence and his punishment which might fall upon people who failed to practice such virtues.[10] The two volumes treated the public as well as the private virtues of the noble, in addition to topics and examples drawn from every land: natural nobility, spiritual (clerical) nobles, secular (political) nobles, inherited nobility, and noblewomen (featuring the Amazons). The *Adelspiegel* offers relatively little personal insight into the problems of the German nobility at the end of the sixteenth century; Spangenberg provided little analysis of the contemporary noble's actual situation or of the currents in society which had been altering his status throughout the course of the sixteenth century. Spangenberg actually seems to have possessed a more sensitive understanding of the peasantry's situation and of the threats which the nobles could represent to the well-being of their subjects than he had for the nobles whom he was defending. Among the several dozen topics which could be analyzed from the *Adelspiegel*, the duties or responsibilities of the nobleman are treated below.

Spangenberg framed his understanding of the duties of the nobleman within Luther's concept of the callings of offices assigned by God within the structure of his earthly kingdom.[11] In the beginning of his first book Spangenberg described the estates assigned by God to his human creatures for carrying out his will. God instituted the estate of temporal authority order to prevent tyranny, murder, and the use of force in ungodly ways, and to provide protection, assistance, counsel, and justice to people in the temporal realm. Governmental authorities—the *"Wehrstand"*—are responsible to create the order within which the other two estates can function—that is, in which the households of the *"Nehrstand"* can provide the things necessary for this body and life, and in which the *"Lehrstand"* can proclaim law and gospel. This understanding of the structure of human life and responsibility provided the basic orientation for Spangenberg's discussion of general societal obligations in the "Table of Duties" which he published in book form in 1558; he used it again in his *Mirror of Marriage* of 1570.[12]

In his introductory discussion on the opening pages of the *Adelspiegel*, Spangenberg drew critical implications for noble living from his concept of the nobleman's calling. He raised the warning that those with authority should not regard others with contempt because of their own majesty, riches, power, or might, for every noble line arose in the beginning from the level of the common people. Instead, they should humble themselves before God and use the power which God had given them in humili-

ty and fear of God for the benefit of those in the other estates.[13]

Spangenberg's broad outline of the duties of the nobleman
was based on Romans 13.1-7, and it specified that the governing
powers execute God's wrath against evil doers and approve and
support the good. In his comparison of the noble *(Adel)* and the
eagle *(Adler)*--one of his demonstrations of the literary and
linguistic skills he had acquired at Wittenberg--Spangenberg developed this two-sided understanding of the duty of the nobleman. His sword, like the sharp beak of the eagle, punishes evil
subjects and neighbors, but it also protects his own subjects.
His rule is necessary because without it the peasants would be
so wild that nothing good could be accomplished. But his rule
must bring benefits to those peasants by preserving order, halt-
ing unnecessary wars, and exercising justice.[14]

As a theologian Spangenberg was of course concerned about
the application of this power to the religious realm, but he
certainly did not neglect to remind the nobles of their responsibilities in regard to the temporal aspects of their subjects'
lives. They are to govern first of all with reason, according
to written laws, not according to their own whims or desires.[15]
They are to govern with justice, without regard to the person
and his station. They are to govern with love, with a fatherly
regard which listens to their subjects and cares for their
needs.[16]

Spangenberg condemned merciless tyranny against subjects.
Specifically, lords were warned against burdening their subjects
with new taxes and new forms of required service which add to
the customary obligations of the peasantry. Such new imposi-
tions of financial and/or labor burdens are neither praiseworthy
nor even excusable. For prosperous subjects enrich even a poor
lord. Suidas reported Tiberius' observation that the well-being
and prosperity of a land's subjects is its best resource and
greatest fortune. Paul wrote that those who will not work shall
not eat; the opposite is also true: those who work should certainly have enough to eat. Wolfish, tyrannical *Juncker* who take
that away from their people will be held in dishonor when foreign visitors observe the depressed state of their villages.[17]
Spangenberg did not limit his appeal strictly to the noble and
godly side of his nobleman's mind and heart.

Furthermore, overlords should not permit their lieutenants
to gouge the subjects under their jurisdiction. Spangenberg expressed the common suspicion and antipathy which courtiers received from preacher and peasant alike in the early modern period; he quoted his friend, Johann Stolz, court preacher at Wei-

mar, to the effect that young nobles come to court as well-
behaved and devout as angels but within a few months the court
makes them as wild and ill-disciplined as if they were living
devils.[18] Noble lords should not listen to every flatterer or
rumor monger who approaches them, especially those who are enemies of the common people. They should administer justice according to an orderly process, and their punishments should not
damage the common weal. Spangenberg condemned tyrannical punishments and those which exacted ruinous fines from subjects.
Officials should punish on the basis of the law, not on the basis of their own greed for the sake of collecting bribes or
fines, and the punishment should fit the crime. Nobles should
neither permit criminals to go unpunished, nor shield their own
children and servants from just correction of their misdeeds.
Spangenberg condemned lords who command their subjects to do the
impossible, who abuse their subjects and treat them like dogs.
Such contempt, along with tyrannical penalties, had caused the
Peasants Revolt in 1525, Spangenberg noted.[19] It is interesting
to observe that Spangenberg shared Luther's initial criticism of
the lords at the beginning of the Peasants Revolt without reit-
erating the Reformer's later condemnation of the peasants' use
of violence. Armed peasants obviously posed no threat to Spangenberg in the 1580's. Indeed, Spangenberg acknowledged the
justice of a number of the grievances presented by the peasants
in 1525.[20]

Lords have a special calling from God to care for the poor
in their lands, particularly for widows and orphans, according
to Spangenberg. They are further obligated to provide certain
basic services for their people, among them upkeep of roads and
bridges, schools, hospitals, and libraries.[21] In a number of
chapters Spangenberg stressed the obligation of secular authorities to promote and support education for their own children as
well as for their subjects. He was echoing his mentors in Wittenberg. With citations form both Luther and Melanchthon and
with a warning based upon papal successes through Jesuit
schools, he urged nobles to promote education: to support in-
structors, provide school buildings, and give clothing to poor
students.[22]

Linked to such secular duties were the religious duties
which Spangenberg believed God had called nobles to exercise.
The *Adelspiegel* made it clear that nobles were not to interfere
in ecclesiastical affairs to the detriment of the preaching of
God's Word. They did not have the right to command or forbid
whatever suited their fancy in the ecclesiastical realm. They
were not permitted to stipulate what was to be taught and what

was to be criticized by the pastors of their lands; they were
not to put a bridle in the Holy Spirit's mouth. Instead, they
should recognize that God had called them to be the church's
nurses and guardians (Isa. 49.23), who extend protection and
fatherly and motherly care to the church and to its faithful
teachers and servants.[23]

The fifth book in Spangenberg's second volume treats "the
fifth crown of honor, which bestows upon the nobility the highest of adornments, namely virtue, and especially true piety in
faith, thanksgiving, and prayer." This piety is the noble's response to the first and second commandments and can be summarized in the fear and love of God. Spangenberg proceeded
through the personal virtues of faith, thanksgiving, prayer,
love for God, fear of God, to the avoidance of false religion
and hypocrisy. He then moved to those virtues of the Christian
noble which affect the churches of his lands.

First of all, reflecting his own personal experiences with
certain princes, Spangenberg criticized rulers who permit the
condemnation or persecution of Christian doctrine and Christian
teachers when they know they should break their silence and defend the true faith. Secondly, the pious noble should not engage in crusades against Christians. Spangenberg's protector,
Count Volrad of Mansfeld, had been attacked by his cousin, Albrecht, in the Smalcald War when Albrecht took the side of Emperor Charles V against the Evangelical leaders for whom Volrad
had fought. Later, Volrad had refused to send troops to fight
for the French king against the Huguenots, unlike other Gnesio-
Lutheran princes who had preferred to fight for the "papists"
rather than for the "sacramentarian *Schwärmer*." Volrad's decision was based on the principle that the Christian ruler could
not participate in the persecution of believers for the sake of
their faith. In 1578 Volrad preferred to be driven from his
lands rather than submit to the pressures exerted by Joachim
Friedrich of Magdeburg, to persecute faithful--i.e., Flacian-
ist--pastors.[24]

Spangenberg urged the German knights and princes to follow
the example of the Bohemian and Moravian nobles who protected
persecuted Christians at the time of John Huss--fifty instances
of German nobles who followed their example by supporting the
Reformation were given. Among them were Franz von Sickingen,
whose antipathy toward the papacy Spangenberg stressed, and Ulrich von Hutten, who accepted the gospel heartily and with great
joy. Listed with the series of nobles who defended the Lutheran
movement in the 1520's and 1530's were the names of several who
supported the Flacianists in Spangenberg's time. He gratefully

recalled that Dietrich von Schlieben had studied the issues involved in the controversy over original sin in 1574, had confessed the truth, and twice had saved Spangenberg's life by
warning him of impending action against him. Spangenberg
praised Eberhart von der Thann for supporting Flacius in ducal
Saxony and Adolf Hermann Riethesel for supporting his friend in
exile and also for helping subsidize the Magdeburg *Centuries*.[25]

Indeed, the pious ruler must exert every effort to cultivate his own personal faith through the reading of the Bible and
Luther, Spangenberg wrote, and must protect and cultivate the
preaching of the truth in his lands, including the abolition of
every barrier to the faithful practice of the Christian faith
and the worship of God--e.g., idolatry, magic, blasphemy, and
the like. Citing Melanchthon, Spangenberg pointed out that this
required the nobles to support the Christian education of the
young.[26]

This education must provide instruction in pure doctrine.
The nobleman's oath of fealty committed him to provide his subjects with pure doctrine since his office as ruler was committed
to him by God. Pure doctrine, according to Spangenberg, was the
Augsburg Confession, and he pointedly warned rulers to protect
their people from those who opposed its teaching. His list of
these opponents was a standard list which any Gnesio-Lutheran
might have compiled: papists, Interimists (probably a reference
to defenders of the Leipzig Interim rather than the Augsburg Interim), teachers of works (a reference to Georg Major), praisers
of nature (a reference either to Philippists like Viktorin
Strigel and Johann Pfeffinger, who had defended a "synergistic"
interpretation of the role of the human will in conversion, or
perhaps to Spangenberg's Gnesio-Lutheran opponents in the debate
over original sin), Osiandrists, Schwenckfelder, "sacramentarian
ravers," and similar sects. Nobles must not show contempt for
God's Word by ignoring the need for their preachers to proclaim
law and gospel; they must not try to subvert the preaching of
law and gospel by diverting pastors into carrying out their own
personal religious programs or by mixing philosophy with God's
Word.[27]

The ruler's other obligations in the ecclesiastical sphere
pale beside this primary obligation to provide faithful preaching of God's Word for his subjects. The ruler must not try to
merchandise the pastoral office through his right of patronage.
He must pay his pastors a sufficient salary. He is obligated to
maintain church buildings and parsonages.[28]

For the Gnesio-Lutherans the question of the right to resist higher governmental authorities had become a religious

question because of their repeated conflicts with secular rulers over the rights of princes to make decisions for the churches in their lands. In general, Spangenberg exhorted noblemen to obey the superiors whom God had placed over them in the structure of his earthly kingdom. However, he also commented briefly on the obligation of the nobleman to resist higher authorities who command something God has forbidden. He condoned disobedience to the commands of the emperor in the spiritual realm and even in the temporal realm if such commands contradict God's commandments. For any oath to a liegelord is superceded by the noble's baptismal oath of faithfulness to Christ, which pledged him to the worship and service of God. On the basis of Scriptural examples he counseled that noblemen must by virtue of their office present their people with a virtuous example, even if that means that they disobey ungodly orders from earthly superiors. In this case Spangenberg was following the ideas set forth by his Gnesio-Lutheran comrades in the Magdeburg *Confession* of 1550. But he did not venture further into the question of armed resistance to higher authorities, as it had been broached four decades earlier in besieged Magdeburg.[29]

Nonetheless, Spangenberg was clearly marching in their train. His attitude toward the *Wehrstand* illustrates in detail the posture of his ecclesiastical party, the Gnesio-Lutherans, toward governmental authority.[30] Spangenberg deeply respected the office or calling which God had bestowed upon the nobles, and he loved and supported those who carried out these responsibilities which God had given them in a God-pleasing manner. For Spangenberg and his fellow Gnesio-Lutherans that meant that the lord was bound to support the preaching of the gospel but was forbidden to interfere in the church--i.e., he dare not cross the clergy who were faithfully proclaiming God's Word. A number of other Gnesio-Lutherans brought exile upon themselves--some more than once--in their defense of that principle, but few others expressed it so clearly in print as Spangenberg did in his *Adelspiegel*.

His comments on the duties of the nobility are often the comments of other people--some of the 750 authorities he cited. German clerics had been both criticizing and praising the nobility for at least two centuries before his birth.[31] Their comments were placed along side biblical injunctions and the observations of classical authors. Erasmus had provided a humanistic model for fashioning mirrors for sixteenth century rulers in his *Institutio principis Christiani* in 1516.[32] Though Spangenberg's and Erasmus' treatment of the duties and responsibilities of the secular authorities differ in the balance of their

concerns, many themes are common to both and are treated in similar ways in these two works--e.g., their criticism of tyranny
and their insistence on the practice of Christian virtue. But
the concepts which lie at the root of Spangenberg's presentation
of the nobleman's responsibilities are also found in Luther.
His understanding of the duties of the noble proceeds from Luther's concept of the two kingdoms and the estates of the earthly kingdom, and they reflect attitudes which Luther had expressed, including concerns for both the spiritual and the temporal
aspects of human life. Spangenberg was nothing if not conver-
sant with the entire corpus of Luther's writings, and his reading of Luther's published treatments of governmental authority
had undoubtedly influenced his own thought a great deal. However, during the final years of his lecture on Genesis, when
Spangenberg was attending the University of Wittenberg, Luther
had also commented frequently on the responsibilities of rulers.
In those lectures he criticized heavy taxation by the princes
and their failure to treat their clergy and to the care for
their churches in a seemly manner.[33] Spangenberg was carrying
on the criticisms leveled by his mentor.

Yet apparently little came of it. The *Adelspiegel* was not
reprinted. In part Spangenberg's ideal for the nobleman's life
did not find a ready audience among the German lords of his day
because it did not really engage the world of their experience.
It was a theologian's view based on a theologian's approach, and
its message was conceived in biblical thought patterns, re-
fracted through Luther's concept of God's call to all men to
serve the secular realm. But Spangenberg did not apply these
insights effectively enough to the actual problems of contemporary nobles to have any influence on large numbers of those nobles. Spangenberg relied on the citation of authorities from
classical, medieval, and contemporary literature rather than the
observation of the actual needs of late sixteenth century nobles, and therefore he did not command their serious attention.
Furthermore, in the ecclesaistical realm Spangenberg's approach
to the relationship between the nobility and their churches was
falling into disfavor, becoming obsolete by the 1590's. The era
of Lutheran orthodoxy had already been inaugurated through the
promulgation of the Formula of Concord in a majority of German
Evangelical lands. That document represented victory for the
main body of the Gnesio-Lutherans (those who opposed Flacius and
Spangenberg on the doctrine of original sin) on most doctrinal
issues.[34] Its acceptance also represented the co-option of most
of the party's leaders into an ecclesiastical structure dominated by those who ignored the Gnesio-Lutherans' prophetic de-

marcation between temporal and spiritual power. Spangenberg
wished to vest ultimate power for the church in the church's own
leaders, not in their temporal, noble overlords. Those overlords would brush aside Spangenberg's sharp denunciations of the
oppression and tyranny practiced by the nobility, together with
his calls for personal repentance. Society was changing in
early modern Europe, but voices like Spangenberg's were muted,
for threats of God's wrath were his only means of correcting
social evil.

Robert Kolb

Center for Reformation Research

III.
STATUS AND VOCATION IN SIXTEENTH-CENTURY FRANCE: THE PROBLEM OF NOBILITY AS A PROFESSION OR FUNCTION--ABSTRACT

The problems historians have encountered in trying to understand how people of the sixteenth century viewed their world socially are well known. Much of what people were saying about their society at the time--as soon as one has moved beyond the usual clichés about the three estates--appears not only lacking in perception but also confusing, contradictory and naive. Some historians have noticed, however, an apparently close relationship between status and vocation in people's definitions of social groups. And I have indeed found in my study of the idea of nobility in the period what looks to be a quite interesting relationship between the two. What I have found specifically is that people in the sixteenth century seemed to view nobility as a profession or a vocation, or as a calling which one fulfilled. That profession was, of course, the military one. In other words, nobility was, in a sense, more something one did than something one was. This view is evident in a wide range of literary and other sources. It becomes especially clear in writings that discuss nobility only indirectly or in passing, indicating apparently that the view was an accepted assumption of the time that people rarely bothered to explain. The evidence shows, also, that the view tended to change and disappear gradually and that it was essentially gone by the middle of the seventeenth century. Understanding this view and how it changed should help us to understand a little better some of the actual social realities of the time; and it might also incidentally suggest that people of the sixteenth century were not as totally lacking in perception on these questions as they may seem to be at first glance.

Ellery Schalk

The University of Texas, El Paso

IV.
NEW WORLD NOBILITY: SOCIAL ASPIRATIONS AND MOBILITY
IN THE CONQUEST AND COLONIZATION OF SPANISH AMERICA

"Tres maneras para medrar, iglesia, casa real o mar"

In the sixteenth century, Spaniards and Portuguese perceived that social mobility existed for them in large measure in
the royal and ecclesiastical bureaucracies and in the opportunities available in the newly-discovered lands in America, Asia,
and Africa. The increasing centralization of royal power in
Spain and Portugal in the sixteenth century created a new demand
for royal servants, and this movement was in part financed and
in part amplified by the demand for conquerors, settlers, and
administrators in the overseas conquests. Great hopes and expectations were raised by the New World which seemed to offer a
wide range of opportunities for a better life. Personal letters
are filled with this concern with the improvement of living conditions and the existence of new chances for betterment. High
among the opportunities perceived or imagined was that of the
achievement of noble or *hidalgo* status. The overseas conquests
of Spain and Portugal seemed to offer broad opportunities to men
(less for women) to carve out a niche with valor and steel just
as the great noble lineages of the peninsula had done in earlier
centuries.
This paper will argue, however, that the opportunities to
attain noble or *hidalgo* status in sixteenth-century America were
far more ephemeral than real for a variety of social and political reasons. Although most people in the sixteenth-century Iberian world did not realize it, the very process of centralization and the development of a bureaucratic state that facilitated
the conquest of the New World at the same time limited the manner
in which individuals might profit from these conquests. America
presented the crowns of Castille and Portugal with real opportunities for social engineering, a chance to create society anew,
but in order to conquer and colonize, traditional forms of inducement and reward had to be used.[1] The formation of a New
World nobility demonstrates the manner in which the crowns at
first manipulated the perception of and aspirations for social
mobility to their own advantage. The political economy of conquest created its own social formations and despite royal reluc-

tance to see the recreation of an hereditary nobility in the New World, an American aristocracy emerged. By the seventeenth century, the Iberian crowns were forced to acquiesce to its demands for legitimacy. While the pace or tempo of this process varied in the Spanish and Portuguese empires, the tendencies were similar and the results parallel.

First let me deal with a subsidiary but related problem. The conquest and exploitation of the New World created new opportunities for the Iberian nobility. Plunge capital had been used by royal and noble investors since the fifteenth-century activities of the Portuguese, and it was certainly not surprising to find intended support for Columbus' venture among a Sevillian noble like the Duke of Medinaceli. Generally, the nobility sought safe and accessible investment opportunities and thus it was the Sevillians who looked especially to overseas profits by financing trade with the Indies.[2] As Tomas de Mercado wrote in 1587, "the discovery of the Indies had presented such opportunities to acquire great wealth that the nobility of Seville had been lured into trade when they saw what great profits could be made."[3] Mercantile investment in the Indies trade was a relatively safe venture for the Castillian and primarily Andalucian noble houses. In Portugal, direct royal investment in maritime ventures dated from the beginning of the fifteenth century and as the various overseas possessions were added, opportunities for investment were increased. To some extent the precocious development of a powerful mercantile bourgeoise in Lisbon and Oporto limited the dominance of the nobility in overseas trade, but there were always those like Antonio Teles de Silva who could amass fortunes as a result of their investments in trade with India and Brazil.[4]

The need to administer newly-won territories also created new opportunities for the peninsular nobility. Ambassadorial posts, military leadership, and positions of confidence and government had long been viewed by the nobility as exclusively theirs by right and obligation. The creation of bureaucratic structures to control the overseas empires of Spain and Portugal presented the nobility with new posts and opportunities for service.[5] The viceroyalties of Peru and Mexico fell almost exclusively to the titled nobility, although not usually to senior members of the great lineages. That fact is reflected in the commotion caused in Madrid when the Duke of Escalona accepted the viceroyalty of Peru in 1601. Rumor had it at the Court that he was deeply in debt and hoped after six or seven years in Peru to have rebuilt his fortune. Nevertheless, one observer stated that it had startled many since "no one of such quality had gone

to those parts before."[6]   The highest Castillian nobility seemed
to prefer positions at Court, the viceroyalty of Italy, or missions to the other courts of Europe rather than the seeming exile of Mexico or Peru.   Still, the titled noblilty continually
served in these seemingly lucrative high American offices and
were often accompanied to their posts by *hidalgo* retainers and
relatives, creating a reflection of Spanish court society in
America.

In the Portuguese world, the same situation held true in
terms of the use of the nobility in the highest positions of colonial governance.   The Estado da India seemed to be a preferred
post and Brazil not particularly sought after.   One governor of
Brazil, Diogo Botelho, complained that "This state is very rich
for the colonist and for His Majesty but for the Governor it is
very poor.   Poor I am and poor I shall depart. . . . My salary
does not suffice for even half the year for this country is most
expensive."[7]

But despite such objections, the nobility of both Castille
and Portugal were jealous of their prerogative of office and
rule.   The sixteenth century witnessed the increasing use of law
graduates *(letrados)* in royal government and the growing influence of this group in all levels of government.   The competition
between the *hidalgo* class and the *letrados* manifested itself in
various ways.   The genre of literature in the sixteenth and seventeenth centuries called "arms vs. letters" is a reflection of
this conflict.[8]   There are also many particular examples.   In
1581 at the Cortes of Thomar the Portuguese nobility demanded
that Philip II fill overseas posts with *hidalgos* like those who
conquered and defend those lands and not with lawyers.[9]   Royal
Councils were usually presided over by a titled noble but staffed
with a mix of nobles and lawyers.   In both Spain and Portugal,
however, the *letrados* themselves were acquiring the insignia and
prerogatives of nobility.   Those sent to colonial posts were
sometimes made knights of the military orders or given patents
of nobility in order to buttress the authority of their office
with social distinction as well.[10]

In short, the expansion of government and bureaucracy created new opportunities and responsibilities for the traditional
nobility of Castille and Portugal that were often unwillingly
shared with the professional magistracy.   In America, then,
there were always some titled nobles and royal officers with
claims to social distinction as representatives of both state
and "high society."

A second and related issue that has concerned scholars is
the social origins of the conquerors and colonists.   There was a

time when a great deal of attention was given to the problem of whether many *hidalgos* participated in the opening of the New World, and the implications of their presence or absence on the "mentalité" of the conquest.[11] It is now clear that the great titled families were little interested in the Indies, that some cadet lines and second sons did hold high office in the Indies, and that the *hidalgos* sometimes staffed administrative and military offices in the New World. Recent research on immigration to Spanish America has demonstrated that *hidalgos* were only 2.0 percent of the immigrants between 1520 and 1538 (289/13,262) and through the sixteenth century those who styled themselves *dons* were generally about 5.0 percent of the immigrants.[12] The problem here is the thin line that separated the *hidalgos* as a class or estate from their traditional function as men of arms. Many men who had lived by, or knew the use of arms in Europe, came to the Indies in the sixteenth century and acted like or proclaimed themselves to be *hidalgos*. Thus, there is no conflict between the low percentage of *hidalgos* represented in the immigration statistics and the statement of Viceroy Canete that most men coming to the Indies were "soldiers, knights, and the poorest *hidalgos*."[13] More important is what men became, not what they had been. A Viceroy of Peru had perhaps put the matter into perspective when he said in 1582 that "in the Indies everyone is a gentleman and this is the thing that most populates them [the Indies]."[14]

The Iberian crowns and individual leaders of conquest and colonization realized the potential utility of offering opportunities for noble status to stimulate individual effort. James Lockhart has demonstrated how this process worked in the conquest of Peru and how the men of Cajamarca (those who were present when the Inca was captured) were rewarded with honors and distinctions such as escutcheons, habits in the military orders, the title of *Don,* and other rewards of office. The fact remains, however, the number of rewards of this nature was small and with few exceptions tended to fall on men whose social standing was already high enough to make the transition smoothly with no public scandal.[15] Moreover, existing distinctions of rank were maintained in awards since those who had been *ciudadanos pecheros* (taxpaying commoners) could become *hidalgos,* but those who already enjoyed that status could be "armed" as caballeros.[16] The maintenance of such distinctions was a general practice throughout the Indies. It should also be noted that the crown was moved to grant such rewards not only in recognition of services, but also to encourage the recipients to continue "to serve, populate, and remain in the said land."[17]

The efforts of the Spanish crown to colonize the island of Hispaniola demonstrate the manner in which the promise of noble status was manipulated as a way to attract colonists. In 1518 a royal order listed certain privileges and liberties to be enjoyed by agriculturalists who would go to the Indies.[18] This did not have the desired effect and as the Iberian population of the Caribbean islands was destroyed by disease and warfare, other remedies were sought. In a long memorial of 1528 two royal administrators suggested that to stimulate colonization the crown should grant tax exemptions, perpetuity or awards, the right to import Blacks and also to grant the titles of *hidalgo* or *caballero* to those who come as colonists. The people receiving these titles would enjoy the same privileges as those of Castille and would be addressed and recognized as such in representative bodies (*ayuntamientos generales*).[19] The crown responded positively in 1529 using almost the exact language as that employed in the proposal of the previous year. Moreover, the crown promised to facilitate the creation of entails (*mayorazgo y vinculado*) and it pledged that in return for the efforts of the first settlers that they would be created "hijosdalgo de solar conicido," with the titles they wished and would be granted the coat of arms of their choice.[20] These promises became more or less a standard formula in the Spanish Indies as a means to stimulate colonization. They are found in the Ordinance of Population of Hispaniola (1560), and were later incorporated in the general Ordinances for New Conquests in 1573.[21]

Such policies seem to promise access to *hidalguia* and noble status through service to the crown in the Indies. But, in reality, very few individuals derived much benefit from the stated policies.[22] The conquest and colonization of the New World did offer considerable opportunities for upward social mobility, but it was usually obtained by personal military and then economic success in the Indies and rarely legitimatized by the traditional ensignia and attributes of the peninsular nobility, at least in the sixteenth century.

In order to examine the historical process of the creation of the American aristocracies, let us turn to four of the attributes of the traditional nobility: the status of *hidalgo*, titles of nobility, memberships in the military-religious orders, and the right to establish entailed estates (*mayorazgo*). Through the prism of these phenomena the patterns and process of the formation of a New World nobility can be seen.

The general policy of the Spanish crown in the sixteenth century was to oppose the creation of a legitimate nobility in the Indies. Despite the process described above in which the promise of noble status was used as an inducement to service, reasons were always found to prevent full compliance. The members of the Council of the Indies generally opposed efforts to create *hidalgos* in the New World. The traditional *capa y espada* councillors disliked the creation of a new nobility whose origins were often obscure and whose claims were based on deeds rather than "blood." The *letrados* in government, ever jealous of royal prerogatives and centralized authority (which is as much to say their own), opposed the possible creation of any force that might diminish these. Even in the 1580's when the crown was in dire need of funds, projects to sell *hidalgo* status were rejected. It was not until the really difficult years of the 1630's that the crown began to acceed to such proposals.[23] Even so, when in 1644 a list was compiled of knights of the military orders in Peru only thirty-four were recorded in Lima and twenty-seven in the rest of the viceroyalty from Quito to Buenos Aires.[24] The sale of titles and insignia carried out on a large scale by the Count-Duke of Olivares and later by Charles II in Spain never reached similar proportions in the New World although it did have some effect.

The hierarchy of Spanish nobility ran from the bottom rungs of the threadbare *hidalgos, caballeros* of the military orders to the titled nobility whose wealth and rank assured them sound and political power. It is clear that few titled nobles *(títulos de Castilla)* were created as a result of the conquest and exploration of the New World. The exceptions are so atypical that they tend to prove the rule by their singularity. Cristóbal Colon received extensive privileges as Admiral of the Ocean Sea and his descendants enjoyed the title of Duke of Veraguas. Francisco Pizarro became Marques de la Conquista (of Peru) and in the most famous example, Hernán Cortes was created Marques del Valle de Oaxaca and granted extensive wealth and seigneurial powers.[25] There were other instances, too, of promises to create such seigneuries included in the contracts for conquest *(capitulaciones)*, but in general they were never fully enacted. Once granted, the subsequent history of these early grants of nobility was generally one of legal arbitration in a continuing effort to reduce their powers. Reasons were always found for limiting the creation of noble titles in the Indies in the sixteenth century.

Peru provides an excellent example of the process. After the creation of Francisco Pizarro as Marques de la Conquista in 1537, the crown did not grant another title of nobility until 1618 and that was given to an Indian noblewoman in reward for her family's loyalties to the crown. In other words, only one grant of noble title was made for the whole viceroyalty of Peru in the sixteenth century. In Mexico (New Spain), aside from Cortez, only Miguel Lopez de Legaspi, discoverer of the Philippines, received a title (Adelentado de Filepinas) with noble-like rank in the sixteenth century. Aside from two titles granted in the period 1616-27 the other titles awarded in the seventeenth century all came in the period 1682-92. In total, there were eighteen titles awarded in the two centuries and fifteen were made in the decade ending in 1692.[26] By the seventeenth century, the Spanish crown in need of support and money had acceded to the demands of the colonial aristocracy for titles as an American inflation of honors began to take place.[27] From 1650-1700 forty titles were created and between 1701-1800 another seventy-eight (See Table I).

TABLE I

GRANTS OF NOBLE TITLES IN PERU, 1537-1810

1532-1600	1
1600-1630	3
1631-1660	10
1661-1690	18
1691-1720	28
1721-1750	26
1751-1780	25
1781-1810	11

Source: Luis de Izcue, *La nobleza titulada en el peru colonial* (Lima, 1929).

As Table II demonstrates, this inflation simply reflected the similar patterns in Spain itself but never reached the same levels. The distribution of habits in the Spanish military-religious orders followed the same course. Despite the seemingly great opportunities for military service and heroic exploits, few of the early conquerors and settlers won these coveted honors. Membership in the military orders was not in and of itself proof of noble lineage, but it did testify at least in theory to "purity of blood" and was usually associated with the other insignia and attributes of nobility. In theory only those who already had claims to *hidagluia* could enter the military orders, but in reality the reverse was true and entrance into one of the orders became in itself proof of *hidalgo* status.[28] Thus, the habits of the military orders were coveted. Little research has

been done to date on the role of the Indies on entry into the
military orders, but we do know that of the first 168 conquerors
of Peru, only four obtained the cross of the Order of Santiago.[29]

TABLE II

CREATION OF NOBLE TITLES IN SPAIN AND PERU

	Dukes		Marquises		Counts		Viscounts	
	Spain	Peru	Spain	Peru	Spain	Peru	Spain	Peru
Philip II (1556-98)	18	0	38	0	43	0	0	0
Philip III (1598-1621)	0	0	20	1	25	0	0	0
Philip IV (1621-65)	0	0	67	9	25	2	0	1
Charles II (1665-1700)	0	0	209	13	78	14	5	0

Sources: Izcue, *La nobleza titulada en el Peru colonial;* Stanley
Payne, *Spain and Portugal* (Madison, 1973), I, 298.

The habits of the military orders were highly prized, however. The chronicler Antonio de Remesal reported that when Pedro
de Alvarado first arrived in Mexico he wore an old velvet doublet
of his uncle that still bore traces of a Cross of Santiago and in
derision the other men mocked him as the "Commander" *(comenda-
dor)*. After the conquest when Alvarado returned to Spain, one of
the first rewards he sought was the legitimate right to wear the
habit of the Order of Santiago.[30] Alvarado's desire was shared
by many.

Colonial administrators, sometimes speaking for themselves
and sometimes serving as spokesmen for the colonists, pointed out
to the crown the advantages to be gained from disbursement and
manipulation of these honors. The Viceroy of New Spain, Don Luis
de Velasco, wrote in 1553 urging the crown to grant habits of
Santiago to deserving gentlemen and cavaliers because it would
oblige them "to be faithful vassals, live a virtuous Christian
life, and remain firm in your Majesty's service; because if the
important people remain firm, it will go far toward keeping those

who are lower from becoming restless."[31] Yet, despite such advice, the crown rarely acceded.

Perhaps some gauge of the minor effect of the Indies on entrance into the Orders is reflected by the fact that between 1526 and 1600 only sixteen American-born Spaniards were rewarded with habits in the military orders.[32] Throughout the sixteenth century few American-born Spaniards gained admission to the military orders and it appears that few Spaniards were able to use their service in the Indies to justify the acquisition of the honorary gowns. Table III demonstrates that as with the granting of noble titles, we can note a significant rise in the number of habits granted to Americans in the seventeenth century, especially in the period after 1630, once again part of the general trend in seventeenth century Iberia.[33]

TABLE III

AMERICANS IN THE SPANISH MILITARY-
RELIGIOUS ORDERS

	Order of Santiago	Other Orders
1600-1630	43	18
1631-1660	100	37
1661-1690	96	53
1691-1720	81	54

Source: Adapted from Lohmann Villena, *Los Americanos en las Ordenes Nobiliarias*.

Like the other traditional attributes of nobility, the entail of *mayorazgo* also experienced an attenuated development in the sixteenth century and even at the end of the colonial regime observers commented on its relative lack of importance in the New World.[34] A study of Mexico has identified only sixty-two entails and many of these created in the eighteenth century. In Chile, a poorer and less important colony, only nineteen have been traced.[35] Unlike Spain where eighteenth-century reformers made the *mayorazgo* a major target of their attack on the ancient regime, in Spanish America no such campaign was mounted in the colonial period.[36] Still, *mayorazgos* were highly valued and desired by Spaniards in the New World and promise of the right to establish them was used as a means to promote military service and settlement. The promises to grant *hidalguias* were accompanied by similar pledges to allow the founders of towns to establish *mayorazgos,* but once again it was in the exceptional cases like that of Hernan Cortes that such pledges were finally honored.[37]

The desire for *mayorazgo* in the Indies was real enough. Spanish patterns of partible inheritance made the establishment of entail based on primogeniture a privilege which was sought as a way of insuring the honor of family name and the solidity of family fortune, or as the traditional form of the grant stated: "that there remain a greater memory of you and of your wife. . . and that your descendants may be more honored and may have the wherewith better to serve the royal crown. . . ."[38] But in the first two hundred years of the colonial regime these grants were few in number and strictly limited by the crown. The general pattern that emerged in Spanish America, then, is the concession of noble status and symbols as a technique for stimulating further service. The crown, however, unwilling to see the creation of a neo-feudal group in the New World, closely guarded its prerogatives and severely limited the attempts of the conquerors and settlers to constitute themselves as a noble estate. It was not until the mid-seventeenth century that Philip III began to accede to the demands of the American aristocracy for the symbols of *hidalguía* in an attempt to generate both loyalty and revenues.[39]

Royal policy in this regard emanated from a strong desire to forestall the creation of a class with feudal status. Control of the Indian population was granted to individual Spaniards *(encomiendas),* while limitations were placed on their jurisdictional and tributary powers and on the hereditary nature of their grants. Though the crown modified its stance to accomodate various pressures as it did in the 1550's, the underlying policy of containing the growth of a hereditary nobility with control over vast numbers of Indian subjects remained in essence unaltered. This policy was not without its costs. The *encomendero* class, limited in their rights and privileges, were also limited in their "feudal" responsibilities, especially those of military service. By the seventeenth century the *encomenderos* no longer served an effective military role nor could the crown count on their service.[40] As a class the *encomenderos* were left (in the trenchant phrase of Mario Gongora), "in a half-way house between tributary feudalism and a patrimonial and bureaucratic state."[41]

Thus far our argument has been based on the desire of the Spanish crown to limit the centrifugal tendencies of a New World nobility and the chronology of change has been closely tied to the fiscal fortunes of the Spanish monarchy. But this is perhaps viewing an historical development upside down.

The factors limiting the granting of titles of nobility, seigneurial rights, and the right to entail property were not only generated by the political and economic needs of the crown. A major element in the formation of the American aristocracy was its own perception and evaluation of what constituted wealth and status. In an area of seemingly endless available land, it was labor that became the important factor of production. Control of Indian tribute and labor became the *sine qua non* of success in the Indies. Acquisition of *encomiendas* was preferred over the older ensignia of noble status. Not that the latter were unwanted, but simply that for those who remained in the Indies, the holding of an *encomienda* brought more direct and immediate benefits, especially in the sixteenth century. For example, the fiscal distinction between tax-paying *pecheros* and *hidalgos* who were free of these and other obligations was not carried to the Americas. *Hidalgo* status in Castille carried benefits equal to about 5000 *ducats*. In America its value was much reduced.[42]

The struggle between the conquerors and colonists and the crown thus revolved around the perpetuity of the *encomienda* rather than over the more traditional forms of entail and perpetuity of property. In effect, the *mayorzgo* symbol of noble status in Castille was replaced in the Indies by the *encomienda* of Indians, but the two institutions really had a parallel significance for the creation of a New World aristocracy.[43]

Without recounting the history of the struggle for perpetuity of the *encomienda*, it can be said that the conquerors chose to fight their battle over this issue, a battle that they waged with silver and lawyers in Spain and on a few occasions with steel and bravado in the Indies. The ultimate solution of limited perpetuity (the law of two lives) represented at best a holding action by the *encomendero* class. By the close of the sixteenth century the rights to inheritance of *encomiendas* in the core areas of Mexico and Peru were coming to an end, and the crown was beginning to reassume its control over the Indian population. Moreover, the catastrophic demographic decline of the Indian population in the Caribbean, central Mexico, and parts of Peru also made the *emcomiendas* in these areas far less valuable and appealing as a means of insuring family wealth and name. Thus the increasing acquisition of landed property and the demand for the more traditional attributes of noble status in the early seventeenth century came as a time when both the legal foundations and the economic value of the *encomienda de indios* was in crisis. By this time, the social prominence of the *encomenderos* came under increasing competitive pressure from bureaucrats, courtiers, and merchants. The complaints of representatives of

the *encomendero* class as distant from each other as Gomez de
Cervantes in Mexico and Pineday Bascunan in Chile underline the
same social transformation.[44]

By the early seventeenth century both the older *encomendero*
class and the newly important bureaucratic and mercantile groups
were seeking formal legitimization of their dominant position in
society. Their control of land, local office, and other forms of
wealth had created them as an aristocracy rather than a nobility,
and they continually sought ways to bring about their transformation from the former to the latter. The crown continued to see
advantages too. Philip III wrote to the Council of the Indies in
1621 that the award of titles to the most noble and wealthy persons in the Indies would be beneficial because "those with the
most obligations and holdings would care for the welfare and conservation of their lands."[45] Despite this more lenient attitude,
wild schemes such as that of D. Pedro de Rado Angulo y Velasco
to distribute (sell) 150 titles and 1000 habits in the military
orders in Peru were rejected as unrealistic in a land where the
majority of the population could not hope for such honors and
where there were few estates permanent enough to support the
"luster" of a noble house.[46] Even by the eighteenth century
when such grants and rewards were more common, they were never
made on a wholesale basis.[47]

The social formation of a nobility in the Spanish Indies de-
pended on the early reluctance of the crown to see the recreation
of a feudal class and the primary interest of the conquerors and
colonists themselves in forms of juridical control and economic
benefit not encompassed in the traditional institutions of the
peninsula. At the same time, the Spanish in the New World began
almost immediately after the landing of Columbus to assume the
lifestyle, attitudes, and self-conception of the *hidalgo* class.
In a colonial situation where important distinctions between subjects and rulers were based on racial criteria, it became easy
for every Spaniard no matter what his origins to justify claims
to "noble" status. As Alexander Humboldt was to put it at the
end of the colonial regime, "every white man is a gentleman (To-
do blanco es caballero)."[48] The conquerors, colonists, and *encomenderos* perceived their functions in defense, governance, and
maintenance of society as those filled by the nobility in Europe,
and thus they saw no reason why they should not assume or be
awarded the traditional ensignia that went with such obligations.

The image of the conquest of the Indies as an extension of
the reconquest has been often used by historians and it was certainly present in the writings of contemporary Spaniards. The
new conquests did seem to offer opportunities for the winning of

name and honor through service and valor; hence *conquistadores* were quick to point to their exploits and services in hopes of rewards and recognition by the crown. Thousands of *probanzas de servicios y meritos* attest to the belief that a just monarch rewarded heroic and sometimes more mundane service.[49] The interest in social ascendancy and nobility among the New World colonists is attested to by the phenomenal demand for and success of popular novels of chivalry in the Indies.[50] Amadis and Palmerim dominated the imaginary landscape of the Indies just as Pizarro and Cortes held the political stage.

While we must discount the usual invective directed at *arrivistes*, the noble pretensions of the Spaniards in the Indies became proverbial. "They are all gentlemen, sons of magnificent fathers,"[51] said Viceroy Nuñez Vela ironically. One author deflated them with even more sarcasm when he stated:

> On landing in Panama, the Chagres River and the
> Pacific Ocean baptizes them so that arriving in
> this city of Lima all are dressed in silk, descen-
> dants of Don Pelayo and the Goths and Archgoths:
> They go to the palace seeking fees and offices
> and in the churches . . . they order masses said
> for the honored Cid.[52]

The Englishman Thomas Gage was even more acerbic in his description of the Creole gentlemen of Chrapas whom he described as presumptuous "and arrogant as if the noblest blood in the court of Madrid ran through their veins," yet in reality poor and ignorant.[53]

Status incongruence led to a fixation with titles, honors, rank, and status that became a supposed characteristic of the Americans. As one royal counsellor put it, "the inhabitants of the Indies are naturally included to every sort of honors."[54] The drive for *hidalgo* status and the ensignia that normally accompanied it was great indeed, and the pretensions of the *conquistadores* unbounded. Yet, when confronted with a man of some claim to nobility in the peninsula, they seemed to melt in their efforts to curry favor.

The tale of Don Alonzo Enriquez de Guzmán is instructive in this regard. A young man of good family but poor estate, Enriquez de Guzmán fell out of favor at Court and was forced to go abroad. He chose the Indies because there gold and silver as well as dangers and diseases were to be found, and because it was a place "where there is much to gain [and] there is also much to lose." On arriving at Santo Domingo he was lodged by a royal

official "as if he had been the Constable of Castille." He was
soon provided with the post of Captain-General of Santa Marta
with nothing more to recommend him than his name and lineage.
Unable to accept the post, he was soon off for Peru. His reception was far in excess of his merits. As he approached Lima,
the whole town council turned out, with forty-six of the principal people of the city including the Governor's chamberlain who
then lodged the new arrival in the Governor's own house. Not
long after, Pizarro gave Enriquez a large sum of money and a
position as one of his captains. *Hidalgos* of such lineage were
rare in the Indies and they generally received great consideration and pampering from Spaniards who aspired to similar status.[55]

Spaniards in the New World reacted to the incongruence between their function and power and their lack of legitimate status by creating or assuming their own marks of distinction.
James Lockhart has demonstrated the ways in which the first generation of Spaniards in Peru hesitantly began to assume prerogatives and lifestyle usually closed to them in Spain. The first
generation was too tied to Spanish usage and distinctions of rank
to lay claim to honors such as the use of the title *Don*, except
in rare cases.[56] The sons of the conquerors and *encomenderos*,
born to power and position in the New World, were far less reti-
cent. The title was still tied to social or economic standing
but its symbolic meaning of high-born lineage was lost. By 1664
the title of *Don* could be, like the other distinctions of nobility, bought at a price of 200 *reales* for one lifetime, 400 *reales*
for two lives, and 600 *reales* to place the title perpetually
within a family.[57] The acquisition of such distinctions seemed
only proper to the elite of New World society.

The control of land, Indian labor, mines, commerce, and office created a New World aristocracy. The Spanish monarchy's
efforts to forestall the development of a noble estate in the
Indies with its own economic base and political prerogatives expressed through municipal councils or representation in assembly
was to a great extent juridically successful in the sixteenth
century. But, what the bureaucratic state would not concede the
New World aristocrats assumed unto themselves. By the seventeenth century, the crown was willing to legitimatize the aspirations of people in the New World in return for money, service,

and loyalty. But by then, despite the continuing demand for honors and distinctions, the basis of power was well established on other criteria. Eighteenth- and nineteenth-century genealogists reached imaginative heights constructing validating lineages for the New World aristocracy, but as such titles became emptier the more they were pursued.[58]

Stuart B. Schwartz

University of Minnesota

V.

PATRICIANS, NOBLES, MERCHANTS: INTERNAL TENSIONS AND
SOLIDARITIES IN SOUTH GERMAN URBAN RULING CLASSES AT
THE CLOSE OF THE MIDDLE AGES

"...like the gods of Epicurus in the intermediate worlds of
the universe," wrote Karl Marx, merchant capital in Europe between the fourteenth and the sixteenth centuries existed between
the feudal world and the capitalist one. Despite the praise
heaped by Liberal historians on the medieval bourgeois as the
ancestor of the modern capitalist, the urban merchants of medieval Europe did not evolve directly into the capitalist class of
modern Europe. Modern research tends, on the contrary, to con-
firm the relationship between the urban merchants and the nobilities that Maurice Dobb outlined some thirty years ago:

> One feature of this new merchant bourgeoisie that
> is at first as surprising as it is universal, is
> the readiness with which this class compromised with
> feudal society once its privileges had been won.
> The compromise was partly economic--it purchased
> land, entered into business partnerships with the
> aristocracy and welcomed local gentry and their
> sons to memberships of its leading guilds; it was
> partly social--the desire for intermarriage and
> the acquisition of titles to gentility; and it was
> partly political--a readiness to accept a political
> coalition (as often happened in the government of
> Italian and other continental towns between the
> wealthy burghers and older noble families) or to
> accept ministerial offices and a place at Court. . . .
> The degree to which merchant capital flourished in
> a country at this period affords us no measure of
> the ease and speed with which capitalist production
> was destined to develop: in many cases quite the
> contrary.[1]

From this revision has come the concept of "the feudal
city,"[2] the idea of the urban bourgeoisie as a class in the feudal
social order,[3] and the interpretation of the "guild revolts" of
the thirteenth through fifteenth centuries as power struggles be-

tween civic factions rather than foretastes of modern bourgeois revolutions.[4] The outcome of the guild movement, whether total defeat for the guildsmen, as at Nuremberg, or near total victory, as at Basel and Strasbourg, did not bring a new class to power and did not transform the town-land relationships.[5] When these struggles were over, there began the reintegration of mercantile and traditional elites based on the "compromises" identified (and lamented?) by Dobb. So unexpected does this process appear in the light of the traditional view of the medieval merchants as the vanguard of modernity (whose ghosts haunt our textbooks in the guise of "the rising middle classes") that Fernand Braudel has labelled it "the treason of the bourgeoisie."[6]

The South German medieval city experienced three waves of upheaval. First came the communal movement for independence in the twelfth and thirteenth centuries, followed by the guild revolts of the era 1250-1400, which attracted much attention from German Liberal historical scholarship.[7] The third wave, the anti-feudal movement of the Reformation era, remained for long the province of scholars on the academic fringe, until the establishment of the German Democratic Republic stimulated the emergence of the topic as a central theme of Reformation historiography.[8] But what had happened between the guild revolts and the popular movement of the Reformation era? How had the urban ruling groups, so badly divided against themselves around 1400, gained the inner cohesion and solidarity to withstand--in most cases successfully--the popular storms of the early Reformation?

What had happened between the guild revolts and the Reformation was that the processes outlined by Dobbs welded the South German mercantile elites and noble patriciates into cohesive urban aristocracies. The continuing social tensions within them, deriving from the ties of the urban nobles to their rural counterparts and kin and from the economic ties of the merchant fraction to its fellow guildsmen, were greatly outweighed by the economic, social, and political bonds and solidarities which bound the fractions together. A group of recent monographs on the South German urban ruling groups at the end of the Middle Ages composed with the methods of modern social history, makes it possible to delineate the characteristics of this social alliance. The paragraphs that follow attempt to do just this, drawing on studies of the principal towns of South Germany--Augsburg,[9] Ulm,[10] Constance,[11] and other Upper Swabian free towns,[12] Swabisch Hall,[13] Strasbourg,[14] and, occasionally, Nuremberg.[15]

Some terminological precision is in order. The term *merchants* is clearest, denoting as it does here the families engaged in long-distance trade and its natural complement, large-scale banking, with connections to the major centers of international trading, Venice, Genoa, Antwerp, and Lyons.[16] Patricians are here the groups of families outside the guilds, who, through their wealth and property, dominated the regimes of their towns until a specific date and afterward shared power with the guilds. This term came into general use very gradually due to humanist influence, and it expressed an analogy to the Roman ruling class rather than a notion of homogeneity of origin.[17] *Nobles* causes no trouble except just at its lower edges, the sector of the category that is here important.[18] Although the lesser nobles tried at times to exclude urban patriciates from their own ranks, the patricians of the South German free towns belonged to the noble stratum comprising those eligible for knighthood *(rittermässiger Adel)*, which did not yet constitute a fixed layer of the noble hierarchy.[19] At Strasbourg, for example, there were ennobled merchants in the guilds and patricians whose only claim to nobility was the reputation of nobility and a noble style of life.[20] These were perhaps as good as an imperial patent, for living nobly was still a fundamental mark of a gentleman.

The economic interpenetration of patricians and merchants took place both in pursuits associated with the nobles and in those associated with the merchants. An extreme case is certainly Nuremberg, where the "nobiles Norimbergenses" were merchants, as were most other families of the ruling group.[21] At Augsburg, as Strieder showed many years ago, at least six of the leading commercial families were nobles from the land, while seven others made up the patriciate, including such families as the Imhof, the Baumgartner, the Rehlinger, the Herwart, and the Welser.[22] The nobles of Schwäbisch Hall were simply a town-dwelling fraction of the local nobility, but they traded heavily in wine and in salt, the foundations of Hall's prosperity.[23]

The patricians of Strasbourg and Ulm were formally barred from trade, but at Strasbourg they could and did invest in trading firms and banking syndicates. Furthermore, they could also evade the trading prohibition by joining a guild instead of a patrician *Constofel*--which several families did.[24]

Movement in the other direction in the form of investment by urban merchants and bankers in rural properties, rents, peasant debt, country houses, and fiefs, is known all over Europe around 1500. Although systematic study of this process in South Germany is still lacking, there is much evidence to indicate that here, too, urban investors brought much land and many peasants under their control.[25] Around Augsburg, Ulm, and Strasbourg, the rich merchants acquired feudal tenures and country places with great ease.[26] The scanty material available on the purchase of

peasant debt by urban usurers indicates that all propertied lay-
ers of society participated in this form of enterprise.[27]

In the leading South German towns around 1500 there were no
mercantile and banking sectors in which the urban nobles did not
have some interests. On the other hand, every source of income
and type of property common among or proper to the nobles was
also open to wealthy commoners.

An account of the social consolidation of the rich urban
merchants with the patricians must begin with the oft-stressed
anti-merchant sentiment expressed by members of the German lesser
nobility.[28] Many nobles feared the collective power of the great
urban business firms and supported the anti-monopoly movement in
the Empire. The spread of this resentment among the lesser nobles reflects perhaps a weakening of old-fashioned, family-and-
fief noble power, the result both of mediatization and of the
failure of seigneurial incomes to keep pace with prices.[29] Such
sentiments undoubtedly lay behind such acts of social vengeance
as the exclusion of urban gentlemen from the Heidelberg tourna-
ment in 1485, but it must have disturbed relations between rural
nobles and urban merchants elsewhere as well. The extreme case
may again be Nuremberg, whose patricians and other wealthy families were denied the right of connubium with the Franconian nobility.[30]

In the cities, however, relations between noble patricians
and rich guild merchants displayed a high degree of alliance and
acceptance, even where, as at Strasbourg and Schwäbisch Hall, the
noble patriciate was simply a town-dwelling fraction of the rural
nobility.[31]

Intermarriage is ever a sign of relative social equality and
social acceptance, and the South German merchants commonly married their children to the progeny of urban and even rural noble
families. At Strasbourg the patricians married readily into rural noble families up to, but rarely including, the comital rank,
and just as commonly into wealthy guild families.[32] Conrad Joham
(d. 1551), for example, was a silk and silver merchant, the son
of an immigrant merchant from Saverne (who also happened to be a
knight). He bought two fiefs and then a patent of nobility in
1536, married one daughter to a rich Frankfurt patrician, others
to a Swabian patrician and a noble of Strasbourg, and his two
sons to daughters of Nicolaus Ziegler, imperial secretary and
Lord of Barr. Similar marriage patterns occurred at Ulm, Augsburg, and some other Upper Swabian towns.

Except for the Nurembergers, the South German merchants
formed one social reservoir from whose ranks the patriciates and
rural nobilities were partly replenished through ennoblement.

Armigerous status or ennoblement could be had in the Empire by paying the appropriate fee to the imperial chancellery and meeting certain minimum social qualifications.[33] From the mid-fifteenth century onward, a small but constant part of the ennobled were rich merchants from the major South German towns, family after family of whom left trade, bought country houses, castles, and fiefs, and lived like gentlemen. This upward mobility of merchants into the urban patriciates and the feudality was known all over Europe at the end of the Middle Ages, although occasionally the opposite occurred with the movement of a gentleman into commerce.[34] The rich merchant who wanted to be a gentleman was a common social type, and his ambition was neatly described by Hans Armbruster in der Brandgasse, a Strasbourgeois who abandoned trade for a patrician Constofel around 1475: "He whom God has given wealth, also wants honor."[35] The pursuit of honor, that quality possessed by a noble even if he had nothing else, led generation after generation of sons of merchants into the gentry, either through the urban patriciate or directly to the land.

This mobility was promoted by the natural rates of extinction of patrician lineages. Either there were continued emigrations after the guilds broke the patrician political monopoly, or patricain families simply died out. About 37 families were enrolled in the patrician Grosse Zunft of Memmingen around 1450, but only 22 around 1500.[36] At Strasbourg, the two Constofeln numbered about 100 adult male patricians in 1444, but they dwindled by about two-thirds before the Reformation; and, for a short time after the Smalkaldic War (1546-47), the Constofeln could not fill the one-third of civic offices alloted to them.[37] And the Augsburg patriciate numbered only eight families when the guild regime decided in 1538 to open it up to other wealthy families.[38]

Sometimes the patricians resisted pressures from below, sometimes not. The case of Strasbourg is instructive. Here the two Constofeln defined their own terms of admission, in which, at least since 1509, the regime supported them,[39] and sometimes the impeccable credentials of the newly ennobled were refused. In 1514, for example, Philips Hagen, grandson of a merchant who had secured ennoblement from the Emperor Frederick III in 1478, sued a Strasbourg Constofeln for admittance and was refused, despite his patent of nobility and despite his marriage and those of other Hagens to patricians and other nobles. Or the Mosung brothers, sons of an ennobled guildsman, who waved their patent in the faces of the same patricians in 1535 and demanded admittance. The patricians muttered about silk purses and sows' ears, the civic regime backed them, and the Mosungs stayed in the country. But these parvenues were exceptional, for the other side of the coin is represented by the cluster of international trading and banking families in Reformation Strasbourg, every one of whom entered the Constofeln before 1600.

In most South German free towns, even the small ones, the patricians had one or more social organizations, and sometimes they formed their own guilds within a guild regime.[40] These *Stuben* varied in their levels of exclusivity, but the very formation of patrician guilds suggests a measure of social accomodation by the patricians to the typical forms of the guild movement.

A final feature of social consolidation, which can only be mentioned here, was the opening up of common career opportunities for rural and urban nobles and the sons of merchants in the form of service to the territorial principalities. The subject has barely been studied, although research on the social origins of the jurists and others who served South German princes during the sixteenth century suggests that education served to aid greatly the amalgamation of the various sectors of the South German aristocracies into a well-integrated class.[41] The topic of education opens up, of course, the reverse side of our topic, the embourgeoisement of the nobility which naturally complemented the incorporation of the mercantile elite into the world of the nobility. But the flocking of young aristocrats into the German universities tor training for lay careers in the sixteenth century suggests the importance of education as a relatively new form of aristocratic cultural capital, the rise of which is one gauge of the process of embourgeoisement.[42]

Political alliances between remnants of defeated patriciates and the richest strata of guildsman are the surest sign of merchant-patrician solidarity. Except for Nuremberg, the major South German towns all had guild regimes, though the constitutional position of the patriciate varied greatly from town to town. Then, too, there were towns where the guild movements were not quite spent by 1500 and where the Reformation broke in upon unresolved struggles between patriciate and guilds. At Basel the final struggle began in 1499, the year of the Swabian War, and ended in the wholesale expulsion of the urban nobility.[43] In other smaller towns, such as Esslingen, the Reformation erupted into political arenas in which the patricians still fought to maintain their power.[44] At Augsburg, finally, the Reformation overlapped unresolved tensions within the upper classes, which briefly took an anti-patrician tendency in the form of the regime of Jakob Herbrot.[45] In most towns, however, the patricians survived the early Reformation years simply because their alliance with the rich guildsmen allowed a united front on the issue of

reform and the acceptance of an ecclesiastical reform trimmed of
its socially dangerous elements.

The political alliance of patricians and guild merchants
rested on the non-revolutionary character of the guild revolts;
for, as Philippe Dollinger has expressed it, "afterwards as before
[the guild revolts], the governments of the German towns rested
in the hands of the richest citizens."[46] It is no surprise to
find an almost perfect correspondence between wealth and political power at Nuremberg, a merchants' stronghold conveniently innocent of guilds. But essentially the same was true of the
guild-dominated free towns of Upper Swabia and of Strasbourg.[47]
The origins of this semi-plutocratic oligarchy go back, as Erich
Maschke demonstrated in a seminal study published fifteen years
ago, to the abilities of the patricians and rich merchants to
dominate the crucial posts in the guild constitutions from their
institution. This domination produced the oligarchies of the era
after 1450, recognized long ago by such historians as Gierke and
Schmoller.[48] Wherever the social complexion of these oligarchies
has been studied in detail, the guilds' share of civic offices
proves to have been nearly monopolized or at least dominated by
the richest guilds in the social hierarchy of guilds, as Maschke
recognized, or, as at Strasbourg, through the invasion of the
poorer guilds by politically ambitious sons of rich merchants and
rentiers.[49] Thus the "little people" finally paid for the victory of the guilds, for the transformation of the guilds into
political corporations had, by destroying their economic coher-
ence, opened them to political invasion by the rich. In all of
these towns, the key to oligarchical control of the guild regime
lay in the wealthy guild merchants, who, although they lived like
the patricians, intermarried with them, and shared many patrician
economic interests, still served this alliance most effectively
by maintaining control of the guilds' political offices.

Reflecting on the results of nearly a generation's study of
the South German urban ruling classes at the end of the Middle
Ages, we need not be so surprised--as Maurice Dobb was--at the
scale and quality of amalgamation of the urban merchants with the
urban and rural nobles--i.e., what in a phrase may be called "the
feudalization of the urban merchants." Whether this constituted
a form of social treason, as Braudel thought, depends on one's
point of view. But of the historical reality of the process itself, there can be little doubt.

Two important qualifications must nonetheless be made to
this picture of the integration of the urban merchants into the
feudal order and its implications for the classic question of the
origins of European capitalism. The first point is that South

Germany at the end of the Middle Ages, like Braudel's Mediterranean world in the later sixteenth century, was losing its role in the vanguard of European economic development and would become, within three generations, an economic backwater, part of the periphery of the nascent world economy developing under control of the Atlantic powers. It is thus in western and not in central Europe that one must look for a mercantile class able to maintain and enhance its economic power and its social separateness from the nobility. Secondly, the South German evidence teaches us--if we needed another lesson--that it is mistaken to identify the city with capitalism and the land with feudalism. The reciprocal process of what I have called "the feudalization of the urban merchants" was the embourgeoisement of the nobility. It is in the economic and social interpenetration of city and land, of urban and rural classes that the beginnings of a different social order must be sought. Immanuel Wallerstein has put it very succinctly: "Bourgeois and feudal classes . . . should not be read, as it usually is, to mean 'merchants' and 'landowners'."50

Thomas A. Brady, Jr.

University of Oregon

VI.
CITIZENS OR SUBJECTS?
URBAN CONFLICT IN EARLY MODERN GERMANY

Historians of Germany have probed deeply into the medieval roots of the urban Reformation. In doing so, they have, quite rightly, concentrated on the autonomous cities of the Holy Roman Empire--both imperial cities in the formal sense and those cities which in fact, if not in name, owed allegiance only to the Emperor. For it was these communities which enjoyed the greatest freedom of decision in their response to the Reformation. In attempting to understand why most of these cities adopted the Reformation, scholars have asked how the inhabitants conceived of civic life and how they believed communal decisions should be made.

The most influential of these scholars is the Göttingen historian Bernd Moeller. According to Moeller's analysis, the attitudes which explain the occurrence of the urban Reformation were rooted in traditions of urban politics which stretched back to the high middle ages. The popular agitation which ushered in the Reformation in many cities represented a desperate attempt by ordinary citizens to revive a traditional conception of community life under which all citizens, rich or poor, stood as equals before God. And the willingness of magistrates in most of these cities to accept the Reformation, after some initial hesitation, reflected their persisting sense of an obligation to heed the will of their fellow-citizens--an obligation implicit in the conception of a "commune" to which many German burghers were still loyal in the early sixteenth century. In short, it is argued, the urban Reformation must be understood in terms of continuity with a medieval past.[1]

Certainly this point of view is entirely valid. Yet the concern for continuity shown by Moeller and his disciples is remarkably one-sided. While they have looked deeply into the pre-Reformation history of German cities, they have scarcely glanced at post-Reformation developments in those same communities.[2] For to them, the Reformation marks the end of an era in the history of German cities. Moeller himself has put this argument most forthrightly:

The Reformation had only retarded the slow break-

down of old city community; it had not been able
to stop it. The burghers no longer felt bound
to each other or to the city. . . . Gradually city
dwellers changed from participating citizens, responsible for the vigor of the commonwealth, into
mere subjects, owing obedience to the city government; and the city governments in turn no
longer saw themselves as instruments of the urban
community.[3]

Moeller's views have been assimilated by a number of other
Reformation historians. By now it is a widely accepted doctrine
that the "civic and communal sense" in German cities, though
briefly revived by the Reformation, came to end soon thereafter.
From the 1550's onward, we are told, "the powers and pretensions
of city magistrates and councillors grew," while citizens increasingly came to be regarded as mere subjects rather than participants in the process of urban government.[4] For the Reformation had marked "the last outburst of activity on the part of
the autonomous city of the middle ages."[5] The urban uprisings
of the 1520's, in this view, were the last links in a chain of
such movements which began in the late thirteenth century.[6]
After the Reformation, it is said, such uprisings subsided, as
the once-free cities of Germany either came under the sway of
princely states or adopted absolutist principles of government
inspired by them.[7]

But is this true? Did the Reformation in fact mark the end
of an era in which popular impulses played an important role in
the government of German cities? Did urban citizens turn into
"mere subjects," passively submitting to the rule of increasingly
authoritarian magistrates? Did the communal spirit die out in
German cities after the Reformation?

The answer to all of these questions is no. It is true
enough that magistrates attempted to increase their powers and
prerogatives--but this was an old problem in German cities, hardly limited to the post-Reformation era. And the citizens of
post-Reformation cities were no more willing than their ancestors
had been to let magistrates assume unaccustomed powers. Indeed,
the history of Germany's autonomous cities between 1555 and 1800
was animated by a constant succession of conflicts between citizens and magistrates--conflicts which were sometimes violent, always bitter, and often remarkably prolonged. This paper will
describe, in broad outline, the causes and characteristics of
these urban conflicts of the post-Reformation era--and in doing
so it will attempt to suggest a somewhat different perspective

on the urban Reformation itself.

The first point to be made is that many of these conflicts revolved around differences in religion. In many cities the magistrates had not succeeded in imposing a single religion on their fellow citizens by 1555, and the principle of *cuius regio, eius religio* did not apply to those communities which were religiously divided at the time of the peace of Augsburg. In some cities, Catholics and Protestants worked out an effective modus vivendi which minimized religious conflict. But in many cities no such agreement proved possible. Tiny Dinkelsbühl, for example, was riddled with religious conflicts for almost a century after 1555 as an overwhelmingly Protestant citizenry struggled to assert its religious rights against the wishes of a predominantly Catholic city council. Only after 1648, with the introduction of "parity"--the rule that each city office would be jointly administered by members of the two confessions--was some semblance of harmony between magistrates and citizens made possible.[8]

In Dinkelsbühl at least the Protestant citizens never resorted to open violence. It was different, however, in Aachen.[9] There, after years of jockeying between Protestants and Catholics for control of the city government, the Emperor himself intervened in 1598 to eliminate all Protestants from the city council. The following decade saw increasing resentments emerge among the largely Protestant citizens of Aachen against the behavior of their Catholic magistrates--not only because the magistrates introduced the Counter-Reformation, but especially because they frequently violated municipal law or custom in doing so. In 1608 matters came to a head when a group of citizens seized their arms and assembled on the marketplace to demonstrate against the council's policies; a committee was quickly established to press their demands in a more formal manner. These actions were sufficiently menacing to bring about the dismissal of some council members and a temporary relaxation of the magistrates' anti-Protestant measures. Three years later, however, the arrest of five Protestant citizens led to a new outbreak. Once again armed citizens gathered in the marketplace to voice their discontent, and this event ushered in months of political agitation in Aachen--agitation which only ended in 1612 when the existing council was entirely replaced by one consisting of Protestants. In fact the new rulers only lasted two years: in 1614 a Habsburg general arrived to restore the Catholic magistrates. But the events of the early seventeenth century in Aachen illustrate how vigorously burghers of the post-Reformation era could fight in defense of their religious rights and communal traditions.

Nor were conflicts of this sort confined to cities in which

Catholics and Protestants competed for civic power. In many communities, especially in the Rhineland, struggles between Calvinists and Lutherans spilled into the political arena. And in many cities of northern Germany the theological conflict between orthodox Lutheranism and Philipist "crypto-Calvinism" embittered civic life in the late sixteenth century. Brunswick, for example, was the scene of recurrent conflicts between a strictly orthodox citizen majority and a council suspected of crypto-Calvinist sympathies. In 1593, a burgher demonstration, during which a visiting Dutch Calvinist was almost stoned to death, forced the council to reverse its religious policies; when the popular orthodox pastor decided to leave Brunswick anyway, his last sermon evoked tearful scenes of regret from the citizens who attended.[10] The resulting alienation between citizens and council was one of the major factors in the violent struggles for power which erupted in Brunswick after 1600.

A century later, theological conflicts in Lutheran Hamburg played an equally important role in generating tensions between citizens and magistrates. Differences between orthodox and Pietist ministers led to violent popular disturbances in the 1690's and to attacks by orthodox citizens on the authority of a senate which was suspected of Pietist sympathies. Although the struggle between citizens and senate eventually turned into a purely political conflict—one which was only resolved with the promulgation of a new constitution in 1712—the initial impetus had come from religious disputes.[11]

In short, the legacy of the Reformation to Germany's cities was hardly a settled one. By eliminating the privileged status of ecclesiastical institutions, magistrates who adopted the Reformation eradicated one of the most persistent sources of tension in late medieval urban life. And by bringing these institutions under lay control, the magistrates naturally increased their own power within the community. Yet in doing so, the councils introduced as many problems as they eliminated. For by making themselves the ultimate arbiters in religious matters, they also made themselves the targets of attack whenever citizens were dissatisfied with the religious situation. And the citizens of post-Reformation communities were often as passionately moved by religious concerns as their forefathers had been. In a celebrated article, Franz Lau once argued that the popular impulse behind the urban Reformation in northern Germany did not die out in 1525, but persisted on into the 1530's.[12] This is true enough, but it must be added that in many cities the popular impulse lingered on long after that. A passionate desire to protect the Protestant message as *they* understood it could lead citizens of a much later day into situations of bitter conflict with their own magistrates.[13]

It is when we turn from religious disputes, however, to conflicts of a more general nature that the full extent of political unrest in the post-Reformation city becomes apparent. Such unrest was not too evident in territorial cities, whose governments lay closely under the control of their princes.[14] But the autonomous cities present a very different picture. A great wave of urban unrest in such communities can be observed in the decades before the Thirty Years War: between 1550 and 1618, bitter and often violent struggles between citizens and their magistrates took place in Aachen, Brunswick, Bremen, Frankfurt, Lübeck, and Stralsund, to name only some of the most prominent cases. In most of these cities the burgher uprisings led to major revisions in the municipal constitution or changes in the structure of government.[15]

During the Thirty Years War, power struggles of this sort were less evident--or perhaps they are simply harder for us to distinguish from the general manifestations of unrest which threatened the security of many urban governments under the strain of war.[16] Once the war was over, however, direct confrontations between citizens and magistrates over specific constitutional and political issues began to break out again, and they continued to occur right down to the end of the Empire in 1806. The conflicts of this era were less prone to erupt into open violence: in struggling against their magistrates, citizens were now more likely to appeal for intervention by the Emperor or his courts than to resort to mob action. Yet these conflicts were no less intense for their being fought out through political channels. One need only look, for example, at the tenacious twenty-seven-year struggle of the citizens of Frankfurt against their magistrates in the early eighteenth century to sense the bitterness that lay behind these confrontations.[17] Nor were such episodes confined to the largest imperial cities. Little Weissenburg, for example, underwent a constitutional conflict which divided the community into two factions in the 1690's and which continued to generate disputes deep into the eighteenth century.[18] Indeed, it has been estimated that fully two-thirds of the imperial cities experienced significant constitutional conflicts in the seventeenth or eighteenth century,[19] and many of these cities (notably Lübeck, Frankfurt, and Hamburg) experienced two or more major confrontations at widely separated intervals.

This is not the place to look at individual conflicts in detail--nor, in fact, is it necessary·to do so. Obviously the conflicts that arose in each city were shaped by local issues

and traditions. Yet in broad outline the urban conflicts of
post-Reformation Germany show a remarkable degree of uniformity.
It is possible, therefore, to answer in a general way the questions that inevitably come to mind about popular uprisings in
any epoch: How did these conflicts begin? Who participated in
them? What were the participants' goals? And did they succeed?

In many cases, as we have seen, the crisis was triggered by
a conflict over religious policy. In other cases the issue was
foreign policy. Not generally in the imperial cities as such,
but in those cities which had ambiguous links to a territorial
overlord, the council's policies towards that prince could easily engender opposition. In early seventeenth-century Brunswick,
for example, the council was sometimes accused of undermining
the city's independence by excessive friendliness to the Duke of
Brunswick-Wolfenbüttel and at other times of threatening the
city's peace by excessive hostility to the Duke.[20] By far the
most frequent sources of conflict, however, were economic. For
example, there might be resentment that the magistrates were not
protecting merchants or artisans from foreign or domestic competition: in seventeenth-century Lübeck the artisans accused the
council of not acting firmly enough against unguilded craftsmen
outside the city walls; in eighteenth-century Frankfurt retailers
were angered by the magistrates' tolerant attitude towards Jewish
merchants within the city itself.[21] But the most important single cause of citizen resentment was, not surprisingly, that
grievance which has engendered so many rebellions in history:
taxation--not customary taxation, sanctioned by law or tradition,
but excessive or extraordinary taxation which had been introduced without the citizens' consent.[22]

Not all of these grievances automatically caused an open
conflict. Indeed, the citizens' first step was normally to petition their magistrates for redress of grievances, and often
such petitions were heeded. When the paternalistic council of
Nördlingen acted in 1698 to protect local weavers from exploitation, the magistrates were rewarded with a fervent expression of
gratitude and loyalty from the affected artisans.[23] And even
when the citizens' grievances could not be rectified, as was often the case with special taxes imposed on the cities by occu-
pying armies or imperial authorities, shrewd magistrates knew
how to deflect or minimize the inevitable unrest. The council
of Nördlingen, for example, accompanied each announcement of a
new tax with an explanation of its causes and an assurance of
sympathy for the citizens' plight. "It grieves the honorable
council and breaks our hearts"--so runs a typical proclamation--
"that once again our loyal, beloved citizenry . . . must and will

be unavoidably troubled and burdened with heavy contributions. . . ."24

In many cities, however--and not only in large ones--the magistrates were less careful about dealing with possible sources of unrest. Yet the price they paid for rejecting petitions from the citizens or ignoring signs of discontent was often a large one. The citizens' original complaints, if neglected, had a way of ballooning into a more general attack on maladministration, nepotism, peculation, and corruption among the council members-- charges which were, all too often, entirely justified. Typically, angry citizens would form an *Ausschuss*--an *ad hoc* committee-- and demand for it the right to review financial affairs or participate in council decisions. And these demands would be backed up by demonstrations in the marketplace, by disruptions of council meetings, or, most dangerous of all to the magistrates, by an appeal to the Emperor to intervene on the citizens' behalf and reorganize the municipal government.

It is important to recognize that these struggles were more than just quarrels over specific issues. As Otto Brunner has emphasized, conflicts of this sort often involved a confrontation over the basic question of who had the right to govern a city. Was the council sovereign, ruling over a population of subjects? Or did it merely represent, and was it responsible to the citizens themselves? To take mass action was one way in which the citizens could oppose the magistrates' notion of their own sovereignty. But by appealing over the council's head to imperial authority, thus emphasizing their right to approach the Emperor directly, the citizens posed a more subtle, yet ultimately more damaging challenge to any presumption of magisterial sovereignty. The endless commissions, investigations, briefs, and judgments associated with cases of *Rat contra Bürgerschaft* represented more than just a typical tangle of *ancien régime* quarrels over privilege and prerogatives. For by setting these inquiries in motion, the citizens were expressing their commitment to a conception of communal self-government and mutual obligation which, despite what Moeller says, did not die out after the Reformation but instead retained its vigor right until the end of the old Empire.26

But who exactly participated in these challenges to the councils' authority? One thing is clear: the sub-citizen stratum of servants, journeymen, and semi-privileged denizens hardly ever took part in these movements.27 But the participants generally did include a broadly representative group of citizens, and the citizenry of a German city included virtually all of the householding artisans and tradesmen as well as merchants and professionals.28 Leadership for the citizen opposition was normally

provided through the existing institutions of the community. In
one city, the prominent guildmasters might assume the dominant
role; in another community, where the guilds were less influential, the captains of the burgher militia might organize the opposition. Certainly it is true that the leadership of these
movements was generally drawn from groups of relatively high social standing. In a city whose council consisted of a *rentier*
patriciate, the opposition leaders were typically wealthy merchants. In a smaller city, where merchants themselves controlled the council, the richest craftsmen would tend to dominate
the opposition.[29] Being close to the top, these men were often
particularly resentful of their exclusion from the magistracy
and particularly contemptuous of the council's mismanagement.

It would be misleading, however, to argue from this that
political conflicts in the post-Reformation city were merely
struggles for power within the municipal elite. In this defer-
ential society, it came naturally to the poorer artisans and retailers to let wealthier fellow-citizens act as their spokesmen.
But if their leaders proved too timid, they sometimes took more
direct action or made extreme demands. In many cities, especially before the Thirty Years War, one can trace the emergence
of more radical--and often more violent--tendencies within the
opposition movement.

The most famous such case was the uprising led by Vincenz
Fettmilch in Frankfurt in 1612-14. The opening months of this
episode conformed to the conventional pattern for such confrontations: the citizens formed an *Ausschuss* to articulate their
grievances and press for reforms, and after some months of negotiations a series of constitutional changes were successfully
worked out. But a number of citizens, led by Fettmilch, were
left dissatisfied by these concessions and pressed with increasing vehemence for more substantial changes. The entire episode
reached a climax in 1614 when angry citizens stormed the city
hall and held the council captive for three days until the members resigned *en masse*. A new council was elected, while Fettmilch raised himself to "Gubernator" of Frankfurt.[30]

In most cases, however, such tendencies towards radicaliza-
tion were held in check by more moderate citizen leaders.[31]
Movements which completely displaced the existing elites were
almost always doomed to failure. In Frankfurt, for example,
Fettmilch was eventually deposed by his fellow-citizens and
handed over to imperial commissioners for trial and execution.
By contrast, burgher leaders who used more moderate methods and
made more moderate demands enjoyed a high rate of success in
bringing about political changes. In some cities the *Ausschuss*

was institutionalized as a permanent agency to review financial
and other policies. In other cases, the municipal constitution
was revised to reduce the amount of nepotism and give opposition
leaders access to council membership. In fact almost every autonomous city experienced some substantial change in its system
of government between the Reformation and the end of the Empire
in response to a citizens' movement.

The real significance of these conflicts, however, lay not
in the specific constitutional changes they brought about but in
the message they communicated: if pushed too far, the citizens
were prepared to rise in defense of their right to participate
in municipal affairs. In one city after another, magistrates attempted to emphasize their sole right to rule the community. In
Hamburg in 1602, for example, the Bürgermeister exploited Lutheran political doctrine to argue that as "subjects" the citizens
would owe their government unquestioning obedience even if it
behaved in a tyrannical fashion.[32] In Frankfurt in 1706 an in-
discreet syndic declared before a burgher delegate, "What Emperor? We are emperors here and the Emperor is emperor in
Vienna."[33] But to say, as Moeller does, that such statements reflect the growing influence of absolutist ideas in the imperial
cities[34] is to present only one side of the picture. For this
trend was met by constant outbursts of resistance on the part of
the citizens themselves. Far from passively accepting their decline into "mere subjects," the citizens fought back with both
words and actions. On the theoretical level, they marshalled
arguments in defense of their rights which easily rivalled in
depth and sophistication the absolutist notions of their magistrates. Opposition leaders in seventeenth-century Lübeck, for
example, cited classical expositions of the "mixed constitution"
or Calvinist theorists like Hotman and Althusius in defense of
their rights.[35] And on the practical level, citizens took actions which, as we have seen, often led to modifications of the
urban constitutions in their favor. In short, the history of
Germany's autonomous cities after the Reformation offers no justification for a picture of steady increases in magisterial powers. Instead, it involved a constant tug-of-war between magistrates and citizens in which neither side had conceded defeat
before the Empire came to end in 1806.

But the most remarkable feature of these urban conflicts of
the post-Reformation era has yet to be mentioned: their striking resemblance to that great wave of uprisings in late medieval
German cities known traditionally as the *Zunftkämpfe* or "guild
struggles." Between the late thirteenth and late fifteenth century almost every large city in the Holy Roman Empire—and many

a smaller one--had experienced an outburst of bitter conflict
between members of the citizenry and the ruling city council.
The history of these medieval conflicts is well known--far better known, certainly, than that of the post-Reformation con-
flicts--and it is necessary here only to draw attention to their
most salient features.[36] In the first place, it is by now generally accepted that the term "guild struggles" is misleading.
Although support for these movements often came from a broad
spectrum of the citizens, including members of the craft guilds,
the leadership almost unfailingly came from the upper stratum of
urban society--from among the merchants or (occasionally) wealthy
artisans who ranked just below the council patriciates in the
social order. The uprisings were sometimes triggered by opposition to the foreign policies and military commitments undertaken
by the councils, but more often by the extra taxes levied to support these policies. In most cases, moreover, the conflict soon
assumed the character of a struggle to replace the existing council wholly or partly with members of the opposition, and in many
cases the burgher leaders did indeed succeed in gaining power
from or sharing it with the old patricians. Thus was formed the
nucleus of a new council oligarchy.

It will be clear from all this that the urban conflicts of
post-Reformation Germany were similar in many respects to the
civic struggles of the late middle ages. But these similarities
are not just apparent to us in retrospect: they were fully appreciated by burgher leaders in the seventeenth and eighteenth
centuries. In many cases opposition leaders felt they were defending rights and privileges that their ancestors had achieved
centuries before. With the assistance of professional jurists,
who usually retailed their expertise as willingly to opposition
leaders as to the magistrates themselves,[37] the burgher spokesmen were quite capable of bolstering their claims with detailed
reference to the charters, privileges, or agreements of an ear-
liar time, in some cases going right back to the medieval era.
In seventeenth-century Lübeck, for example, burgher leaders asserted their rights on the basis of the settlement of 1416 which
had ended the *Zunftkampf* in that city; in Weissenburg the burgher
opposition of 1692 charged the council with violating the civic
agreement of 1377.[38] In actual fact, the successful opposition
leaders of an earlier day were as likely as not the ancestors of
the magistrates of the seventeenth or eighteenth century. But
no matter. Burgher leaders of the post-Reformation era naturally
identified with earlier opposition leaders and felt they were
waging but the latest battle in a long struggle to defend citizen rights from magisterial encroachment.

But what of the urban Reformation? How does it fit into this framework? We know that popular agitation in the cities for introduction of the Reformation involved more than just enthusiasm for Protestant doctrines. In addition, it reflected the conviction among many burghers that only by adopting the Reformation could the traditional peace and communal unity of their cities be preserved: "ultimately this passionate activity of the Protestant townsmen stemmed from the conception which the medieval city had of itself." For this insight we are, of course, indebted to Bernd Moeller.[39] Yet much as he emphasized the intellectual and political traditions which underlay it, Moeller still interpreted the urban Reformation essentially as a religious movement. In the fifteen years since his book was published, however, it has become increasingly apparent that the religious changes the burghers sought--and generally achieved--were only part of a much wider set of reforms which German townspeople were demanding in the course of the 1520's.

This belated emphasis on the broader framework in which the urban Reformation occurred can be attributed to two basic causes. First, recent years have seen a growing interest among Western historians in the Marxist concept of a *frühbürgerliche Revolution*--the notion that an explosive (though in the end unsuccessful) revolutionary movement arose among both peasants and townspeople in Germany during the 1520's.[40] Second, the four-hundred-fiftieth anniversary of the Peasant War caused fresh scholarly attention to be directed not only to the peasants' revolt itself but also to the burgher uprisings which occurred at the same time in many communities.[41] What this research has made clear is that during the 1520's the authority of magistrates in many cities was challenged by burgher movements which demanded a broad spectrum of reforms not only in doctrinal and ecclesiastical matters, but also in the economic and political system. This wave of citizen unrest in the 1520's was by no means a sudden phenomenon, somehow triggered by the Reformation itself. To the contrary, it was preceded by decades of burgher uprisings all over Germany--uprisings in which all the classic resentments against exclusive and arbitrary rule by the patricians continued to be voiced alongside the growing chorus of anticlericalism.[42] There is no doubt, however, that the urban uprisings reached a pitch of intensity in the turbulent 1520's. Some of these movements, it is true, were immediately suppressed, and others succeeded in dominating their city governments for only a matter of weeks; but still other movements, especially in northern Germany, managed to gain control of the towns and hold power for a number of years before being overthrown.[43]

In the end, then, the political and economic changes sought by these burgher opposition movements came to nothing. Only the demands for religious change were permanently adopted, and the reason for this is not hard to find. While the political and economic demands would generally have reduced the power of traditional council elites, the dissolution of the ecclesiastical system and adoption of Protestant doctrines were hardly likely to do so; if anything, they served to increase the magistrates' own powers. Yet the failure of these movements to achieve the political and economic reforms they sought by no means diminishes their significance. For the burgher movements of the 1520's not only brought about the Reformation in the cities; they also formed part of that persistent pattern of opposition to magisterial rule which runs as a constant thread in German urban history from the beginning of the fourteenth century to the end of the eighteenth.

We need only look at the repeated uprisings in Frankfurt am Main to sense the continuity between burgher movements of one century and the next. For example, the Forty-Six Articles put forward during the burgher uprising of 1525 not only called for extensive religious changes, but also revived demands for guild autonomy and council reform which had first been articulated during the "guild struggle" in fourteenth-century Frankfurt.[44] In 1612 the Fettmilch Uprising broke out in Frankfurt shortly after these Forty-Six Articles had been re-published and circulated in the city; many demands put forward in this period echoed those of 1525.[45] Though the Fettmilch Uprising was crushed, it left the city a legacy in the form of two important constitutional documents: the Citizens' Agreement of 1612 and the *Stättigkeit* (a code to regulate the Jewish community) of 1616; and the great constitutional conflict of the years 1705-32 began as an effort to force the magistrates to adhere to the letter and spirit of these two agreements.[46]

To speak of continuity in this way is not, of course, to suggest that a specific tradition or ideology of opposition to council rule was handed down within burgher families or groups from one century to the next. After all, the line that divided magistrates from citizens was a flexible one, and a family which produced burgher leaders in one generation might easily produce a *Bürgermeister* in the next. Rather, to refer to continuity in this way is to suggest that there was something inherent in the structure of German urban government which made the recurrence of such conflicts, century after century, almost inevitable. The specific grievances of burghers in 1350 were sometimes different from those of their descendents in 1700. But the method of re-

dress they sought was remarkably consistent: some form of institutional change which would guarantee citizens greater participation in the government of their communities. These goals were
hardly "democratic" in the modern sense: the burghers always
believed that government by their betters was meet and proper.
But at the same time, they believed that magistrates were obliged
to heed the will and serve the interests of their fellow-citizens. And when they felt that this obligation was being neglected, they never hesitated to demand appropriate reforms.

For this reason, efforts to pinpoint a specific period when
German urban governments became more "oligarchical," or when citizens turned into "mere subjects," are doomed to failure.[47] So
are attempts to argue that specific intellectual doctrines, such
as those of the Reformation, tipped the balance in favor of one
or the other side. The temptation among urban magistrates to
rule in an arbitrary and self-interested manner was always pre-
sent--in the fourteenth centruy as in the eighteenth. But at the
same time, the impulse of citizens to demand that their interests
be respected was an equally persistent feature of urban politics
until the end of the Holy Roman Empire. The arguments which magistrates used to defend their conduct were available to the other
side as well. Both magistrates and citizens in the sixteenth
century proved themselves able to exploit Protestant doctrines
to justify their behavior; just as both magistrates and burghers
of a later generation could quote sophisticated sovereignty theory to defend their conduct. These doctrines, after all, were
but the latest weapons in an old war. There were truces in this
war, of course; when magistrates were cautious in their behavior
and citizens were restrained in their expectations, the tension
between them might be muted or "smothered."[48] But in the political and intellectual context of the old Empire, that tension
could never be permanently resolved. Seen in this light, the
"urban Reformation" appears neither as a unique set of events nor
as the culmination of a medieval trend. Instead it appears as
only one phase, albeit a very important one, in a recurrent pattern of internal conflict in German cities which stretched from
the end of the thirteenth century to the end of the eighteenth.

Christopher R. Friedrichs

University of British Columbia

VII.
URBAN POOR IN THE SIXTEENTH CENTURY:
THE CASE OF STRASBOURG

The magistrates of a sixteenth-century city shared common problems with the urban administrator of today. Faced by spiralling inflation, constant in-migration of unskilled workers and endemic unemployment, the sixteenth-century magistrates were forced to stave off the tide with emergency welfare programs for which there was never adequate public support and certainly never adequate tax revenue. Indeed we might well ask whether the present urban crisis is not a major example of the *longue durée*.

Until recently historians who have looked at the records have tended to focus their attention on the institutions established to take care of the poor and on the problem of begging. We have tended to assume that sixteenth-century contemporaries had little understanding of the fundamental causes of poverty, the complex interaction between inflation, overpopulation, the pressure on the land, and urban immigration. Since their solutions to the problem were often presented in a theological vocabulary, the secular historian of the present tends to regard them as sometimes quaintly naive.

Who were the urban poor in the sixteenth cnntury? Erich Maschke in a recent study identifies them as that segment of the population living at a level of minimum subsistence.[1] While the head of the family usually received a regular income, it provided only enough to live on from day to day.[2] These workers had neither money nor the property which would enable them to purchase citizenship. They were politically powerless and economically immobile, although they might comprise as much as two-thirds of the population of a given city.[3] Many of these men and women were recent immigrants from the countryside, pushed into the city by the diminishing availability of farmland and crop failures. Despite the fact that the city offered only a marginal chance of improvement, the movement out of the country continued throughout the century.

Demographic studies now being completed estimate that the city of Strasbourg sustained an increase of some 25 percent in its population during the course of the sixteenth century,[4] despite a death rate which was always higher than the birth rate. This increase was the result of immigration. From 1523 to 1529, there was a spectacular influx as the violence accompanying the Peasants' War led many citizens of small Alsatian towns and villages to seek the protection of the city walls. This was repeated in 1544 through 1565 when the religious wars again left the countryside vulnerable. In these years the average number of artisans arriving with enough money to purchase burgher rights totaled 165 persons per year.[5] How much greater was the total of unskilled workers and journeymen unable to pay the purchase price and for whom we therefore have no record?

The flood tide of immigration from country to city was further aggravated by the movement of political and religious refugees--indeed it is hard to distinguish between them. According to one chronicler, refugees began to appear in Alsace in 1525, during the Peasants' War, when up to 3,000 poor people, widows, and orphans came into the city and were lodged in various ways, but mostly in the Franciscan friary.[6] Daniel Specklin wrote that the first religious refugees, the Anabaptists, arrived the following year.[7] By 1530, he reported that 1,600 persons were given shelter in the former Franciscan friary which had been converted into a refugee center.[8] By 1538 the persecutions had reached such a point in Spain, Italy, and France that "many pious people were deprived of their goods and possessions and some 1,500 people came to Strasbourg."[9] Johann Wencker, a chronicler who served as *ammeister* of the city in the seventeenth century estimated that 23,548 persons were sheltered in the *Elend Herberge* of the city during 1530,[10] probably meaning that they were given shelter for the night and then sent on to the next city. Sixteenth-century writers did not have the same attitude towards figures as the modern observer and it is impossible to make any definite estimate of the refugee population from these numbers. The figures serve rather to show the magnitude of the problem as it appeared to the contemporary observer. Specklin's figures of 1,500-1,600 meant that the city was faced with a yearly influx, no matter how temporary, equal to 6 percent of the total population. The 23,000 figure meant that temporary relief was offered to as many souls as lived in the city.

To meet the needs of the immigrants, the refugees, and the poor who were already resident in the city, the Strasbourg magistrates had a set of institutions which had grown up gradually since the thirteenth century. The first lay welfare institution, the *Spital*, was founded in 1263 and functioned as an old people's home. By paying a specific sum of money to the city for a definite time, donors to the *Spital* received care and lodging when they were too old to work. Later foundations provided a hospital for lepers and the *Elend Herberge* for destitute travelers.[11]

Begging in the city was carefully controlled and limited to certain brotherhoods and guilds. The policy of the magistrates was
to help only the neediest poor and to eliminate unnecessary begging. Any person wishing to beg had to be authorized by the
overseer of beggars who granted the privilege to those who were
established residents of the city.

Since alms were given only to residents and begging was
similarly limited, the definition of residency assumed central
importance. Closely related was the question of responsibility
for the foreigner or outsiders. Before 1450, foreigners were
permitted to beg but as the numbers increased it was decided that
the city would support only those immigrants who bought *schult-
heisbürgerrecht*, which granted no political rights but permitted
these secondary citizens to receive alms.[12] With the steady flow
of refugees during the sixteenth century the feasibility of retaining the special status of the *schultheisbürger* had to be
closely examined.

In 1522 before the Reformation was underway in the city,
the magistrates undertook to reorganize the existing welfare system and to extend the services provided. A Common Chest was established: all donations to the poor were to be given directly
to the civil authorities and were to be administered by them.
This included not only donations by individual citizens but any
contributions made by cloisters, chapters, and other religious
foundations.[13] In short, all welfare funds were pooled and administered by an official responsible to the city magistrates.

Appointed to the new post of welfare administrator was a
former chaplain and Latin teacher named Lucas Hackfurt. Early
attracted to the reform, Hackfurt was later an Anabaptist, although his official position constrained him to recant.[14] From
the moment of his appointment as welfare administrator in 1523
until his death in 1554, Hackfurt kept a weekly record of his activities, including payments made to particular cases. He also
incorporated into his records the memoranda he directed to the
Rat explaining the problems he faced, exhorting them to use the
resources of the city for a godly purpose.[15] These records reflect Hackfurt's understanding of the problems which came before
him and provide a description of the social and economic conditions of the city at the time. How did he identify the poor?
What groups did he see as most needy? What solutions did he offer? Did he recognize the complexity of the issues or was he
content simply to provide food and clothing and prevent urban unrest?

At the beginning of his administration, Hackfurt had an all-
embracing view of his mission. He believed he should care for

all the needy and the sick who presented themselves at the city
gates in addition to the resident poor. On December 25, 1527,
making clear mention of the anniversary of the nativity of Our
Savior, he urged the *Rat* to be less rigid toward foreigners.
They should not be driven out into the neighboring villages to
be rid of them. Similarly the *Rat* should not discriminate
against the *schultheisbürger* who arrived in the city and then
fell ill: they should receive the same care and treatment as
citizens.[16]

By 1530 his attitude began to change. He realized that the
city would be overwhelmed by the number of "foreign" or outside
beggars. In August 1530 he recommended that no foreigners be
permitted to enter the city in order to beg.[17] The *Rat* accepted
his advice and in an ordinance of September, 1530, decreed that
no beggars would be permitted within the gates. Wagonners, driv-
ers, ship's people, and fishermen were warned of the new policy
and informed that their vehicles would be checked against smug-
gling. To appease the city's conscience, small loaves of bread
were to be distributed at the gates.[18]

Illness was another cause of poverty and raised particular
problems among the foreign poor. Hackfurt was much concerned by
the city's liability towards foreign women who came into the city
while they were pregnant and who, on giving birth, were eligible
for six weeks on the welfare rolls. Servants, both young men and
young women, could become infected with the *blätter* (syphillis)
and thus were unable to leave without danger of harm to others.
They could then become a permanent responsibility of the city.
These examples demonstrated the need to restrict the influx of
foreigners.[19]

By 1531 Hackfurt began to synthesize his ideas and to for-
mulate a policy with regard to the *schultheisbürger*. These secondary citizens, he pointed out, siphoned off funds which should
be directed to the needs of the real poor. They purchased citizenship, at the low price, purely for the purpose of collecting
welfare. "Once they are allowed to nest here," he said, "there
is no way to prevent them from agitating and stirring things
up."[20] They ignored the oath they had taken to the city and
therefore should be punished. Hackfurt recommended that if a
schultheisbürger were found begging in the streets two or three
times, his oath should be considered dissolved and he should be
banished from the city. Relieved of the burden of the *schultheisbürger*, the welfare program could provide for those whose
needs were genuine, people incapacitated by illness or other mis-
haps which had brought "disorder into their lives."[21] Hackfurt
then proceeded to spell out the groups which should be given

priority.

One of the first responsibilities of the magistrates was for the young. They should be hired out to established artisans to learn a trade or a skill. Responsible young married people should be helped to establish themselves in the trade for which they were trained and should be given work. Other crafts people should be helped in times of crisis lest they fall into pauperism.[22] Apprenticeship arrangements should be made for young boys whose families had little money to prevent them from becoming beggars. Similarly girls of marriageable age from these families should be aided with dowries to keep them from unmentionable occupations.[23]

In a massive memorandum in 1532 Hackfurt repeated his admonitions and defended himself from the criticisms lodged against him:

> The citizens complain that young boys and girls go up
> and down the streets begging so that no one can eat in
> peace. One boy pulled the bell off of some one's
> house. . . . But who has offered to take these young
> people during this harsh period of inflation when
> even those who have had servants for a long time dis-
> miss them and give them leave? I know of no rich
> man so generous as to take half a dozen such chil-
> dren into his house. Where can the parents go with
> them? Even if they should find a job, they do not
> have the clothes they would need--and what citizen's
> wife (assuming they were given a servant's position)
> would let herself be followed by such a rag-a-muffin,
> or would give him an old coat? Nor is there any
> craftsman who would teach such a lad for no pay.
> That is why it is so difficult for the welfare board
> to hire out young boys for trade. . . . This is why
> they must become miserable beggars, because they
> receive no help in their youth. . . . We give care
> to the *schultheisbürger* to the detriment of these
> young people.[24]

Hackfurt was clearly conscious of the particular problems of those who were not yet established--the unskilled workers and the journeymen whom he recognized as having too little protection within the economy. He was also aware of the burdens which pressed on the rural population, and he believed that the city should attempt to relieve the problems of the villagers as well as those of the urban community. In 1530 he wrote to the *Rat* with regard to the great increase of migrants into the city as a result of the Peasants' War. The war itself, he said, had created many widows and orphans and had brought all kinds of people into the city. The heavy taxes levied as penalties on the villages after the war fell on everybody--the guilty and the innocent, the good and the bad. Many were forced to surrender everything they had to pay the required damages and thus had to take refuge in the city to begin a new life.[25]

Hackfurt felt responsible to the peasants although they could be considered to be citizens of the city only in those villages which were in the direct possession of the city. In 1532 he wrote: "it has troubled me and my heart aches that I have not been able to go to the villages, that I cannot help them, provide funds for them and give them a little pleasure."[26] He acted in terms of this concern. In 1527 when he first appealed to the *Rat* to admit foreigners, he had argued that it was unfair to drive them away since the result was to burden the peasants in the villages who had less with which to meet the needs.[27] In 1529, again asking for funds, he stated that money for the poor should come from the rich, not from the peasants in the villages.[28]

As he carried out his duties as welfare administrator, Hackfurt developed a firm grasp of the economic realities. He realized that poverty stemmed from economic insecurity, that many of the working class, artisans, servants, and women wage earners had no margin to provide for any sort of personal crisis. He was also aware of the relationship between local conditions and the phenomenon of broad scale and escalating inflation--the "thürung," as he referred to it. The high cost of living meant that those men and women living on the margin of the economy could never be sure of obtaining adequate food for themselves or their families. And it meant particular hardship among all the working class during the winter when both the price of grain and firewood went up. In 1531 he outlined the final cause of the problem:

> What drives the poor here in such numbers? The
> answer--the great need and the dearness of all
> things. And where does the dearness come from?
> From God. Why did he send it to us? Because of
> our disbelief and sins, our ingratitude and self-
> ishness, from which develops great cruelty and
> unbrotherly hardship for our neighbours.[29]

Yet the remedy was close at hand. God had given wealth and property to the monastic orders who had misused them. Now He wanted this wealth to be dispersed to the poor for their needs.[30]

Hackfurt identified the underlying causes of the welfare problem as inflation, unemployment, immigration, and the diversion of welfare funds to the *schultheisbürger*. While he could offer advice, admonitions, requests, and exhortations to the *Rat*, it was their responsibility to provide the remedies. Their edicts and protocols reflect a clear-headed understanding of economic conditions as well as a concern for the common man and the poor.

They, too, were acutely aware of the dangers of inflation. A series of ordinances from 1515 to 1597 attempted to control the circulation of debased currencies in the city--first Lorraine coinage, later coinage from the Netherlands.[31] A 1578 ordinance forbade the use of the Netherlandish thalers on pain of confiscation and other punishment. The 1580 law explained the exact reasons for this proscription. The circulation of debased silver currency had caused the price of grain to go up and alloyed coins were, in themselves, a means of cheating the common man. The *Rat* ordered every burgher who had such money come into his hands to take it to the officials at the city treasury and have it weighed to find out its true worth so that the city could move to eliminate it from circulation.[32] The *Rat* believed that the purchase of grain or wine in advance of the harvest contributed to the rising price of goods. The rich were able to buy whatever they needed, leaving the workers and the poor with less food at a higher price. The *Rat* tried to regulate this by a series of market ordinances which made it illegal to buy grain or wine in the fields or in the villages. All produce had to be brought into the regular, appointed markets.[33] In a year of particularly serious shortage, they ordered that no one, rich or poor, was to buy more than what he needed for one week in order that there be enough for everyone.[34]

The impact of the streams of refugees was reflected in two protocols, one in 1554, the other in 1575, which forbade Strasbourg burghers and inhabitants to provide shelter, aid, or protection to any foreigners, excepting only merchants who came in for the annual fair.[35] These were both enacted during periods of civil war in Germany and France when the city simply could not absorb the numbers. But the *Magistrat* were aware that overcrowding could come from other sources as well. Ordinances forbade the buying up of several houses to combine them into a larger house. This, the *Rat* said, pushed up property values and made it impossible for the common burgher to buy a house. Furthermore it removed these houses from economic productivity as workshops and shops for artisans, handworkers, and craftsmen and restricted their usefulness to a single family.[36]

The magistrates recognized the shortage of jobs and attempted to meet the needs of the unemployed. A public works project was already underway in 1532 to improve the fortifications of the city. The purpose was to provide work not only for the poor but also for day laborers who could find no other work.[37] At the end of the century, a flannel weaving industry was established to provide employment for the poor and their children. A *Rats-protocol* of 1594 forbade the manufacture of this type of textile by any other citizens of Strasbourg since it was to be a monopoly of the poor.[38]

The core of the welfare system was in-house relief—direct welfare payments to those in need—disbursed by the welfare administrator and his four assistants. Due to Hackfurt's incessant requests, by 1530 there was also a doctor attached to the welfare board who took care of the poor who were sick. In addition to in-house relief, the welfare administration provided food and, in the winter, firewood. Food meant bread which was distributed at the gates to the itinerant poor or to certain families within the city. The preparation of the bread was let out by contract to certain bakers and Hackfurt supervised these men constantly to see that fair weight was received.[39]

Lucas Hackfurt saw the ordinances and welfare institutions as a response to the immediate problem. They were the finger in the dike, to be sure, and were designed to relieve the overt misery and discomfort. The long-term solution would necessitate the redistribution of the economic resources of the community. God, he said, had provided the city with more of the wealth of this world than the rural areas. Thus the city was obliged to carry a greater burden in terms of welfare. To fulfill these obligations, God had given the city the properties of the church and the monastic establishments, again in greater number than in the rural areas. The property was there because God wanted it to be distributed by the secular authorities to help the poor.[40]

Hackfurt's plan for reapportioning the wealth of the church began with what he called the "surplus supplies" of the chapters and convents.[41] In 1529 he recommended that all chalices, pyxes, and other ornaments be taken from the convents, together with the surplus food in their cellars and storerooms. The food should be distributed to those in need, the treasures and the vestments should be used as collateral for cash funds for the poor.[42] At the same time he recommended that the buildings of one or two of the wealthiest monastic establishments be taken over by the city and given to the welfare office. It would then have room for grain storage, flour storage, a bakery, and a place to store household furnishings for the poor.[43] By 1530 the city had initiated the process suggested by Hackfurt. The Dominican friary, one of the largest in the city, became the welfare headquarters. Yet this was not enough. Hackfurt urged that all the monastic revenues be reallotted to the poor.[44] The monastic and mendicant orders, both male and female, he argued, had removed resources that belonged to the whole community. Now was the time to redress the imbalance and give back to the poor that which had been taken from the common fund.

> People say that the sack of the beggar has no bottom. How is it that we are so stingy with the poverty sack and yet the sack of the priests and monks to this very day [1532] are still regarded with honor and no one touches them in this time of need? If one took the cloister properties as collateral . . . it would be a useful way to use them and the common, poor citizens could be kept from disaster and wretchedness.[45]

Hackfurt's memoranda and the *Rat's* protocol reveal a society sharply divided on economic lines. The urban milieu offered a large measure of political and economic stability for the patricians, and the middle class. The lower levels of the economic pyramid, however, lived out a marginal existence. They were rarely able to purchase citizenship; they had no economic security. They were caught by the competition of new, unskilled workers coming in. Whatever they earned was absorbed by inflationary increases in price. The *Rat* were genuinely concerned by the plight of these men and women, in part because they realized the potential for urban unrest. Lucas Hackfurt was more than willing to inaugurate any program which promised to alleviate their insecurity and their misery. He did not believe that the poor should remain poor, nor did he look on them as inferior morally or socially. Poverty, Hackfurt realized, was caused by the unequal distribution of wealth, but no one was ready to face the implications arising from this imbalance.

Miriam U. Chrisman

University of Massachusetts

VIII.
SELF-IMAGE AND AUTHORITY OF PARIS THEOLOGIANS
IN EARLY REFORMATION FRANCE

Clearly the Middle Ages are no longer defined and evaluated
by the point of view of humanist academics seeking to discredit
their predecessors and academic rivals. The *medieval* University
of Paris and its theologians have benefited as much as any other
institution or group from this happy development.

Unfortunately, the University of Paris of the sixteenth century and especially its Faculty of Theology (which we sometimes,
though erroneously, call the Sorbonne) still suffer from that old
bias which historians of French universities still adopt from the
humanists and reformers. Happily, ecumenism and objectivity have
largely eliminated the sectarian causes for such prejudice. And
there are other hopeful signs. Sixteenth-century scholasticism
and humanism are no longer seen as the inveterate enemies which
many humanist diatribes made them out to be. And there is a
better appreciation of sixteenth-century scholasticism in Paris
in its Thomist revival and in the creativity of the *via moderna*
of Nominalism. But the university corporation, or institution,
is still usually dismissed as ceremonious, self-serving, archaic,
logic-chopping, oppressive, inefficient, and ineffectual. It is
often denounced for failing to embrace the new forms of piety and
politics coming from the expanding population and the increasing
social self-assurance of the layman. Jacques Le Goff, attempting
to evaluate the French conception of the University during the
Renaissance, has said that French universitues in general were
in a rapid state of degeneration as corporations, of decline as
professional centers, and of retrenchment as centers of social
formation.[1] Jacques Verger, in commenting on the Paris theologians' attempt to resist the growing authority of the monarchy
in France, has concluded that "the theologians lacked true political sense, resisting or rather failing to grasp the implications of modern politics, and they were therefore condemned to
inefficiency and gradual effacement as a social force."[2] A completely opposite view, however, is expressed by Franco Simone.
He has said that the Paris theologians around the year 1500 were
indeed

     aware of the importance of the historical period in

which they lived and concerned about the ever-increasing difficulties which Christianity was called upon to overcome, and they fully grasped the need to face the new circumstances with new methods. They sought from the centuries of experience of the Church not the rejection of the bolder elements of contemporary thought or social requirements or material progress but the assimilation of every original element, while rejecting only that which might be harmful to the life of the Spirit.[3]

It is neither my intention nor my desire to defend the social, political, or theological views of the theologians of Paris. I personally believe that Simone's blanket defense of them is too extreme, but I also believe that Le Goff's and Verger's far more typical criticisms of them are also intemperate. For example, given the consequent history of the Valois monarchy from Francis I to Henry III, who could fail to wonder if the theologians' opposition to the king and his lawyers was not, indeed, a wise plea for a political order based on subordination and morality? As for the theologians' view of the Church, its doctrines and its role in the changing sixteenth-century society, why cannot we be content to recognize their view as a conscious, deliberate choice of highly educated--if rigidly trained--men for stability and traditionalism, without letting our own aversion or approval of that choice interfere with our first duty which is to understand them?

My own work over the past several years has involved research into the University of Paris' Faculty of Theology (with a capital F: the institution) and the faculty (with a lower case f: the personnel).[4] In the present essay, I would like to examine one small aspect of this, the Faculty's understanding of itself, of its authority, and of its role in the Church and society, and to see how it attempted to implement these. To this end, we shall look at three particular aspects of this self-image and role: the Faculty as a consultant in matters of faith and morals, the Faculty as an inquisitor and censor, and the Faculty's interaction with other institutions of Church and State.

Regarding the first of these aspects, theological consultant, the theologians of Paris in the year 1500 stated a general policy towards such consultations. They said that it was incumbent on them to be

by their office and profession ever ready, in keeping with the precept of Peter, the Prince of Apostles,

to give an account of the Faith to everyone who asks
it and to oppose nascent errors everywhere with determination and vigor in order to build up the Church
Militant and to elucidate the truth under the guidance
of most holy Mother the Church and the holy apostolic
see.[5]

Elsewhere in this volume, Ellery Schalk defines the nobility
as a *profession* for those who bore arms. The theologians here
speak of *their* profession as explaining the Faith and defending
it against error. This is reminiscent of a passage from Johan
Huizinga in which he says that "long after the Middle Ages a certain equivalence of knighthood and a doctor's degree was generally acknowledged. . . . By being knighted the man of action is
raised to an ideal level; by taking his doctor's degree the man
of knowledge receives a badge of superiority. They are stamped,
the one as a hero, the other as a sage."[6] We could also cite
the position of Erasmus here. Despite his satirical references
to doctors of theology in the *Praise of Folly,* Erasmus considered
the doctorate in theology as the highest professional dignity--
and he resented Noël Beda's refusal to address him as a doctor
or even as a theologian.[7] In 1514, the Paris theologians said
that it was their duty, by virtue of their profession, "to ren-
der an opinion in matters pertaining to the faith, hope etc. to
all those seeking it from them, and to put at rest any scrupulous
or disturbed conscience. . . ."[8] These were not empty claims.
Over sixty cases of consultations between 1500 and 1542 have been
discovered. These included consultations by kings, 7 times; by
princes and dukes, 4 times; by bishops, 18 times; by abbots and
religious orders, 6 times; by universities, 3 times; by cathedral
chapters, 4 times; by city magistrates, 3 times; by inquisitors,
3 times; and by private groups and individuals, 10 times. There
was also a frequent and close collaboration between the Faculty
of Theology and the Parliament of Paris. These consultations involved a wide variety of issues. Some examples are the famous
cases of Martin Luther, referred to the Faculty by the Duke of
Saxony and by Luther himself; the issue of Johann Reuchlin; the
case of Henry VIII's marriage; the question of the poor-relief
laws of Ypres in Flanders; Cajetanus' book on papal authority;
the Franciscan Order's quarrel about which faction was most
faithful to the intentions of the founder; the liceity of taking
interest on loans;[9] the salvation of a child dying without baptism; and so on. In Henry VIII's consultation about his marriage, it is quite clear that he considered the decision of the
Paris theologians to be the most important one of all the univer-

sities he was consulting, and he expended an enormous quantity
of resources on this.[10] There is, of course, ample place to argue about the appropriateness of particular decisions of the
theologians. But the wide range of clients and of subjects submitted to the Faculty leaves little room to doubt that the Faculty of Theology of Paris of the early sixteenth century still
claimed--and still held--a place of importance as advisor and
arbiter in the minds of all levels of sixteenth-century society.

The theologians did not always wait for problems or questions to be submitted to them by others. They frequently acted
on their own initiative, especially when they felt that other
authorities or institutions were failing to take proper steps.
This inquisitorial activity became very common, especially in
the first years after 1520--the year Martin Luther was first
mentioned in the Faculty's proceedings and the year that the in-
defatigable Noël Beda assumed the direction of the Faculty. But
it is not my intention to trace here a history of the Faculty's
reaction against heresy. I think it is more important to examine the theologians' reasons for undertaking this activity and
to see what this reveals about their understanding of their authority and their relationship vis-à-vis other institutions such
as the papacy, the episcopacy, and the monarchy in France.

In the statement formulated in the year 1500, quoted above,
we have already seen that the theologians of Paris saw it as
their professional duty "to oppose nascent errors everywhere
with determination and vigor." The canonical basis for such action is not clear, but the Faculty of Theology always considered
its own authority as older and superior to that of canonists.
Certainly the historical precedents for it go back to the early
years of the university. A group which considered itself the
foremost faculty of theologians of Christendom and which had
successfully challenged the authority of the papacy itself in
the previous century could understandably be expected to assume
the role of defender of the faith when it felt that other agen-
cies were not fulfilling this task. In respect to the papacy,
Paris theologians did posit a certain primacy of the pope over
other bishops. But they were still strongly conciliarist at
this time.[11] In several concrete decisions, the theologians
sought to limit the power of the pope in France. It perennially
opposed the claims of the mendicant orders, based on a papal in-
dult, to exercise sacramental functions in French dioceses.[12]
It strongly fought against implementation of the Concordat of
1516 between Pope Leo X and King Francis I, and appealed to a
future council when threat of physical force was applied.[13] It
only reluctantly abandoned its support of the schismatic Council

of Milan-Pisa-Lyon in the face of the papally-convened Fifth Lateran Council.[14] The Faculty condemned the Roman Breviary of 1535.[15] It had a hostile view of the Council of Trent,[16] even though a number of Paris theologians had more or less prominent roles in the Council in their own right as bishops. Later in the century, the Faculty of Theology of Paris was to subject the papal Index of Prohibited Books to examination by the Faculty before allowing publication in France.[17] It should be remembered, too, that the real question in the divorce consultation of Henry VIII centered on one's view of papal authority--i.e., "Whether the pope can dispense a brother to take or accept as wife the widow from a marriage consummated by his pre-deceased brother." Fifty-seven Paris theologians ruled that the pope did not have that authority, while only fifty-two ruled that he did have it.

In regard to the authority of bishops, the theologians of Paris were traditionally champions of bishops' jurisdiction and prerogatives. But in 1525, during the Parliamentary inquiry into the famous reform experiment at Meaux, the Faculty of Theology clearly attempted to set aside Bishop Guillaume Briçonnet's authority on the basis that he was permitting heretical preaching in his diocese. During the Parliamentary proceedings, the bishop's lawyer compared the theologians' attempt to usurp the rights of the bishop to a crow trying to fly like an eagle.[18] The theologians' lawyer retorted that the Faculty of Theology of Paris was the "salt of the earth" in France, that, while the theologians could err as men, God would hardly desert his people in France by allowing this light and doctrine to fall into error. He further asserted that no bishop could teach anything contrary to the determinations of the Faculty of Theology, that the Faculty did not have to justify itself to the bishop, who ought to know that the Faculty is aided by God.[19] At no other time, however, did the theologians ever claim this quasi-infallibility staked out for them by their lawyer in 1525. At the height of the Faculty's campaign against Gérard Roussel in 1533, the theologians petitioned the bishop of Paris, Jean Du Bellay, to lend his support to them since the Faculty by itself could do nothing "except give judgment on doctrines concerning the Faith and guide those who are its own members to walk rightly in faith and morals."[20]

The theologians did not hesitate to challenge the king of France himself. From 1522 to 1534, there was almost unbroken opposition of the Faculty of Theology to the king's "soft" position on innovation in church teaching. The Faculty of Theology consistently pursued men who enjoyed royal favor but whom the

Faculty considered to be heretics--Lefèvre d'Etaples, Erasmus, Louis de Berquin, Pierre Caroli, Gérard Roussel, to name only a few. In 1523, for example, several strong anti-royal statements appear in the proceedings of the Faculty. The theologians protested that the king's protection of Lefèvre d'Etaples "impeded in many ways the implementation of the declaration of truth and the extirpation of error." Shortly thereafter, the Faculty declared that the king's policy was "dangerous and pernicious" and that "the king did not understand what he was doing."[21] The Faculty directly refused to obey a royal order to leave Louis de Berquin alone, telling Berquin "The Faculty has considered the tenor of the two letters of our lord the King, and humbly thanks him for them; and it will act as it seems best, and it will give an answer to our lord the king which the Faculty hopes he will find satisfactory."[22] When the Queen Mother Louise of Savoy consulted the Faculty about the spread of Lutheranism in France, the theologians told her that "persons in high places" were responsible for this. In its actions against the group of Meaux reformers, the Faculty took advantage of the king's imprisonment in Madrid to attack those whom the king would have protected had he been free. In 1529, the theologians took a significant part in the trial of Louis de Berquin which led to his execution-- again, in the absence of the king.[23] The papal legate in Paris, Salviati, had only recently heard the king threaten to send the theologian-judges in the case to the galleys; he said that he had many complaints against "these theologians and their unjust sentences."[24] A year later, when the theologians refused to come to a speedy decision in the divorce consultation of Henry VIII, Francis I wrote that if he were ever at war with the pope he would first have to assure his defense at home against the Faculty of Theology of Paris.[25] Despite these and other threats, the Faculty of Theology was unrelenting in its pursuit of men it considered to be heretics. Thus, when the king abruptly changed his orientation after the famous *affaire des placards* in 1534, he and the Parliament of Paris began to look more favorably on the theologians whose consistent opposition to heresy was now largely vindicated. The crucial factor here, though, is that it was not to a submissive, "rubber-stamp" Faculty that they turned. Rather, it was to an independent-minded group which had maintained its institutional integrity and single-mindedness in spite of two decades of threats and ridicule. The new royal attitude towards the Faculty reached its high point in 1543 when King Francis I accepted and ordered published throughout the kingdom twenty-five Articles of Faith drawn up by the theologians of Paris. The king ordered French bishops to insure that every curé, vicar, monk, and friar receive a copy of the Articles and observe them, and to punish anyone who did not abide by them. Laymen, too, were expressly forbidden to preach openly or secretly anything contrary to the Articles under pain of imprisonment for sedition. Judges, lawyers, procurators, and other officers were ordered to enforce the Articles of Faith under pain of forfeiture of office. Finally, the king expressly ordered enforcement in the Parliaments of Paris, Toulouse, Bordeaux, Rouen, Dijon, Dauphiné, Provence, Savoy, and Piedmont.[26] Nor did the Faculty's Articles of Faith die with King Francis I. They were expressly renewed and reaffirmed by King Henry II in his Edict of Châteaubriand of June 25, 1551. Article 41 of the Edict ordered all bishops to have the Articles read in all the parishes of the kingdom and to admonish the people to observe them. Article 43 specifically forbade preachers to contradict the Faculty's Articles of Faith in any way.[27] Eleven years later, in 1562, every person connected with the Parliament of Paris, from the six presidents down to simple clerks--several hundred in all--had to swear to uphold the Articles of Faith of the Faculty of Theology of 1543. This process was followed by a solemn procession to Notre-Dame de Paris of thousands of Parisians, comprising royalty, princes, cardinals, bishops, Parliamentarians, ecclesiastics, and students. In July of that year, all the officials of the University had to take the oath to follow the 1543 articles.[28] These oaths and processions must surely be seen as a kind of show of solidarity, a massing of the forces of orthodoxy within the period immediately after the outbreak of the Wars of Religion.

The censure of books was a prerogative which the theologians of Paris claimed and exercised even before the advent of Martin Luther. This, too, often involved the Faculty in disputes with other authorities, especially in the case of humanists such as Erasmus and Lefèvre d'Etaples who enjoyed royal favor. But in the 1540's the Faculty began to issue catalogues of prohibited books. These catalogues enjoyed royal privilege and sanction. The Faculty's struggle against the famous printer Robert Estienne, culminating in his sudden flight to Geneva, is well known.[29] Such an incident illustrates why Roger Doucet judged that the Faculty of Theology of Paris assumed "the intellectual direction of the kingdom"[30] and why Elizabeth Armstrong said that a system developed which gave the Faculty the power to determine policy and the Parliament the power to carry it out.[31]

We have, therefore, surveyed several activities of the theologians of Paris: consultant in matters of Faith and morals; inquisitor; and censor. We have also looked at the theologians'

self-image and their conception of their authority vis-á-vis
other institutions of Church and State. From all this it seems
clear that the Faculty of Theology of Paris was not merely ceremonious and self-serving, not inefficient and ineffectual.
Rather, the theologians' conservatism and determination to preserve unity in faith, subsidiarity in authority, and a political
order based on morality allowed them to play a substantial role
in the political and ecclesiastical affairs of sixteenth-century
France.

James K. Farge, C.S.B.

University of St. Thomas

IX.
THE IMPACT OF THE REFORMATION ON
STUDENTS AT THE UNIVERSITY OF TÜBINGEN

Prior to May 1534, the University of Tübingen was a strong
supporter of the faith of Rome and the Bishop of Rome. Yet, ten
years later, with the addition of Erhard Schnepff to the faculty,
the school became more Lutheran than Luther. By the end of the
second decade following the introduction of the Reformation, the
theological faculty was composed of second generation Protestants, thus symbolizing the end of the Reformation and the beginning of a new era. In the intervening period, the faculty included Roman Catholics, Swiss Reformed, humanists, Lutherans, and
one man who began the period as a Roman Catholic and changed with
the trend of power. The influence of Roman Catholicism and the
Reformed tradition waned during the first decade of Protestant
political control, and their strength in the theological faculty
of the territorial university is probably indicative of their
influence throughout the duchy of Württemberg.[1]
    The students who attended the University of Tübingen during
this period found a number of changes in the transition from Roman Catholic to Protestant, with the students who studied theology encountering the greatest change. This paper will survey
briefly the statistics of student enrollment, look at changes
in curriculum and student life, consider the foundation of a new
approach to student support, and examine those students who maintained their Protestantism during the Augsburg Interim and who
subsequently joined the faculty of the university.
    The Reformation was introduced to Tübingen and the Duchy of
Württemberg when Duke Ulrich successfully recaptured his duchy
after a fifteen year exile. The Restitution of Ulrich was accomplished through political intrigue on an international scale,
under the direct leadership of Ulrich's cousin, Philip of Hesse,
and with the financial backing of Francis I of France.[2] Ulrich
lost no time in initiating changes in Württemberg. Upon the recommendation of Strasbourg reformer Martin Bucer, he called upon
Ambrosius Blarer from Constance to assume the task of overseeing
the institution of the Reformation in the southern half of Württemberg. Blarer was a Protestant of the Swiss type, though clos-
er to Bucer than Zwingli. The northern half of the duchy was
entrusted to a strong advocate of Lutheranism, Erhard Schnepff.

Ulrich apparently had some hope of uniting the two forms of Protestantism in Württemberg--a hope spurred by his dual loyalties. He had been converted to the Protestant cause by Oecolampadius and Zwingli,[3] and restored to his lands by the Lutheran Philip of Hesse.

Blarer's responsibility for the establishment of the Reformation included the reformation of the University of Tübingen, where he concentrated on the theological faculty. Blarer found great resistance within this group, not only because of his own theological position, but because one not an academician was seeking to effect a change in the academic community.[4] After an unsuccessful invitation to Melanchthon to assume the leadership of the university, Duke Ulrich brought Simon Grynaeus, the Greek scholar from Basel. Grynaeus helped Blarer prepare the first reforming ordinances of the University of Tübingen, which were promulgated in January of 1535. These ordinances mark the constitutional reformation of the university, moving from Roman Catholicism to a church-university under Protestant influence and control.[5] Ironically, given the later position of the university as a major bastion of Lutheran orthodoxy, these early stages were the work of what we now call the Reformed tradition.

Contrary to what one might expect, there was no great reduction in students matriculating at Tübingen following the institution of the Reformation; indeed, there was a rather substantial increase during the first ten years, from 1535 to 1545. From 1525 through 1534, 529 matriculated at Tübingen for an average of 52.9 per year, while the next ten years, dating from the first reforming ordinances of the university, saw 868 matriculate for an average of 86.8 per year. This amounts to an increase of 65 percent after the institution of the Reformation.[6] As to what happened to the total student population, it is very difficult to say since total enrollment figures were not maintained. There are epistolary references to numbers of students fleeing Tübingen for the security of Freiburg, along with some faculty. This was occurring as early as two months after the arrival of Reformer Ambrosius Blarer in Tübingen. Ulrich Zasius reported from Freiburg to Boniface Amerbach of Basel that on account of the "Lutheran treachery" masters and students were arriving in Freiburg, having fled Tübingen in order to avoid the introduction of such "detestable" teaching.[7] Also, preliminary studies indicate that little change in geographical origins of students took place with the coming of the Reformation. The vast majority matriculating at Tübingen both before and after 1535 were native Schwabs.

Students remaining in Tübingen after January of 1535 were

receiving a Protestant university education--a situation which
meant some changes and some difficulties at the very beginning.
The difficulties included the problem of the office of the chancellor, which was of utmost importance to the legal position of
the university and any degree granted by the university. Because
the university received its legal status through both ducal and
papal decrees, the pope's representative within the university
played a significant role in determining the status of the university. By custom dating back to the founding of Paris and
other early universities, the highest church official in the re-
gion became the papal representative. In Tübingen this was the
prior or provost of the Tübingen *Stiftskirche*. He was also the
chancellor of the university, an appointment made by the pope.[8]
The right to nominate for papal approval the chancellor of the
university (a lifetime appointment to be negated only by act of
the pope or the abdication of the office holder) was given to
the *Landesherrn* in 1492. Under this papal decree only one chancellor was named, Ambrosius Widmann in 1509-10, who remained in
the position into the years of the Reformation in Tübingen.[9]

The approval of the chancellor was required for the granting of each degree. Thus, when in 1535 Chancellor Ambrosius
Widmann fled Tübingen for the nearby bishopric of Rothenburg,
the university was confronted with the problem of what to do
about students who had completed all requirements for degrees.
The chancellor's seal and signature were necessary, and Widmann
had been careful to take the university seal with him.[10] As a
result, the granting of degrees by the University was delayed
briefly while the faculty and court searched for a solution--a
situation which apparently gave little concern to entering students, although it was a constant worry for the faculty. The
archives of the university abound with discussion of the matter,[11] and even though several attempts were made at solving the
problem, including many different offers to Widmann, no completely satisfying conclusion was made until his death, in August
of 1561. At that time, the university and the then Duke Christopher of Württemberg were able to name a new chancellor without
recourse to papal authority. In the interim during the fifty
years of Widmann's control, doubt was cast upon the validity of
all degrees from Tübingen. And this doubt was not ill-placed.
Widmann, for example, refused to grant a master of arts degree
to one Jakob Jonas because his baccalaureate degree--the pre-
requisite for the master of arts degree--was from the University
of Wittenberg, and he regarded the degrees granted there to be
invalid.[12]

To relieve the situation the faculty sought and received

advisory memoranda from Luther and Melanchthon in November of 1538. These stated that the duke as *Landesherrn* had the right to replace Widmann who had abandoned his responsibilities and refused to follow the ducal requirements for a territorial church. This argument, however, ended neither the distress of the university nor of the dukes of Württemberg. Nevertheless, with the support of the theologians at Wittenberg, the decision was made to resume the granting of degrees under the authority of Johann Scheurer, who was promoted from his position as Deacon of the Stuttgart *Stiftskirche* to fill the post left vacant by Widmann's departure. Widmann repudiated this arrangement, although in 1555 he agreed that the rector and senate of the university could assume the authority of his office, and sent along the seal. He refused, however, to give up his position as Provost and Chancellor, and signed the letter granting the use of his authority to the university with these titles.[13]

Regardless of the serious questions raised about the legality and validity of the degrees conferred by the university, students continued to come to Tübingen in increasing rather than decreasing numbers. The changes in the university were obvious to all observers. The mass was abolished by March of 1535, and curricular changes were instituted at once.[14] For the students in the liberal arts curriculum the primary changes were twofold. First of all, the faculty had to be at least neutral on religious issues, if not of the Protestant party. Secondly, the Renaissance emphasis on classical languages was re-introduced, with great efforts being expended on Greek and Hebrew, languages of direct use in biblical studies.[15]

The most significant curricular changes confronted by students were to be found in the theological curriculum, as would be expected. Ordination was no longer required for recipients of theological degrees. The traditional textbook, the *Sentences* of Peter Lombard, was thrown out in favor of studies rooted in biblical exegesis. The final goal was to base the study of the Bible on the Hebrew and Greek texts.[16] Philip Melanchthon played a part in this reformation of the curriculum. Although he could not return to his alma mater as a teacher, he did spend a few days as a consultant on university matters for Duke Ulrich in the fall of 1536.[17] He gave his approval for the direction of the changes underway, and encouraged the move towards the systematic study of biblical theology. Melanchthon was also instrumental in aiding the Lutheran faction in Württemberg in overcoming the influence of the Reformed theologians.[18]

The rights and privileges of the students and faculty were reaffirmed by Duke Ulrich, although some changes in administrative structure and regulations were made very early in his reign. The traditional division of the Bursa between the *via antiqua* and *via moderna* was finally eliminated, and traditional concerns about the moral depravity of students were voiced, accompanied by threats of dire consequences in this world and the next. Other than a public announcement of intentions to purify the lives of the Tübingen students, however, there appears to have been little qualitative change in living conditions for most of them.[19]

The most profound change in the university for students came not so much in terms of overall university reformation, but in the opportunities which were open to a portion of the students through the establishment of the Tübingen *Stift*, an endowed scholarship program which provided financial support for students and eventually included regular housing arrangements. This later development saw the *Stift* become something of a communal organization for some of the students attending the university. Although not at first limited to theologians, the Tübingen *Stift* eventually became similar to what is known today as a theological seminary, providing education to those going into church vocations. In this form the Tübingen *Stift* continues to the present, and is housed in the same building which it has occupied since 1547.[20]

The basic idea of the *Stift*, a somewhat new approach to the financial support of students in early modern Germany, apparently originated out of two sources. First of all, there was a similar movement about the same time at the University of Marburg, the Protestant university founded by Duke Ulrich's cousin and benefactor, Philip of Hesse.[21] Sceondly, Martin Bucer and Jacob Sturm were seeking the support of the Strassburg city council for a foundation with essentially the same purpose, goals, and structure as that which developed in Tübingen.[22] The essential concept involved provision by the state for endowments and subsidies for the support of a certain number of students at the university. One of the new features was the attempt to combine funds from several sources. First of all, some church lands that were being expropriated by the state, particulatly monastic lands, were given to the *Stift* as endowments. Also, parishes in Württemberg were to provide over the years some small amount of support based on a variety of formulae, including the ability of the parish to pay and the number of students from the parish in the university or the number seeking the services of the *Stift*.[23]

Initially, the *Stift* was open to all students who were in need and were from the duchy of Württemberg. But there were conditions attached to receiving aid from the *Stift*. Students who received a degree from the University of Tübingen through the assistance of the *Stift* were required to spend a number of years in service to the Duchy of Württemberg with the number apparently dependent upon the level of support received. Once the *Stift* became exclusively the domain of theological students, service to the duchy was seen in the three areas of parish work: teaching, and administrative work for either the church or state. This became a regular source of educated personnel for positions in the duchy, and also provided some amount of control by the government over the education of its bureaucrats.[24]

The *Stift* was first mentioned in 1536 in a document issued by Duke Ulrich in which he reaffirmed the traditional privileges of the university.[25] The first *Stipendiaten* received support in early 1537, and they were housed in the Bursa Moderna. These students received a total of twenty-five florins which, if very carefully managed, would have meant that their basic living costs (except for bread and wine) would be provided for. University fees were waived. However, at first the funds were delivered directly to the individual students who were then to disperse them as needed.[26] It was not long before the disadvantages of this system were seen and corrected!

Initially, the activities and studies of the *Stipendiaten* were supervised by masters serving as Magister Domus, Beadle, and similar roles. However, by 1541 the Swiss theologian and professor of Bible, Paul Phrygio, was made superintendent of the *Stift*, with responsibilities over all aspects of life of the *Stipendiaten* in Tübingen.[27] After ten years of existence, the *Stift* was moved to the former quarters of the Augustinian chapter in Tübingen--a massive building rising up from the bank of the Neckar. It remains in use to the present as the home of the *Stift*. When first taken over by the *Stift*, there was room for forty students at a time in the former monastery. By the end of the first decade of the *Stift*, 120 men had been *Stipendiaten*, including some who will be discussed later as successors to the first generation reformers.[28]

In the early years of the Reformation in Tübingen, the *Stift*, in flux, was seeking its way and identity. By the middle of the century very few other than theology students were admitted to the *Stift*; and, by the end of the sixteenth century, it was exclusively for theologians. For students, the *Stift* provided a community within a larger community, a place where common interests and concerns could be shared with other students, a place where influence could be gained and used both for the present and for the future. The shape and nature of the Lutheran Church in Württemberg was largely determined by men who received their university education, including their liberal arts education, through the Tübingen *Stift*. Further, during the crisis that struck with the imposition of the Augsburg Interim, the *Stift* provided a means of quiet resistance and subversion on the part of the Lutherans. With the Peace of Augsburg, the *Stift* became one of the great centers of moderate Lutheran Orthodoxy.[29]

At the same time that the *Stift* was taking shape, a change in administrative procedures was quietly insuring the longevity and successful takeover by the Lutherans. In 1538 the position of Deacon of the Theological Faculty was created, and among other duties the Deacon was to have general oversight of the "orthodoxy" of the teaching and opinions of students and faculty, in both public and private. Students, according to the 1538 statutes, were to abjure all forms of heresy, keeping themselves to the "true Christian religion" alone. Beyond this, as indicated above, there were few changes from regulations in force prior to the introduction of the Reformation.[30]

The university continued to prosper under the Protestants, although the last of the Swiss theologians was lost to the theological faculty in 1543, when Paul Phrygio succumbed--possibly to the plague.[31] The next several years saw an intensifying of the position of the Lutherans in Tübingen. Erhard Schnepff, noted as a "strenge Lutheraner" by friend and foe alike, replaced Phrygio and saw to it that the university was loyal to Wittenberg in as many aspects as possible.[32] Students continued to come, in increased numbers. However, with the Schmalkaldic wars, the students and faculty of the University of Tübingen found the situation changed radically. Schnepff was forced to flee the city, and the city and the university were saved from being plundered by the Spanish troops of Charles V only by a direct order from the Emperor himself.[33]

With Schnepff gone, the one remaining faculty member in theology was Balthasar Käuffelin, a murky figure who had been a Roman Catholic priest, and had simply swayed with the winds of power. Although he was a master at "going along," he had never been trusted by the Protestants.[34] Käuffelin now took an active role in returning Tübingen to Rome. His efforts, however, were as short lived as the Interim--perhaps of even briefer duration. Although Schnepff had been forced to leave Tübingen, other men of equally strong Lutheran convictions were in residence. Some of these were banished Lutheran pastors who had come to Tübingen as a safe and profitable haven in which to wait out the storm of the Interim, perhaps with hopes of soon returning to their former parishes. Among these were Jacob Andreä, who had been a deacon at Stuttgart and would in later years be chancellor of the University of Tübingen and the pre-eminent leader of moderate Lutheran Orthodoxy; Jacob Heerbrand, who, having used his "enforced vacation" as an opportunity to study Hebrew in Tübingen, would soon join the theological faculty of the university as a professor of Hebrew; Sebastian Rockeln, former deacon in Goppingen, who also took advantage of the opportunity for further study.[35]

When Käuffelin reinstituted the Mass in the chancel of the *Stiftskirche*, students and some of the younger faculty of the university continued Protestant preaching services in the nave of the church. Conflict between the two groups was frequent and regular, until an agreement in September of 1551 was reached which allowed the two forms of worship to exist side by side. In addition, because the Protestant preacher in the *Stiftskirche* was not as strong as the Provost of Tübingen desired, Jacob Andreä, once again a student in the university, was given permission to preach in the nearby St. Jakobskirche, much to the chagrin and dismay of the Roman Catholics. Andreä preached regularly to overflow crowds, and drew complaints from the Catholics that the Interim was not being properly observed in Tübingen.[36]

Duke Ulrich's policy was to observe the letter of the law of the Interim whenever--but only whenever--it was absolutely necessary. Through a series of intricate bureaucratic procedures, he effectively stifled any major triumphs for the Interim in the short run. When a suit was being filed against him by Archduke Ferdinand, Ulrich's death terminated the legal procedures and the duchy was passed on to his bright and capable son, Christopher.[37]

Throughout this period the university remained open and Protestant theological education continued underground. This was accomplished largely by the use of students as unofficial teachers. Martin Frecht, the former pastor at Ulm, was brought to Tübingen ostensibly as a student, but actually as a teacher, He was made the Magister Domus of the *Stift*, and he lectured on biblical works. He could not be openly appointed to the faculty for fear of offending Emperor Charles V, who had imprisoned Frecht for his Protestant beliefs and activities as the reformer of Ulm.[38]

A similar though more straightforward course was followed by Jacob Beurlin. Pastor to the congregation of the village of Derendingen, just outside of Tübingen, he also continued his studies in the university according to the wishes of Duke Christopher. On April 22, 1551, he received the Doctor of Theology degree from Tübingen and soon thereafter was named to be professor of theology along with Käuffelin and the unofficial professor, Martin Frecht.[39] Beurlin represented a new generation of Protestant leadership. He had matriculated at Tübingen in November of 1533, just a few months prior to the arrival of the Reformation, and was only 14 years old when Duke Ulrich returned to Württemberg. He had had a difficult time accepting the new religion, especially since his parents very much opposed it. Nevertheless, he remained in Tübingen to become the first graduate of Protestant Tübingen to return to his alma mater as a professor of theology.[40].

As soon as it was obvious after the signing of the treaty of Passau and the Peace of Augsburg that the period of the Interim was over, Duke Christopher moved quickly to eradicate Roman Catholicism from his duchy. In Tübingen, Käuffelin was retired. This vacancy was filled, on recommendation of the theological faculty,[41] by Dietrich (Theoderich) Schnepff, son of the former theology professor Erhard Schnepff. Like Beurlin, Dietrich was a student of Protestant Tübingen, having matriculated in 1539.[42] He was joined in his university appointment by Jacob Heerbrand who came as a replacement for the late Martin Frecht.[43] Heerbrand had studied in Wittenberg under Luther and Melanchthon, and received his Doctor of Theology degree from Tübingen sometime around 1550 after having matriculated in 1543.[44] Together, Beurlin, Heerbrand, Schnepff, and Andreä represented a theological faculty which was totally and completely composed of second generation Protestants, all former students at Tübingen.

The Protestant students at the University of Tübingen helped save the Protestant character of the institution during the Interim. They were rewarded with positions of responsibility once the struggles of the early 1550's were over. Thus the University of Tübingen during the Reformation discovered that a university can survive a period of profound political and intellectual and economic unrest, and survive with integrity. And it was the students who attended Tübingen during this period who returned to Tübingen some of the grandeur which had been lost after the early decades of Gabriel Biel and, briefly, Johannes Reuchlin. The decades on either side of the introduction of the Reformation were periods of pronounced mediocrity in the university. With the Augsburg Peace, Tübingen began to establish a reputation for substantial scholarship and theological leadership.

Richard L. Harrison

Eureka College

X.
THE THEOLOGY OF EXILE:
FAITH AND THE FATE OF THE REFUGEE

In order to understand the religious experience of exiles
and the theological reflection of this experience on the Christian church, it would to be sure be proper to begin with a description of banishment or flight in its political, sociological, psychological, and domestic aspects.[1] Space does not permit me to do this. Instead two quotations from outside the ecclesiastical sphere will at least indicate the gravity of the
problem. The Roman poet Ovid, banished to the Black Sea by Cae-
sar Augustus in the year 8 A.D., lamented: "Exile is death."[2]
The French novelist Victor Hugo was compelled by Emperor Napo-
leon III to escape to the English Channel island of Guernsey
(1851-70). There he wrote over his door: "Exile is life."
The first could not bear the separation from interchange with
the cultured; the other perceived his situation as the realiza-
tion of freedom for opposition. But common to both is the orientation to things of the spirit, which give life its meaning.
Little wonder that in the domain of the Bible banishment is much
more than a change of residence: it always has to do with God's
guidance and will.
God's revelation in the Old Testament appears in two streams
of tradition which often stand in opposition to one another in
human history: (1) legislation and priesthood build and preserve law and homeland; (2) the exodus motif and the preaching
of the prophets revitalize society and the state. Later, in the
New Testament, the discipleship of Jesus and the message of the
kingdom of God give a radical significance to the essentially
transient nature of the Christian's sojourn in this world: he
is in a state of permanent exile. The persecution of the early
church allowed this to be concretely experienced. But with Ori-
gen and Augustine, the Christian estrangement developed a com-
prehensive cultural creativity.
A few words on Augustine are in order. He was a loyal citizen of the Roman empire. The decline of the empire and the
conquest of Rome by Alaric in 410 affected him so deeply that
until his death he was agitated by convulsions of grief. Yet
much as the Christians were drawn into the catastrophe, Augustine taught them not to set their hearts on the *civitas terrena*,

but to contritely accept the breakdown as a victory of Christ.

> The *civitas caelestis*, the citizenry of heaven, can
> not have communion in religion with the earthly, but
> must in this respect go its own way. At the hands of
> those antagonistic thinkers to whom they prove them-
> selves an annoyance, the heavenly citizenry suffer
> wrath, enmity and the assault of persecution. . . .
> This heavenly citizenry, as long as it is still on
> the earth, calls its citizens out of every people and
> gathers its pilgrim company from among all languages,
> untroubled by all differences in customs, laws and
> institutions which serve the establishment or mainte-
> nance of earthly peace. . . . This earthly peace is
> brought into the service of the heavenly. . . .[3]

Thus the catholicity of Christians not bound to an earthly home
promotes at the same time a humanistic community on earth which
overcomes cultural particularism.

Augustine had a disciple, a Spanish secretary and presbyter
by the name of Orosius,[4] who narrowly escaped the Vandals. As a
supplement to the *De civitate*, Augustine allowed him to write a
book about tragic moments in world history--hardly a work, by
the way, of a critical spirit. But Orosius hit upon the precise
situation in the experience of the Christians of his generation
when he wrote: "Everywhere is my homeland, everywhere law pre-
vails, everywhere I find my pattern of worship." That was the
dictum of a good citizen of the Empire and an expression of admiration for the *pax Romana*. Now in a time when within the empire men fled from one land to another, it found that Christians
were indeed homeless but nevertheless could find their home anywhere. Little remained of Ovid's nostalgia for home. Exile lost
its terror. An unknown Christian wrote: "Exile is in exile."
It was the consciousness of the *civitas Dei* that brought this
about.

Throughout the entire history of the church up to this day,
refugee and minority congregations often reflect in an exemplary
manner the inner Christian dynamic between renunciation of the
world and the will to shape it. Meanwhile the individual refugee often interprets his homelessness as a manifest union with
the rejected Jesus. These elements, which were manifest in the
period of the early church, became important again in the Reformation era.

Among the Reformers the activity of Heinrich Bullinger, the
successor of Zwingli in Zürich, combined both tendencies in ex-

emplary fashion. Although he was himself the model of a bourgeois conservative churchman,[5] he developed into an organizer of
large scale refugee aid for the exiled of Locarno and England, a
spiritual advisor to unnumbered oppressed visitors and corre-
spondents throughout Europe, and a theological consultant who
trained the persecuted and exiled to understand and accept their
place in God's design for salvation in history and in church
history. Bullinger's letter to the Hungarians under Mohammedan
rule (1551)[6] reads here and there like an exhortation to Christians in Eastern Europe under non-Christian governments today.
Bullinger's book on the history of the persecution of Christians
brings his reader to a conscious identification with the persecuted in the early church and in the Middle Ages.[7] The same is
true of the widely read *Acts and Monuments* of the refugee John
Foxe. The *Book of Martyrs*, reissued innumerable times since
1563, gave birth in all denominations in the English speaking
world to the conception of the Reformation as a movement of martyrs.[8] At the same time it strengthened the inner bonds between
Anglican traditionalism and the catholicity of the early church.
It never became the justification for sectarianism, as did the
comparable *Unparteiische Kirchen und Ketzerhistorie* by the Pietist Gottfried Arnold (1699). Especially noteworthy for the
understanding of the refugees as individuals are the letters and
songs of the hunted Anabaptists. As early as 1527 at Zürich,
Felix Manz compares his own road to death with the life history
of Jesus in his poem *Bei Christo will ich bleiben*.[9]

Luther's Reformation strove for the "righteousness, which
is valid before God." The monk and professor preserved for the
religious life the separation from the world which made it possible for a Christian to criticize from within in a conserva-
tively conceived society. Melanchthon's apology for Roman law
would reinforce this tendency for centuries in Lutheran state
churches. The Lutheran doctrine of the two kingdoms did not attempt to divide Church and State but to discriminate between the
spiritual and the secular. The secular remained the sphere of
law and reason.[10] Thus the two kingdom doctrine could be used
to justify statism. Luther and Melanchthon did advocate the execution of Anabaptists (and the expulsion of the Jews) yet not
as heretics, but rather as disturbers of the political order.
The individual was meant to accept the power of the state.

The Reformation in South Germany and Switzerland strove for
the Christian renewal of town and village communities and thereby appeared at first sight to be even more conservative in motivation. Nevertheless the prophetic preaching of Zwingli, Bucer,
Oecolampadius, Blaurer, and Calvin contains pneumatological and

eschatological elements which fundamentally transcend the earthly
and religious life and point to the kingdom of God.

In the free cities of the Empire[11] a humanistic individual-
ism influenced the educated among the upper classes. But the
citizenry, along with the increasingly self conscious peasantry
in the villages, lived and thought with a strengthened sense of
Christian community. They wished to deliver the political, judicial, and economic orders from an archaic ecclesiastical tute-
lage and entrust themselves to a direct guidance of the Holy
Spirit. The communes of the *Devotio moderna* and the Brotherhood
of the Common Life were expressions of this general trend. There
were further evidences of this pneumatological emphasis in South
German and Swiss Reformation theology in the stress on the fundamental unity of the civic and the Christian communities; in
the principle of the democratic brotherhood; in the Zwinglian
and Bucerian doctrines of the Lord's Supper which start from the
celebration by the congregation, not from the remission of sins
for individuals.

The conservative stability of this way of thinking was
hardly compatible with the needs of uprooted exiles. In fact
the history of the reception of refugees was just as sad in the
sixteenth century as in the twentieth. The needs of the community were placed before those of the individual and the exiles.
Furthermore, with the military and political suppression of the
towns by Charles V (1545) and the consequent check upon the
South German-Swiss Reformation tradition, success fell to the
patriarchal-absolutist order rather than to the elements of
brotherhood. Both Lutheranism and Calvinsim contributed to the
same end by their identification of paternal authority (expressed
in the fifth commandment) with the Sovereign and the State.

In the Anabaptist movement, kindled by Zwingli's preaching
and then developing independently, the biographies of innumerable
preachers and brethren fully demonstrate once again the homelessness and liberty of the Christian. This liberty is carried even
to anarchism. The refusal of the Anabaptists to perform military
service or to take up a civic office or even to take oaths,
placed them even while they were still in their homes in the position of the homeless. The magistrates in villages and towns
were thrown into the greatest perplexity[12] since, apart from the
scribes in the larger cities, there were no paid officials in
towns and villages. It was necessary in a community that every
healthy man twenty years old and over should perform some civil
service several hours almost daily as official, counsellor, administrator of justice, guildsman, guard, committee member, con-
troller of fire, forest, field, food, or merchandise, etc. The

Anabaptists by refusing these duties clearly appeared as anti-
social.

The origins of South German spiritualism lay also in human-
ism--a cosmopolitan humanism, which was oriented to the individual. The experience of many representatives of Italian Evan-
gelism and the short duration of the Italian refugee congregations were indicative of a separate rather than a communal religious development. Their sufferings embodied the problems which
came with uprooting, with alienation. As in our time, so in the
sixteenth century exile hid in itself the danger of psychological and spiritual tension, pretentious claims, frustrated quar-
relsomeness, and general demoralization. Bullinger's difficulties with the exiles from Italy and Tessin, the difficulties of
Calvin and Knox with the refugee congregation in Frankfurt am
Main, the family calamities among the Pilgrim fathers offer vivid examples of the trauma shared by all those who were persecuted for the sake of their faith.[13]

John Calvin, himself a refugee, evolved a theology in Geneva for a prohibited and rejected minority in France--a theology
which was adaptable to other refugee communities as well. The
crucial elements of his thought--election, pneumatology, sanctification, and church discipline--were adapted to the pragmatic
situation of the exile. He trained congregations for self suf-
ficiency and constructive social activity. Sanctification
gained a political dimension as progress. Influenced by his own
experience, Calvin required of the Nicodemites the sacrifice of
emigration when necessary.[14] Admittedly, as a humanist scholar,
he himself had a cosmopolitan outlook. But in the crises which
occurred in the refugee congregations of various languages in
Geneva, he was always mindful of the human and material consequences of migration for the laity which quite often involved
renunciation of any hope of reunion with marriage partners, parents, or family. Even more importantly, however, the *Institutio
Religionis Christianae* itself is a cosmopolitan document. Although relating to many contemporary situations and personali-
ties, it is in no way committed to any one nation or its history.
Luther's writings are those of a Wittenberg professor, Zwingli's
and Bucer's those of preachers in imperial cities. But the
works of Calvin could have been written anywhere.

The refugee John à Lasco gave the refugee congregations in
Frankfurt am Main, London, and Emden corporate constitutions as
a defense against internal and external menace. These constitutions have remained until the present day as models for the
worldwide Reformed Church. Among his followers were the Flemish
refugees in the northern Low Countries, who because of their

faith and to preserve their own lives became the instigators of
the war of liberation against Spain. Their homelessmess was
overcome in the founding of new homes. Their progressive orientation soon gave way to conservatism.

These reformed Forms of Discipline trained members of the
refugee congregations to keep together, to be disciplined in
their conduct, and to overcome homesickness and hyper-individu-
alism. The refugee who was excluded from political rights and
obligations in his new place of residence turned his energies to
the religious congregation. In his isolation his life was hence
given a new significance. Now, in his view, the ecclesiastical
order was of higher importance than the political. With the
passing of time refugees frequently managed to improve their
economic status and to become politically acceptable. Then their
offspring struck roots in the new environment and postulated
participation on the "lower" level too--i.e., in civic affairs.[15]
The Reformed·and Mennonite congregations everywhere became fore-
runners of democracy.

The precedent repeated itself on a larger scale with the
Pilgrim Fathers, who built strictly ordered states in the New
World, and whose movement culminated in the North American Declaration of Independence and The Bill of Rights. The Pilgrim
fathers and their descendants offer many examples of the way in
which the trauma of an outlawed and defenseless refugee could
suddenly transform itself into rigid social structures. The sacrifice which the fathers had made for the Word of God obliged
their grandchildren to erect a political structure in accordance
with God's Word.[16] "The historical significance of the Pilgrim
fathers (and the Puritan founders of states in the New World)
rests in their valid and lasting articulation of the Christian
understanding of democracy as the divinely sanctioned form of
government for the North American spirit."[17]

The English refugees fleeing from the Catholic Mary Tudor
were received by Bullinger in Zürich, where the church order was
conservative. But upon their return to England the example of
Zürich's Puritanism gave impetus to the progressive ferment within and outside the established Anglican church. Politically,
the movement led to the English Revolution and thereby to the
Empire. In the theological course of Puritanism[18] from the
vestments controversy to the Westminster Confession and beyond,
the same phenomenon revealed itself. The established Zwinglian
ideal of a more thorough purification of the church (over against
Lutheranism) consolidated itself in Bullinger's Zürich and was
introduced into the Anglican system by the returning English
refugees, where it acquired a long-lasting religious and politi-

cal potency.[19]

This theological trend was strengthened from the beginning by the prevalent apocalyptic ideas, which Bullinger himself did not shun--indeed he became their spokesman. Those who went from England to Zürich were greatly affected by Bullinger's long series of one hundred and one sermons on Revelation. The millenarian emphasis in English Puritanism developed after the Zürich stay. Bullinger's sermons were dedicated to the English exiles and were used extensively in Puritan apocalyptic writing (e.g., by Bartholomew Traheron), and were translated into English in 1561, a second edition appearing in 1573.[20] There is almost no apocalyptic writing among English Protestants prior to their exile under Mary from 1554-58.[21]

Puritan views on church polity were also developed in exile, as George Yule has written: "I am almost certain that Thomas Cartwright the Elizabethan Puritan, and Andrew Melville the Scots Presbyterian worked out their Presbyterian views of church government, which were very doctrinaire, while they were refugees in Geneva."[22] In the same climate Bishop John Ponet while a refugee in Strasbourg in 1556 wrote *A Short Treatise of Political Power*.[23] He was a Zwinglian. He contested absolute monarchy, advocated the legislative competency of Parliament, and asserted not only the right but the obligation to punish a tyrannical prince by death. He was an authentic forerunner of democracy. Four years later there appeared in Geneva the well known revolutionary pamphlets of Goodman and Knox[24]--likewise written with the recklessness of the banished, who had nothing more to lose.

The Huguenots, who with their privileges had been looked upon since Henry IV as obstacles to absolutism, became for their part pioneers abroad of new economic and social forms. In Prussia, where they were taken under the protection of the Elector as civil servants or military officers, they became the champions of the constitutional state in the age of enlightenment and absolutism. The refugee Theodore Beza[25] became the leading theorist of the right to resist. In the countries to which they immigrated they unconsciously converted in a few generations from opponents of absolutism to industrious builders of a patriarchal system in government, economy, and society. The process was made easier because almost everywhere they were allowed to govern their churches independently. The Huguenots[26] have even to the present day preserved in France their spirit of enterprise in ecclesiastical affairs.

Thus Christian refugees by reason of their faith are both extremely progressive and extremely conservative. Every flight is a political criticism, and simultaneously contains indeed an anarchistic element. It weakens the society which one abandons or by which one is exiled. That is particularly true of refugees who in obedience to God's Word leave an order created by men. In the endeavors which regularly follow to organize a Christian community life, the ever new path from Exodus to Sinai manifests itself. Together and in opposition to one another, the law and the preaching of the prophets, Moses and Elijah, witness to the coming King and his kingdom.

The presence of refugees through the centuries has given occasion for a living sympathy of Christians for other Christians--for Christians all over the world, for brothers in the faith in other lands. First with the advent of the closed territorial states of the eighteenth century and then of the national states of the nineteenth, these bonds were broken up. Today we probably live in the age of the most numerous and most thorough persecutions of Christians in all of Church history. The enemy has learned to halt emigration. But in Africa and Asia many flee and seek new homes, new freedom for faith and service. Who among us is mindful of this and takes it to heart? In the World Council of Churches in Geneva a great deal is known about this, but there one has good grounds not to speak too loudly. Thereby the church allows brotherly love to grow weak and gives up the pattern of the self-denying, liberated Christian life.

The young generation, however, is becoming alert. They surmise what an aid and an enrichment it would be not only for the Church but for the nations as well if it were again true as the *Letter to Diognetes* from the third century asserted with regard to Christians: "They dwell each in his own homeland, but as bystanders. They take part in the political life as citizens, and yet stand apart as aliens. Every foreign land is to them a homeland, and every homeland is alien to them."[27]

Gottfried W. Locher

University of Bern, Switzerland

XI.
THE MARIAN EXILES AND THE ENGLISH PROTESTANT TRADITION

The English Reformation is of a different sort than the
Continental Reformation. The Henrican reforms certainly paved
the way for further reforms and Lollardy had left an indelible
mark on the common people of sixteenth-century England. The
choice of people to whom Henry had bequeathed the education of
the long-awaited male heir, Edward, clearly showed Henry's decided interest in reforming the Church of England. The turn of
events, however, went even further than Henry would have allowed.[1]

At the coronation of the nine-year-old Edward, he was presented with the swords of England, France, and Ireland. But
there was to be a fourth: the Sword of the Spirit, the Bible,
was to be the primary sword which would depict the direction the
sovereign state would proceed during the critical years of
1547-53. Under Edward VI, the Reformation would begin to take a
more definite Protestant shape. Archbishop Thomas Cranmer set
the stage for a biblically illiterate clergy by printing for
them twelve practical homilies and Erasmus' *Paraphrases* of the
Bible.[2] In time, Cranmer would bring distinguished theologians
from the Continent to bolster the cause of reform through the
medium of Christian humanism and learning. Martin Bucer and
Paul Fagius were appointed to teach at Cambridge, and Bernardo
Ochino and Peter Martyr Vermigli were to hold the fort at Oxford.
And, of course, there would be the Edwardian Prayerbook which
appeared in 1552 and which was imposed by the king without rati-
fication by Parliament.

The "Church of the Strangers," an ethnically pluralistic
ecclesia in London, was already implementing strong reformed
church polity. It, too, paved the way for a new direction taken
by the church in Edward's brief reign.

But the young king died on July 6, 1553. Mary Tudor had
confessed upon her accession that she would return England to
the religion of her childhood. In September, 1553, Cranmer,
Nicholas Ridley, Miles Coverdale, Hugh Latimer and others were
deposed and some of them imprisoned. The "Church of the Strangers," under the leadership of John A'Lasco, was disbanded on the
17th of September and its parishioners embarked for Denmark.
Peter Martyr obtained a safe-conduct passage and returned to

Strasbourg. In October Mary became queen, and the Mass was re-
established two months later. Her announced marrigae to Philip
II of Spain served only to make the situation more ominous for
those who had basked in the light of Edwardian reforms. From
prison Cranmer exhorted those English people pricked in conscience over the startling reentrenchment to look abroad for a
place to retire where God could be purely served.[3]

This advice was heeded. Many of the greater minds fled
with Peter Martyr to Strasbourg. Others were attracted to Zurich
and the reputation of Heinrich Bullinger. The Duke and Duchess
of Suffolk found refuge at Emden. William Whittingham, William
Williams, and Thomas Wood went to Frankfort, arriving on June 2,
1554, with about two hundred companions. An English church was
thus founded at Frankfort which was later to be a focus of controversy, giving impetus to the flight to Calvin's Geneva of a
more radical group.[4] We shall have occasion to return to this
group below.

A question lurks in the mind of the modern observer. What
prompted and motivated this mass exodus into exile? The answer
seems ready at hand. Christian humanism had created a new cultural force in English society. The concern for excellence in
scholarship, clarity in communication, dependence upon original
sources, and the moral integrity of the human family--all bequeathed by Christian humanism--constituted a framework within
which certain epistemological dynamics were nourished. Preachers
and Christian theologians attracted to humanist circles shared
a common concern for a method as well as a content, and indeed
the latter became important because of the inter-workings in the
methodology itself. Moreover, for these Christian humanists,
the content became as much the focus as the method. The Bible
thus became the main source of values for Christian humanists,
for it provided a philosophy of life, related to antiquity,
which could bring about a true renewal of civilization.

Erasmus was typical in this respect and his pilgrimage in
England left its mark. But the discussions at the White Horse
Inn in Cambridge during the 1520's were not so much about the
"new learning" as about the "new ideas." It was Luther's Reformation and Lutheran theological ideas which were the exciting
issues. While the political and magisterial reforms were taking
place in the reign of Henry VIII, there was an ideological reform already afoot whose content was the Hebrew-Christian scriptures combined with the methods embraced by humanism and the hermeneutic and theological dynamic that characterized Luther's
sola gratia, sola fidei, and *sola scriptura.*

The roots of restitution, renewal, and dissent in sixteenth-

century England touch the ground of many different movements
and *geistes*. The sectarian movements, such as the Wycliffites,
the Lollards or Bible-pushers, provided the accessibility of
Bibles and the drive to be biblical in reform; the humanists,
Thomas More, John Colet, and especially Erasmus, provided the
broad framework in which the question of reform and renewal became relevant; and, preachers like William Tyndale, John Frith,
and Hugh Latimer provided what Karl Barth called "the language
event" by their sermons, their translations of the Bible into
the vernacular, pamphlets. Combined with the social and political turmoil of the events of 1553 and Mary Tudor's policies of a
return to a medieval synthesis of Roman and royal conservatism,
these considerations were more than enough motivation to send
English people across oceans into exile. It was more than a
matter of conscience; for many, it was a matter of survival.

The accuracy of our portrait can be seen in a curious little document, *The Humble and Unfained Confession of the Belief
of Certain Poor Banished Men*, written by a certain Nicholas Dor-
caster, believed to be John Ponet, in May of 1554. This document appeared just after Sir Thomas Wyatt failed in his revolt
and Mary's second Parliament consented to the Spanish marriage.
The author mentions that he and fellow ministers are exiled because of their concern for following the inspired Word of God;
they neither desire to go beyond it nor to do things unautho-
rized by it. The ministers show a concern for the church, uti-
lizing the Augustinian doctrine of the two manifestations of the
church--the invisible universal church, and the visible particular church. The visible church is known by three marks: the
preaching of sound doctrine, the administration of the biblical
sacraments, and ecclesiastical discipline. The trouble with the
church, they contended, was that there was little emphasis on
"good and upright discipline." A tree is known by its fruit
just as the sun is reflected in its beams.[5]

What is needed is a return to the New Testament doctrine
and practice. Paul's enjoinders in *I Timothy* and *Titus* for ministers and their functions should be implemented. The true,
biblical understanding of a sacrament needs restoration; after
all, there are many "outward visible signs in the Bible" which
God uses for his purposes. A sacrament is a sign representing a
holy thing, a seal of God's righteousness. Thus, the partaking
of the outward, visible sign is also the partaking of the reality promised in the sign, the process being certified by the
Holy Ghost.[6] In the sacrament of the Lord's Supper, we receive
the body and blood of the Lord in the visible signs of bread and
wine. That this is no ordinary human operation is clearly evi-

denced by the necessity of faith on the part of the participant and the working of the Holy Spirit. Only within the eyes of faith is this mystery unfolded. The authority for this practice is the New Testament (*I Cor.* 11); no doctrine of transubstantiation is authorized by Paul in this passage, and the language of the people is definitely the language priests ought to use in the service. We need no "printed wafers and such stuff" but "good natural bread." Both kinds are to be given the congregation and there is no mandate to kneel before the elements as if they themselves were something transcendent.[7] The author suggested that there is no need to make an oblation of the sacrament for departed ones or diseases. Anything that smacks of the Roman Mass is a "blind and willfull abusing of the Sacrament."[8]

The three formative factors that make up the restitutionist and dissenting motifs in the English Protestant tradition are quite apparent in this little confessional document. First, there is the Christian humanist emphasis on the necessity of ancient sources and models, coupled with the necessity for renewal and moral integrity. Second, there is the Lutheran notion of *sola scriptura* (and to a certain extent *sola gratia* and *sola fidei*). And, third, there is the overwhelming mandate to restore and renew the biblical pattern. Taken together, they give a very clear picture of a typical early English reformed position: Erasmian and humanist, Protestant and very anti-Roman, biblical and restitutionist.

Our study will be given more substantive direction as we return to the English exiles who settled in Frankfort in 1554, many of whom became the most boisterous voices in exile while in Calvin's Geneva from 1555 to 1560. The story of the Frankfort exilic church has been told in *A Brief Discourse of the Troubles at Frankfort, 1554-1558 A.D.*, attributed to William Whittingham.[9] Without rehearsing the entire scene here, it should be pointed out nevertheless that among the Frankfort exiles there was an incipient radical party under the staunch leadership of John Knox. The split was inevitable, but the focal issue was the Edwardian Prayerbook. The sympathizers of the English Prayerbook were led by John Cox. Knox and the more radical exiles wanted to take the Reformation further than the Prayerbook would allow. A controversy erupted and the Knox group was eventually outvoted and disgraced into leaving. During the controversy, Knox and others had corresponded with Calvin who then offered them the opportunity of setting up an English church in Geneva where they could implement their views on worship, church order, and discipline.[10] As early as June 10, 1555, Calvin appeared before the Council of Geneva to indicate "that certain Englishmen are desirous to repair hither for the sake of the Word of God," and to request that the council would be pleased to grant them a church in which they might preach and minister the sacraments.[11] The council agreed that steps should be taken to provide a proper place for the English, and that conference should be had with Calvin on the subject. Several places were suggested, but nothing final was decided until the arrival of the exiles on October 13. On October 24, Calvin again appeared to remind the council of its former resolution. Three syndics were appointed to examine the situation and recommend a suitable place. On November 14, the council, having heard the report of the syndics, resolved to grant to the English, as well as to the Italians, the use of the church of *Marie la Nove*.[12] They were to meet in the church, also known as the *Auditoire* because Calvin lectured there, and on November 25 Calvin again appeared before the council to work out the details. He recommended that the Italians should hold services on Thursdays, Fridays, and Saturdays, and that they should preach on Sundays at their accustomed hour; the services of the English should be on Mondays, Tuesdays, and Wednesdays, and they should preach at nine o'clock, the minister being chosen by the English after he had been presented for examination and reception to the council. The council agreed, and on Friday, November 29, it was reported that Anthony Gilby and Christopher Goodman were received as ministers of the Word of God for the English inhabitants of Geneva.[13]

John Knox no doubt was the most interesting personality among the exiles. He had come to Geneva to see the pure reformed faith in a realized situation, and to revive and refresh his wearied spirit by communion with like-minded Christian brethren so that "he and his associates might be nerved by what they witnessed for further achievements in the serivce of their common Lord and the good of their native land."[14] It was to Geneva, then, that these exiles brought their own theological ideas to be tried and tested by the teachings of Calvin--teachings with which they found large agreement. Ultimately their ideas were inlaid alongside the ultimate source of their doctrines, the famous annotated Geneva Bible of 1560.[15]

The Forme of Prayers and Ministration of the Sacraments was the creedal statement and church order of these Englishmen exiled in Geneva from 1555 to 1560. It is usually recognized that this 1556 document was an English reproduction of Calvin's *La Forme*, originally written by the Genevan in Strassburg in 1540 and subsequently re-edited and eventually translated into English in 1550.[16] However, the similarity between the two documents is a bit misleading. In their preface, the English exiles

bemoaned that there was no good sovereign in their homeland.
Consequently the day of visitation had come, and plagues were
upon the land.. The English churches of the exile were examples
in doctrine and practice to the fatherland because they were established according to the limits of God's Word. Only ceremonies commensurate with the New Testament were allowed. The
practice of singing Psalms had biblical, historical, and reformed
bases, they believed, and thus they made an apology for setting
them to meter, showing concern for making the rhyme "according
to the Hebrew sense." They could not find a better catechism
than Calvin's and they mentioned that they had received his approval for the church order itself.[17]

The Confession of Faith is a commentary on the Apostles'
Creed in a text replete with scriptural references. The church
has two manifestations, the invisible, universal body and the
visible church "seen to the eye of man." The "tokens" of the
visible church are three: (1) "the Word of God contained in the
Old and New Testament . . . so it is left for all degrees of
men, to read and understand"; (2) the two sacraments of baptism
and the Lord's Supper (the latter shows that God not only feeds
our bodies "but also spiritually nourisheth our souls, with the
graces and benefits of Jesus Christ"); and (3) ecclesiastical
discipline "which standeth in admonition, and correction of
faults." Interestingly, the exiles stated that the political
magistrate belongs within this order as well, although his job
is political and *not* ecclesiastical. He must be honored and
obeyed in all things *unless* they were contrary to the Word of
God. Moses, Ezekiel, and Josiah purged their lands of idolatry;
so too must contemporary magistrates. Thus the Christian magistrate must defend the church from all idolatry, heresy, papistry,
and Anabaptism, and must "root out all doctrine of devils and
men as the mass, purgatory, *limbus patrum*, prayers to saints and
for the dead, freewill, distinction of meats, apparel and days,
vows of single life, presence at idol service, man's merits,
with suchlike. . . ."[18]

The lengthy sections which follow deal with the selection
of church officers, the weekly assembly of ministers (consisto-
ry), confession in several forms, prayers and the church orders
regarding baptism, the Lord's Supper, marriage, visiting the
sick, burial, and ecclesiastical discipline. Metered Psalms,
Calvin's catechism, and devotional prayers conclude the document.
Throughout the exiles were concerned with reordering the English
church after the church of the New Testament *as they saw it reflected* in Calvin's Geneva. For example, in choosing a minister
or pastor, the elders should assemble the whole congregation to-

gether to examine a candidate. He was to be sound in doctrine and able in speech, and he was given a text in order to show his abilities privately. Eight days were spent in the process, the congregation fasting and praying the entire time, especially in consideration of his manner and conduct of life. Finally, if he were acceptable, he was presented at the morning service by the minister, who directed his sermon toward his qualifications and duties, and the congregation received him and appointed him minister.[19] What Professor James C. Spalding has called the "Deuteronomic View of History" is quite apparent also.[20] Among the prayers in the document is the "prayer for the whole estate of Christ's Church." They prayed for the magistrate and ruler, the officials of Geneva, that they all might "maintain the purity of religion, reform manners, and punish sin." They then made special mention of "our miserable country England" which once knew the mercy of God, but now stands in need of his pity because of bondage to idolatry and immorality. They prayed that God would root out the workings of the ravenous wolves and spare those who were being persecuted and imprisoned. Then follows the blessing of *Numbers* 6.8 and *II Corinthians* 12.[21]

The order on ecclesiastical discipline deserves special attention since it is a hallmark of the English Protestant Tradition. Discipline is like the sinews of the body, knitting it together--a bridle to stay the wicked from their mischiefs. It is a spur to prick forward such as are slow and negligent. In short, it is God's way of keeping his church in good order. Why? There should be no men of "evil conversation" in the church. There should be no infection of the good by workers of evil. And, when men are corrected or excommunicated, they can be brought to repentance and their souls saved. These were reasons enough for the Genevan exiles! There was a distinction made between public and private discipline. In private discipline, according to order of *Matthew* 18, first an individual attends to the offender, then if there is no resolution, additional witnesses become involved; finally, if the matter were still unresolved, the offender was to be brought before the whole church, thereby making it a matter of public discipline and ultimately excommunication. To be excommunicated was to be excluded from the sacraments and duties of the church, not from sermons. The expulsed could always listen to sermons![22]

The Confession of the English exiles in Geneva makes it quite clear that the three strands of the English Protestant tradition, adumbrated above, stand intact. The humanist strand is apparent in the on-going search for renewal through antiquity; the Protestant strand stands out obviously in the anti-

Roman, anti-clerical polemic characteristic of Continental reformers as well as in the notions of *sola scriptura, sola fidei,*
and *sola gratia;* finally, the restitutionist strand is perhaps
even the strongest as evidenced by the constant and persistent
desire of the exiles to return to the New Testament pattern of
doctrine, church order, and piety. Calvin's influence was doubt-
less important and crucial, but it should be clear that their
theology and view of history were independently grounded in a
much wider *sitz in Leben.* The heritage of Tudor-Stuart English
dissent was not a monolithic restitutionism, but one whose character was complicated by the cultural milieu which conditioned
it in the sixteenth century and by ideologies which were shaking
the foundations of all Christendom.

It is interesting to see how this tradition developed into
the radical ideas of Knox, Goodman, and Ponet regarding civil
disobedience. It is true that "Anglicans were willing to accept
what history had given and to use their religion to account for
their complete obedience to the state"[23] but that radical Puritans, because of the restitutionist motif so strongly undergird-
ing their theology and view of history, became non-cooperative
with the state and sought even to overthrow it. The key to their
theories of revolution against the state will not be found in
their different views of the church, but in more basic ideological differences. The heart of these differences was hermeneuti-
cal: how to interpret the covenant theology with its many cor-
ollaries of a Deuteronomic view of history, national religion,
religious nationalism, religious independence, and ultimately
religious revolution.[24]

It remains only to indicate how the exiles fared upon their
return to England in 1558. (Some of the Genevan exiles did not
return until 1560, however.) Exile had definitely radicalized
them, but Elizabeth was to wield a strong hand of compromise.
Many erstwhile exiles, now filling ecclesiastical posts in Elizabeth's *via media,* found a new battleground. No longer was it
to be a "Christ against culture" social posture; in the latter
half of the sixteenth century it would become a "Christ within
culture" battle--a battle the Puritans were destined to vacillate
between winning and losing. But that would be another chapter.

I suppose in any scholarly discussion involving the *bonnae
litterae* the last word should be given to the poets. Again to
reinforce the dynamics of dissent presented in this paper, our
discussion will be concluded appropriately by a rather famous
dissenter himself, the young John Milton:

But to dwell no longer in characterizing the de-

pravities of the church, and how they sprung, and
how they took increase; when I recall to mind at
last, after so many dark ages, wherein the huge
overshadowing train of error had almost swept all
the stars out the firmament of the church, how the
bright and blissful Reformation (by divine power)
struck through the black and settled night of ig-
norance and anti-christian tyranny, methinks a sovereign and reviving joy must needs rush into the
bosom of him that reads or hears; and the sweet
odor of the returning gospel imbathe his soul with
the fragancy of heaven. Then was the sacred Bible
sought out of the dusty corners where profane false-
hood and neglect had thrown it, the schools opened,
divine and human learning raked out of the embers
of forgotten tongues, the princes and cities trooping
apace to the new erected banner of salvation; the
martyrs, with the unresistible might of weakness,
shaking the power of darkness, and scorning the
fiery rage of the old red dragon.[25]

Dan G. Danner

University of Portland

XII.
SIXTEENTH-CENTURY EUROPEAN JEWRY:
THEOLOGIES OF CRISIS IN CRISIS

By the sixteenth century, Jews had been exiled from so many lands at so many different times that one may wonder why this century in particular merits special consideration. Jews were probably the first conscious minority group in Europe, aware of the differences separating them from society at large. Indeed, one functional definition of Jewishness was exile and alienation much as European culture and civilization might be characterized as Christendom. Though the terms *Christian Universalism* and *Christendom* may have been fictions, from the viewpoint of European Jewry all the West *was* uniform in isolating the Jew as a special class of people, subject to special laws and considerations because of one central fact: the Jew rejected Christ. Consequently, whatever actual territorial exile may have entailed, European Jewry lived in a far greater cultural exile. Though many Jewish communities were ancient, often founded long before the time of Christ, the Jew was understood as a foreigner and an alien. The crusades, plagues, and their expulsion from most of western Europe intensified and institutionalized the Jewish sense of isolation into a permanent sense of paranoia.[1] Yet, despite such difficulties, the Jewish community during the Middle Ages developed no rationale, no explanation, no intellectual understanding of their own exile.

One area where medieval Jewish existence was exceptional, enduring, and free from restraint was the Iberian peninsula.[2] Political, religious, and economic tensions between Christians and Arabs were so great that concern about Jewish residence was overshadowed. As a result, Jews were nowhere more secure, more prosperous, and more educated than in Spain. For this reason, the expulsion of 1492 was perhaps the most traumatic event faced by Jewry in many centuries. This expulsion, affecting many hundreds of thousands of people, had its first effects in the sixteenth century but its reverberations finally reached a dramatic climax in the seventeenth century.

But who were these Spanish Jews? Actually, there were two groups of people in Spanish society suffering because of their Jewish roots. First, there were those Jews expelled from Spain in 1492 and from Portugal in 1497-98. Choosing exile to apostasy, several hundred thousand Jews made their way to Italy, Greece, Turkey, North Africa, and Israel.[3] A second group of people, however, also suffered alienation though of a different nature; these chose apostasy. From as early as 1391 many Jews were forcefully converted to Christianity. Others, fearing loss of life or property, willingly converted, while still others felt too attached to Spain to leave in 1492 and accepted baptism. All told, several hundred thousand Jews converted. These "conversos" or "New Christians" were often sincere converts to their new religion, but others, perhaps the overwhelming majority known as Marranos, used their Christianity as a social and religious shield behind which they continued to observe their Jewish practices. Though many Marranos held high positions in government, economy, and even the Church, the higher they rose in office, the more they were detested; Marrano, after all, means pig.[4]

If the Marrano was alienated from his Christian environment through enmity and discriminatory "pure blood laws," he was equally cut off from the Jewish community.[5] At first rabbinic authorities referred to these new converts as *anusim*--those who were stolen through forced conversion--but they were increasingly known as *meshumadim* or destroyed ones, the usual term for lost converts. Thus, if the Jew was territorially exiled from Spain, the Marrano was spiritually exiled and psychologically alienated, for though he was a Christian, he could not accept Christianity. Yet, much as the Marrano tried to live the life of a secret Jew, he could rarely do so nor could he receive the support of Jewish institutions outside Spain. The Jew and the Marrano both expressed types of desperation, though their circumstances differed. The Jew maintained his sense of community but suffered from being universally hated and despised. The Marrano remained a subject in beloved Spain, but he was a hypocrite detested by both Jews and Christians and increasingly subject to the rigors of the Spanish Inquisition. Both groups faced psychological, moral, and spiritual crisis, and both groups developed "theologies of crisis" and exile to help them explain their anomalous positions so as to lighten their burden of suffering. Since neither could alter its objective situation, both groups attempted to redefine suffering and exile, for in both cases reality was too horrible to accept.

In 1539 Rabbi Jehiel ben Samuel of Pisa forwarded his rabbinic commentary *Minhat Kanaot* with the following warning:

> And if by chance there will be found some inaccuracies in this book, they should be attributed to

> me and the limitations of my knowledge, but also
> to the worries which now press us, breaking the
> branches and tearing up the roots and blinding
> the eyes of our intellectual judgements.[6]

The author's fears that his generation was losing control were not unfounded, nor would his disclaimer have been misunderstood by European Jewry. During the Middle Ages, Jewry developed stable and powerful communal institutions. Indeed, medieval Jewish communities experienced much autonomy and independence. Rabbinic authority, based on the sixty-three volume codex of Jewish law known as the Talmud, reached a highpoint of political autonomy precisely because the Jew was separated from civil society. Exile and dislocation seriously weakened all communal institutions, especially rabbinic legal jurisdiction. One result of the loss of consistent control was the emergence of an extreme messianism and Cabbalistic mysticism as major intellectual and emotional forces.

Messianism had always been of continuing Jewish interest, especially during hard times.[7] Jewish messianism was more "this-worldly." than its Christian counterpart; the Son of David would liberate Israel from exile and bring vengeance upon her tormentors and opponents. During periods of stability and prosperity the messianic impulse diminished, but during the sixteenth century it became a prime theme of most speculative religious writing. Similarly, Cabbalistic mysticism had many devotees during the Middle Ages but was of secondary importance to rabbinic and talmudic concerns.[8] Cabbalists were traditionally concerned with the nature of creation, the emanations of the Godhead, and a spiritual form of Scriptural exegesis, but they now turned to the theme of national redemption. Significantly, Cabbalists succeeded in expanding their numbers from a small group of mystics into a mass movement, while at the same time their ideology challenged rabbinic authority and talmudic concerns. As one sixteenth-century mystic observed:

> The decree from above that one should not discuss
> Cabbalistic teaching in public was meant to last
> only for a limited time--until 1490. We then en-
> tered the period called "the last generation" and
> then the decree was rescinded and permission giv-
> en . . . and from 1540 onward the most important
> commandment [mitzvah] will be for all to study it
> in public, both young and old, since this and noth-
> ing else will bring about the coming of the mes-

siah.[9]

It is not surprising that Jews all over the world were affected by the results of the Spanish expulsion. Much of German
Jewry was expelled during the 1490's and early 1500's and again
in the 1560's, and Spanish Jews, or Sephardim, often settled in
established Jewish communities, dominating the intellectual
leadership sensitive to the problems of exile.[10] An early indication of this new orientation was expressed by Isaac Abarbanel's fifteenth-century work *The Wells of Salvation* wherein he
explained the rationale for his book: "My entire aim and purpose in writing this book, so very dear to me, is to strength-
en the feeble hands and uplift the stumbling feet."[11] Abarbanel
recognized that prognostication of the messiah's coming was forbidden by Jewish law, but he argued: "Our life is so hard and
our fortunes so unhappy that we are constrained to inquire after
the hour of our release and redemption. Furthermore, the end is
not far off and it is now proper to reveal it."[12] The body of
the work deals with complex numerological and Cabbalistic equations based on the book of *Daniel* and other parts of Scripture.
Using these equations, Abarbanel determined that the messiah
would appear in 1503. Other authors forecast other dates but
all shared Abarbanel's major end-purpose and concern--to determine the date of the messiah's coming so that Jews might have
sufficient faith to maintain their faith.

Certainly events seemed favorable. The fall of Constantinople was understood in apocalyptic terms ·by both Christians
and Jews. The Avignon papacy and the later division of Christianity during the Reformation were still further signs. For
these Sephardic Jews, however, the most important event was the
actual fact of their expulsion in 1492. One author, Abraham
Halevi, noted the pertinence of *Obadiah* 1.20. The prophet had
observed: "And the captivity of this host of the children of
Israel that are among the Canaanites even unto Zarapath and the
captivity of Jerusalem that is in Sepharad shall possess the
cities of the south." Halevi noted that *Zarapath* was Hebrew for
France and *Sepharad* was Hebrew for Spain. Both expulsions had
been completed, and it was only a matter of time before Israel
again settled in the city of the south, Jerusalem.[13] This was
indeed the closing hour of exile.

Not all Jewish authorities were convinced of the new messianism. Azariah dei Rossi, a great sixteenth-century Jewish
humanist observed: "I am aware of a whole group of 'sons of the
prophets' who are waiting for the year 1575 as the day of God in
which God will lead forth His people in joy to everlasting sal-

vation."[14] Perhaps because dei Rossi and others were skeptical
about these attempts to force God's hand, this group--the sons
of the prophets--were very careful not to antagonize Jewish sen-
sitivity. One member of this group, Daniel ben Perachia, defended his speculation with the standard argument that he wrote
only "to strengthen the weak hands and make firm the tottering
knees and not, God forbid, to calculate the end."[15] Yet in the
very same work Perachia reckoned the end would come in 1575. As
one date after another passed without incident, newer dates were
anticipated, but there was no slackening in the prognostication.
To practitioners it was obvious that these tried and true Cabbalistic numerological devices were accurate but that individual
computations were in error. Eliezer Ashkenazi ben Eli Rote noted
such disappointment but observed: "It is apparent that the
prophecies in Daniel show that we are very near the messianic
times."[16] He offered the date of 1594 as the important year
while his colleague Gedaliah ibn Yahya noted that the messiah
would appear in 1598.[17]

The messianic impetus so prevalent in sixteenth-century religious writings was not limited to esoteric intellectual circles
using arcane Cabbalistic numerological devices. Popular enthusiasm for a would-be messiah was so great that the sixteenth
century witnessed a large number of false messiahs who raised
the emotional level of Jewry only to prove equally disappointing
when one such movement after another ended in failure. In all
but one case all such messianic pretenders were either Marranos
or Sephardic Jews. Notably, Asher Lämmlein, the first messianic
pretender in the sixteenth century, was Ashkenazic--i.e., of
German origin.[18]

Influenced by Abarbanel's speculation that the messiah
would appear in 1503, Lämmlein appeared in Istria near Venice in
1502. The contemporary chronicler David Ganz reported Lämmlein's
impact:

> In the year 1502 Rabbi Lämmlein announced the ad-
> vent of the messiah and throughout the dispersion
> of Israel his words were credited. The news even
> spread among the gentiles and many believed in him.
> My grandfather, Seligman Ganz, smashed his oven in
> which he baked his passover bread [matzot] being
> firmly convinced that next year he would bake his
> passover bread in the Holy Land. And I heard from
> my old teacher Rabbi Eliezar Trivash of Frankfurt
> that the matter was not without basis and that he
> [Lämmlein] had shown signs and proofs. . . .[19]

Another chronicler, Joseph HaCohen noted that even leaders in Palestine believed in Lämmlein,[20] and Tobias Cohen noted that 1502 was known as the "Year of Repentance."[21]

Despite Lämmlein's widespread support, his efforts led to nothing other than significant conversion to Christianity on the part of many whose faith and hopes had been shattered. Despite the emotional and psychological dangers inherent in messianic expectation, Jews continued to believe that God's chosen was near at hand. Consequently, David Reubeni of Marrano origin caused great excitement when he appeared in 1522 in Nubia, Egypt, claiming to be the brother of a certain King Joseph, the Jewish king of Khaibar in Arabia.[22] Reubeni asserted that his brother's 300,000 subjects were the descendants of the tribes of Reuben, God, and Menasseh. While not claiming to be the messiah himself, Reubeni said he was engaged in a secret mission to bring about the liberation of Europe's Jews and their restoration to Israel. Reubeni gained great notoriety in 1524 when he presented his credentials to Pope Clement VII along with the proposition that they join forces against the Turks. Similarly, he was well received by King John III of Portugal who promised him military aid in any campaigns against the Turks.

David Reubeni was everything European Jewry longed for. He told a delegation of Marranos:

> Trust in God for you will be privileged to behold
> the rebuilding of Jerusalem, and do not fear. But
> I did not come this time to take you and bring you
> to Jerusalem because we must first wage great battles
> around Jerusalem before you can come there and be-
> fore the land will be ours and before we can offer
> sacrifices there. After that is done we will re-
> turn to you and take you there but at this time I
> came only to announce to you that the time of de-
> liverance is near at hand.[23]

Reubeni's program came to nothing, for once the novelty of a Jewish prince had worn off, Reubeni was seized and tried before the Inquisition in Mantua where he was found to be a fraud. After being sent to Spain as a prisoner, he was never heard from again.

After yet more conversions to Christianity, other false messiahs appeared fulfilling the demands of yet newer speculations. And so the cycle continued. Though both radical Christian sectarians and radical Jews were very tolerant of messianic and apocalyptic failure, there came a time when the focus of

such movements changed. It was obvious that messianic theologies
of "crisis-bred-messiahs" led to little and were even stimulating
a greater sense of crisis through unmet expectations. Consequently, it was logical that if a messiah able to alter the Jewish pattern of suffering did not appear, the only road open to
sixteenth-century Jews was to redefine suffering and exile to
give it greater meaning.

Of the many great centers of Cabbalistic mysticism, it was
the achievement of the sixteenth-century community in Safed,
Israel, to accomplish the important end of redefining suffering
and exile.[24] Indeed, this new Cabbalism, known as Lurianism
after its founder Isaac Luria, soon spread throughout the Jewish
and Marrano worlds and brought about a new wave of pietism. By
redefining the nature of the universe and Israel's relationship
to the world, the Spanish Cabbalists in Safed were about to turn
exile and suffering from an extraordinary and burdensome condition to be eschewed, to a state of cosmic importance where each
act carried great meaning. Moreover, exile and suffering became
the very fount and origin of national redemption. By arguing
that the messiah could not come to redeem Israel before the
world reached a level of perfection as yet unattained, the Safed
Cabbalists disassociated themselves from all previous failures.
More difficult, however, was explaining how a world so obviously
full of evil and corruption might attain a satisfactory level of
righteousness. Luria explained that at the time of creation,
God, the sum total of existence, contracted into His own being
to make room for the universe. But the emanations commissioned
to carry out creation could not contain this concentrated divinity and shattered, sending sparks of divinity throughout the universe. Only when these primordial sparks were again collected
into one entity could true righteousness result and the messiah
come to redeem Israel and the world. The people of Israel were
the agents chosen by God to collect and retrieve these divine
sparks by travelling throughout the world to wherever they
might be located. Consequently, what humans understood as exile
was nothing less than the process through which Israel travelled
the world over to retrieve divine sparks and a precondition necessary for the liberation of Israel and the redemption of the
world. Elucidating upon these views, Chaim Vital of Safed wrote:

> When Israel went out of Egypt all holiness was
> taken from there. For that reason Israel has
> been condemned to bondage among the seventy na-
> tions so that it might extract the divine sparks
> that have fallen among them. Our sages have

taught that if a single Jew is taken prisoner by
a nation, this is sufficient and it is accounted
as if the whole of Israel had been in bondage
there . . . for the purpose of raising all [the
sparks] that had fallen there among that particular nation. Therefore it was necessary that
Israel be scattered to the four winds in order
to raise everything.[25]

Exile was generally difficult to bear but the present times were
particularly hard since only the very last sparks demanded retrieval; these were, however, the most difficult to locate and
collect. Thus, in the final hour of the world, Spanish Jewry
was forced to the four corners of the earth to redeem a world
that rejected them.

This new redemptionist Cabbalism, redefining the collective
Jewish experience, also gave new meaning to individual lives as
well. Luria taught a variant form of traditional Cabbalistic
belief concerning the transmigration of souls whereby only a
soul left incomplete at death was reborn--and would continue to
be reborn until that soul acquired a degree of righteousness acceptable to God.[26] Thus every Jew possessed the soul of some
past sinner seeking fulfillment through personal piety. Individual human suffering, like collective exile, was an illusion,
for the conquest of sin was actually a struggle on an individual
level not unlike Israel's collective mission. If exile was necessary to retrieve divine sparks, personal suffering was necessary for the salvation of individual souls of a fallen humanity.
If the Jew seemed personally unfortunate and collectively afflicted, in reality Israel was personally and collectively the
suffering servant of humanity. It was understandable that Israel was despised, for it was the impious Christian soul that each
Jew sought to sanctify through personal piety. And it was
Christian European history that Jewish exile would redeem.

But what of those Jews who were not part of the Jewish community? Could Marranos partake of their brothers' joy in immi-
nent redemption? Many Marranos followed the false messiahs and
were no doubt equally disappointed in the failure of such movements. But with each generation, the Marrano community was that
much more cut off from its Jewish origin as well as the Jewish
community outside Spain. As a result, each generation witnessed
increased acceptance of Catholicism and increased estrangement
from Jewish circles.

More than any other group, Marranos might benefit from the
coming of the messiah when such terms and distinctions as *Jew*,

Marrano, converso, and *New Christian* would be eliminated. Indeed, given Christian and Jewish antipathy towards Marranos, only so miraculous an event as the coming of the messiah might alleviate their situation. Yet, the undeniable fact was that Marranos, despite the observance of many Jewish practices and rituals, were Christian and might be understood as such by the coming messiah. While it would be helpful indeed to know more about the relationship between Jews and Marranos, existing material is unfortunately inconclusive. Some historians have pointed to cooperation between the two groups where possible, with one major historian concluding that Marranos were Jews in all ways except the observance of all Jewish rituals.[27] At the other extreme, some historians have demonstrated that much of rabbinic legal literature of the age considered Marranos true converts to Christianity and not a special class of people.[28] For their part, Marranos in the sixteenth century have left us little to work with, no doubt because the Spanish Inquisition made the composition of apologetic tracts very dangerous. It is also possible that the first generations of Marranos were more concerned with maintaining the semblance of Jewish ritual rather than with creating their own justifications and theology.

Fortunately, some sixteenth-century apologetic tracts do remain, and the abundance of seventeenth-century material makes the Marrano position fairly clear. The first apologetics often justified the position of the Marrano on the rabbinic dictum that a Jew, even one who consciously sins, still remains a Jew. Others yet (e.g., Diego de Simancas) cited *Deuteronomy* 5.30, "that ye may live," to explain their choice of apostasy.[29] Yet it was important for these thinkers to reconcile apostasy with legitimate Jewish religious expression since so many Jews did not feel the need to convert. In this light, Samuel Aboab argued that only Christian belief was forbidden, but that external idolatry was not important if one maintained true belief in one's heart.[30] Proof for this position was taken from the Letter of Baruch ben Neriah, the Epistle of Jeremy of the Apocrypha, especially verses 5-6.

Defensiveness concerning apostasy soon gave way to its very opposite tendency: the defense of conversion as the highest form of religious expression. The *Book of Esther* became a major scriptural writing in Marrano circles, and a three day holiday was instituted in place of the single day of Purim celebrated by Jews in commemoration of her deeds. Esther, it will be remembered, consciously concealed her religion so that she might marry King Ahasuerus and save her people from the machinations of the evil Hamen.

Marrano thought became even more sophisticated when it employed the developing Lurianic Cabbalistic ideas described previously. We noted earlier that Lurianic thought taught that exile was necessary for the retrieval of divine sparks. Marranos extended this argument to include their own position by teaching that some Jews would be forced into an even greater exile than expulsion and would be forced to become Christians in search of the sparks fallen among those of that religion. Thus, for instance, Abraham Cardoso, a most prominent Marrano apologist in the seventeenth century, argued: "It is ordained that the king messiah don the garments of a Marrano and go unrecognized by his fellow Jews. In a word, it is ordained that he become a Marrano like me."[31]

Cardoso was not the only Marrano to make use of Lurianic thought. Menassah ben Israel held negotiations with Oliver Cromwell concerning the readmission of Jews to England after several centuries of exile but not in order to find refuge for Jewish immigrants. This Marrano firmly believed that the messiah would not come unless there were Jews in every country of the world to retrieve divine sparks.[32] Similarly, Marranos thought it significant that Columbus discovered a new world in the very year Jews were expelled from Spain, for here too was a corner of the world needing spark retrieval by the Jews. Though it is unlikely, there has been speculation that Christopher Columbus was of Marrano background. It is known for certain that much of his staff, including his navigator, translator, physician, and others, were Marranos.[33]

Marrano influence in Jewish circles became very apparent during the seventeenth century in the case of Shabbetai Zvi.[34] This false messiah generated more excitement and anticipation than any previous would-be redeemer. Claiming the loyalties of almost all Marranos and possibly most Jews, Zvi's movement grew dramatically until 1666 when he and several hundred of his followers converted to Islam to avoid execution by Turkish officials. While Zvi's career falls outside the confines of this treatment and has been very well analyzed elsewhere, it is noteworthy that his Marrano followers remained loyal as did a significant number of his Jewish followers. Needless to say, Zvi's apostasy was explained on the basis of previous Marrano apologetics, as was the conversion of the Sabbatean Jacob Frank and three hundred of his followers in the eighteenth century when they accepted Roman Catholicism in Poland.[35]

The Marrano theory of exile and apostasy came full circle where conversion, at first an act to be tolerated, later came to be regarded as a necessary form of behavior on the part of the

messiah--or an act of legitimate Jewish religious expression.
The permanence of Marranism may seem surprising, but Marranos
continue to maintain their quasi-secret religious existence in
Spain and Portugal to this very day.[36] Even Shabbetai Zvi's Is-
lamic followers continued until quite recently to maintain their
own identity as a separate Moslem sect, the Doenmeh.[37] Thus,
a theology of crisis predicated upon anti-Jewish legislation in
the fourteenth and fifteenth centuries has been maintained to
the present time through the careful cultivation of a mysticism
of conversion even where such external pressure no longer exists.
In the theology of crisis predicated upon a state of continual
crisis, rejection and exile become institutionalized into a permanent state of conversion.

Jerome Friedman

Kent State University

XIII.
THE INTELLECTUAL CLIMATE IN PORTUGAL
IN THE FIFTEENTH AND SIXTEENTH CENTURIES

In an interesting article published in *Renaissance Quarterly*, Professor Trinkaus defined the modern world as a "displacement of the consciousness of God as the prime directive force in the universe by a notion of human powers and of 'natural forces' which indeed begins with the Italian Renaissance."[1] There are to be sure other forces at work during the period. Nevertheless, I agree with Trinkaus that the horizontal rather than the vertical world-outlook was the most powerful impulse of Renaissance humanism in the shaping of the modern world.

Whereas scholars of Italian and Northern humanism have found much evidence in support of this thesis, there are relatively few attempts made to relate the discoveries to the same process. Contemporary humanists, on the other hand, were aware of the significance of the adventures in the light of their own intellectual endeavors. In such a spirit Angelo Poliziano of Florence wrote to the Portuguese King John II that he would like to tell the story of the discoveries in Latin.[2] In his *De Disciplinis* Luis Vives endorsed observation and experience as the necessary basis of knowledge. He saw the same experimental stance behind the adventures. In the dedication of the treatise to John III, Vives expressed his admiration for the sailors "who show us," he said, "the course of the heavens and seas of which we have not heard before; truly to the human race has opened its planet."[3] If for many humanists classical Greece and Rome were the golden ages of mankind, others believed that the great events of their own century could stand comparison with the ancients. Lazzaro Buonamico affirmed in a letter to Damião de Gois, the Portuguese humanist, who studied with him: "Do not believe that there exists anything more honorable to our own or the preceding age than the invention of the printing press and the discovery of the new world; two things which I have always thought could be compared not only to Antiquity, but to immortality."[4]

In the first part of this study I will relate the discoveries to some aspects of the humanist movement. The second part will deal with the reform of learning under King John III who ruled from 1521 to 1557. At the end I will add a few words about the changed climate after John III's death.

At the same time when Lorenzo Valla proclaimed man's autonomy in secular matters, Henry the Navigator sent his ships to
explore the Western coast of Africa. It appears to the modern
observer that the Portuguese prince put the Italian humanist's
thoughts into practice. Henry was driven by both secular and
religious motives. About the former Zurara, his contemporary
chronicler, left no doubt. "He wanted to know," he wrote, "the
land beyond the Canary Islands and a cape that is called Bojador;
since up to this time the truth of that which was beyond the
cape had not been established either through writings or the
memory of some men."[5] What was available at the time were the
fanciful geographies of a Pomponio Mela, a John de Mandeville or
a Pliny.[6] Ptolemy, whose *Astronomy* was known before his *Geography*, believed it impossible to sail around the Eastern coast
of Africa. Of more value was the Catalan Raymundus Lullus' report on his travels to the Orient.[7] In 1415 Henry retired to
the Cape of St. Vincent and founded an observatory at Sagres.

In search of the truth of unknown lands and seas--similar
to the humanists' hunting for manuscripts to establish the truth
they were looking for--Henry surrounded himself with Arabic and
Jewish astronomers and geographers and a famous mapmaker.[8] His
brother prince Pedro brought back from his European trip maps
from Italy and Marco Polo's famous book.[9] Henry, like King John
II, inspired scientific research without being a scientist himself. Besides the theoretical preparation, Henry expected from
his captains the highest dedication to the mastery of the sea.
Gil Eannes, for example, a well-qualified navigator who had been
a student of astronomy at Lisbon University, was sent on several
expeditions before he mastered the hostile elements and reached
the dreaded Cape Bojador. It was the beginning of other daring
voyages leading to India, the Far East, and Brazil.

João de Barros and Damião de Gois applied in their respective histories the humanist ideal of *virtù* to the sailors who
bravely met dangers and deprivations.[10] Luis de Camões opened
his epic poem, the *Lusiadas*, not with giving thanks to God for
his guidance, but with praising the endurance of the navigators
which was greater "than could be expected of human nature."[11]
In the Renaissance, on the other hand, *virtù* did not always con-
note such an admirable quality of heroism. Consider Machiavelli's theory of a prince and Cesare Borgia's practice. Like the
latter, the overseas heroes often thought to prove their superior ability and courage by cruel actions against the natives.
For example, João de Castro, the last viceroy of India, had many
women and children killed after he had won a long and bloody

battle at Diu in 1546.

The adventurers' thirst for knowledge matched that of the humanists. Many gave valuable reports of what they had observed in far-away lands. An outstanding scientific work was written by Garcia d'Orta, a botanist and alumnus of the University of Lisbon. He published a book describing the many healing plants and drugs he had found in India.[12] On his return from India, Duarte Pacheco Pereira compiled a treatise entitled *Esmeraldo De Situ Orbis*, a manual of astrological and cosmological data concerning West African navigation. In the judgment of Saraiva, the great cultural historian, Duarte, was aware of the necessity to build a rational understanding of reality on experience.[13] Pedro Nunes in the *Tratado de Defensão de Carta de Marear* developed a theory of the position of the sun at every hour of the day which was tested by João de Castro when he sailed to India in 1538.[14]

Despite the fact that for the humanists secular matters had their own positive values, the human world was not yet severed from the larger cosmos. Consequently, humanists combined a secular outlook with sincere devotion to their faith. The same is true for the Portuguese overseas adventures. Given a mixture of secular and religious motives, the latter were strongly accentuated. Ever since the Portuguese had fought a "crusade" against the Muslims who occupied their country, a missionary zeal had captured their minds. This spirit motivated the overseas missions which the Portuguese kings sent out in the wake of the conquests.

Henry the Navigator's goal was above all to destroy Muslim rule in Africa. He had high hopes to find the Negus of Ethiopia who, since he was supposed to belong to the Christian faith, could assist the Portuguese in their fight against the Muslims. Many fantastic stories about his wealth and power circulated in Europe. His great empire was said to be situated somewhere in Africa and/or the Orient.[15] The long search for the land of the Negus succeeded only after Henry's death under King John II. The disappointment was great, however, when it became known that the Ethiopians were Monophysites and followed many Old Testament rituals. The Ethiopian religious issue, on the other hand, has considerable interest because in connection with it the question of religious tolerance was raised.

Despite their continuous efforts, the Ethiopians were not recognized by the pope as members of Western Christianity. Damião de Gois, the Portuguese humanist and friend of Erasmus, who had met one of the Negus' envoys, was moved by his bitter complaints that his country was treated like a religious outcast.

Imbued with an Erasmian spirit of religious reconciliation, Damião asked the Ethiopian to write down for him the articles of
his faith and promised to translate his account into Latin. The
book, which appeared in 1541, contained a strong plea for religious tolerance based on faith in Christ that, it was said, suf-
ficed to unite all Christians.[16] In Portugal the book was not
allowed to circulate, in part for personal reasons since the en-
voy's way of life had scandalized the authorities. It aroused,
however, much interest among humanists. Guillaume Postel, for
example, read the essay and fully agreed with the broad concept
of Christianity it embodied.[17]

If Ethiopia disappointed religious expectations, the Portuguese had the satisfaction that the ruler of the Congo converted
to Catholicism in 1491. The king, who adopted the name of Alfonso, was eager to establish cultural and economic relations
with Portugal. The Portuguese king sent skilled laborers to the
African country, and members of the Congo's ruling class came to
Portugal for their education.

Portugal's relation with the Congo could be praised as an
example of how a more advanced nation helped a less developed
people, were it not for the fact that Alfonso paid for Portuguese
services with slaves.[18] Slavery was not unknown in Africa, but
the conquerors made it into a lucrative trade. Zurara in the
previously mentioned chronicle of Guinea gives a touching account
of the way the natives were herded together, divided by lot, and,
regardless of family relationship, sold as personal property.[19]
The slave trade was stepped up when the colonization of Brazil
began under John III in 1532. It is difficult to reconcile
slavery with the era's awareness of the dignity of human beings.
To be sure, criticism of the slave trade was voiced occasionally.
Thus Erasmus condemned the harsh treatment of the natives in
Africa.[20] The most impassioned debate concerning slavery was
led by Las Casas, the Spanish Dominican bishop, who had served
for many years in the Indies. As a friend of the Indians Las
Casas tried every possible means to improve the fate of the natives. Although Las Casas had some measure of success in his
time, his views were in the end proved ineffective in his own
and other nations.[21] The present generation understands only
too well that second to no other event that occurred in the age
of Renaissance humanism, colonization and slavery caused the most
serious human and political problems to the modern world. In
one respect, however, the Portuguese had an advantage over other
colonizing powers. They did not know any racial strife and
treated their slaves well. Already Zurara noted this fact.
Gilberto Freyre, the noted Brazilian sociologist, remarked in the

Masters and Slaves: "The terrible slave-driver, who came near transporting from Africa to America, in filthy vessels that could be recognized from afar by their stench, an entire population of Negroes, was, on the other hand, the European colonizer who best succeeded in fraternizing with slaves."[22] Intermarriages with blacks were frequent and left a decisive mark on the social development of the two countries, Portugal and Brazil.

Under Henry the Navigator knowledge and missionary ideals were the overriding motives. But with the progress of the discoveries the economic advantages of the overseas trade attracted the merchant adventurer. Taking the place formerly held by Venice, Lisbon became the center for imports from India, especially spices, drugs, and jewelry. A new class of rich merchants came into being among whom the Portuguese king was the leading entrepreneur. King Manuel celebrated his victories with an ambitious building program that embellished Portugal's metropolis and attracted many visitors up to our own day.

The sixteenth century has been called Portugal's Golden Age not only because of the striking overseas successes, but also because of the flowering of the arts and sciences during this period. Already John II had shown interest in humanistic studies and attracted Cataldo Parísio Sículo, an Italian humanist, to the Portuguese court. He was supposed to teach the king's illegitimate son George and some nobles.[23] It was a modest beginning that gained momentum under King John III, who followed Manuel I on the throne in 1521.

The structure of the Portuguese society was hierarchical with the royal palace the center from which all major activities radiated. The reform of higher learning was thus in the hands of the ruler. This raises the question: What kind of a person was John III? Scholars, puzzled by the king's character, have called him in turn enigmatic, fanatic, and liberal.[24] Those who label him a fanatic Catholic think of the Inquisition which was introduced after the king had put great pressure on the pope to give him the necessary permission. Was John's motive to enforce religious orthodoxy? Against it speaks the king's willingness, as we shall see, to tolerate liberal humanists who freely discussed controversial religious questions. It is true that the High Tribunal kept a watchful eye on "heretics" and *conversos* whose property was confiscated if found guilty. The king repeatedly complained of the empty treasury he had inherited from his predecessor. He may have hoped to improve his finances with the money taken from the defendants by the Inquisition. Such cold calculation has justly aroused strong antag-

onism to the king among later observers of his reign. But it
does not contradict or exclude John's liberal frame of mind in
the intellectual domain. However this may be, some noted Portuguese did not hesitate to express their thoughts freely and, so
it seems, took the king's openmindedness for granted.

One thinks of Gil Vicente, the famous author of many plays
and sermons. After an earthquake had hit Santarem, a city not
far from Lisbon, Vicente sent a letter to the king informing him
of a speech he had delivered on the occasion. He had called together a group of monks who attributed the earthquake to God's
anger because of the impiety of the *conversos*.[25] Vicente reported to the ruler that he had rejected the monks' explanation
of the tragic event since he considered it an act of nature, not
of God.[26] A second point he made was still more courageous. He
described the utter despair of the New Christians when they
heard the monks' accusation and how they were gripped with mor-
tal fear of the people.[27] Most important, Vicente added a stern
warning against persecution of those who were not yet ready to
embrace the Christian faith. "It is more virtuous," he asserted,
"to awaken and convert them . . . than to scandalize and shock
them in order to satisfy the confused opinion of the masses."[28]
One cannot imagine that Vicente would write such comments to a
king who was a fanatic in religious matters. In his many plays
Vicente dealt with the moral conduct of his contemporaries. Although he criticized all strata of society for the concern with
material gains, the worldliness of the clergy provoked him
most.[29] He admonished the upper classes--the king was by infer-
ence included--that they should treat people justly.

Vicente's social criticism was seconded by João de Barros.
Barros, one of the great figures of Portugal's golden age, still
awaits his biographer.[30] He was talented in many ways and combined in his person the humanist, the moralist, the patriot, and
the pious Christian. In addition, he served the king in Lisbon
as treasurer of Indiahouse, a highly responsible position,
for many years. Posterity has celebrated him for his history of
Asia, the *Decadas*, but he was also a thinker who fitted well into the humanist period. As the historian of his country's overseas adventures Barros displayed his patriotic feelings. Whereas in a religious context he rejected warfare, in the *Decadas* he
praised the Portuguese discovery of lands that were unknown to
Alexander the Great.[31] Among his writings that contain his
philosophical and religious thoughts, the *Spiritual Wares* takes
first place.[32] It is a dialogue between Will, Understanding,
and Time on the one side representing human weaknesses, vices,
and heresies, and Reason on the other, the latter being the

leader in the discussion.[33]

In his dedication of the *Spiritual Wares* to Duarte de Resende, Barros explains the purpose of his tract. I am not writing this, he said, for the Erasmians "who are already old, but
for some new Portuguese of whom you and I have heard" [heretics,
sinners and New Christians], who should be converted to Christian values.[34] Saraiva asserts that the *Spiritual Wares* "is the
most complete manifestation of the Erasmian spirit in Portugal."[35] Like Erasmus, Barros ridiculed the scholastic argumen-
tation and advocated a simple faith in Christ.[36] He had a thorough knowledge of ancient authors whom he quotes in support of
his views with moderation. Compared to the light that Christ
brought to the world, both Barros and Erasmus believed the classical writers inferior in wisdom and ethics.[37] Barros further
agreed with the Erasmians in their evaluation of the two Testa-
ments. Whereas the Old Testament, according to Barros, is replete with crimes and wars with the Jews living under the law,
the New Testament embodies a wholly spiritual message.[38] Barros
further joins Erasmus and Vicente in condemning the secular tendencies of the clergy; he had little sympathy for the many orders which in his opinion divided Christianity.[39] Barros was
also the spokesman for lay piety. In view of the fact, he
claimed, that most clergymen were, like the ancient pharisees,
given to a rigid interpretation of Scripture, a layman like himself may undertake the task to explain Christianity to unbeliev-
ers.[40] Barros shared the humanist sense of the dignity of all
men. Vices, he argued, were the result of the cunning of the
few and not of original sin.[41] This was, from an orthodox religious standpoint, a bold statement. His admonition to the upper classes was equally daring. He told them that their large
share in material possessions was against natural or divine law
that gave all men an equal right to the earth and its fruits.[42]
The high society, spoiled by the goods and slaves imported from
overseas, had indeed become decadent; they were averse to any
kind of work—a fact also noted by Nicolaus Clenardus.[43] The
Spiritual Wares sounded a warning to the most powerful people in
Portugal. Interestingly enough, Time has the last word in the
dialogue. It cautions Reason to leave matters in its hands
since any sudden change in a man's life is accompanied "by inner
torment." It is the function of Reason to establish truth.
Time, on the other hand, takes a person's psychology into account: It tells Reason that it is impossible to erase at a single moment of time customs which have a long history behind
them.[44]

The *Spiritual Wares* is a courageous book. It is remarkable that John III tolerated its publication. Under different intellectual conditions it was put on the Index in 1581. One must conclude that John III did not insist on religious orthodoxy. In addition, the king took a more than casual interest in Erasmus and the kind of humanism he represented.

In 1533 Damião de Gois, the diplomat, humanist, and great friend of Erasmus, returned to Portugal for consultation. He brought with him a message from Erasmus whom he had visited in Freiburg not long ago. Erasmus had dedicated his *St. Chrysostom* to John III but at the same time criticized the king's spice monopoly.[46] Far from holding a grudge against the "prince of humanists," the king asked Damião to invite the famous scholar to come to Portugal. He proposed to make him a professor at the University of Coimbra which had been planned since 1531 but did not open until 1537.[47] The king was not only aware of Damião's relations with Erasmus but knew of his visit to Wittenberg in 1531.[48] Nevertheless, John offered him the position of treasurer of Indiahouse in Lisbon, a sign of high confidence. After much soul-searching Damião declined the flattering proposal. He asked permission to continue his studies in Louvain and to cultivate his friendship with Erasmus. John granted him his wishes. The king's high regard for Erasmus is the more remarkable since in neighboring Spain his influence was already waning. Moreover, he was well informed of the debate regarding Erasmus' work at Valladolid in 1527; two Portuguese had taken the lead in condemning his writings.[49]

Second only to Damião de Gois, André de Resende, the humanist and poet, was a great admirer of Erasmus. He gives a lively account of the arduous trip he undertook to Louvain for the sole purpose of meeting Erasmus, who unfortunately had already left for Basel. Resende associated with Nannius and Goclenius, two devoted friends of Erasmus, who taught at Busleiden College. He shared their resentment against the scholastic theologians whose animosity had caused Erasmus' departure from Louvain. Resende composed an *Encomium*--Erasmus had it published without his knowledge--praising the friend he had never met for having restored true learning and wisdom; at the same time he derided the "abstract verbiage" of Erasmus' enemies.[50] After Resende had returned to Portugal, John III asked him to deliver a speech at the opening of Lisbon University in 1534.[51] There is no doubt that the king was aware of the approach Resende would take in his address. It was a passionate endorsement of Erasmian humanism. Resende did not deny that St. Thomas and Duns Scotus were great theologians, but, he warned, this did not justify the utter neglect of the Church Fathers. From the latter one could

learn, he continued, that rhetoric was not a hindrance, but an
advantage to theology. He further admonished the professors to
teach ancient languages because they are like windows opening
the mind's eye to "divine poetry" and "true oratory."[52]

John III's interest in humanism was echoed by his sister,
the princess Maria. In her entourage were several women who
were famous for their learning. Among them was Joanna Vaz who
was credited with the knowledge of five languages. Joanna and
André de Resende composed poems deploring the death of Erasmus
in 1536.[53] In the same year Aires Barbosa published his *Anti-
moria* with the avowed purpose to counteract the "delight" with
which too many scholars read the *Praise of Folly*.[54]

In his *Encomium* Resende had assured Erasmus of the sympathy
the royal princes had for his ideas. He certainly thought in
this connection of Prince Henrique--the archbishop of Braga, future cardinal, great inquisitor, and ultimately king of Portugal. Henrique sent Resende to Salamanca to invite the Flemish
humanist Nicolaus Clenardus to become his teacher of ancient
languages. Clenardus was glad to accept the offer because he
resented the arrogant students at the university.[55] He was an
Erasmian humanist who engaged in a very special mission. Clenardus harbored strong feelings against the forced conversion of
Muslims. He studied Arabic in order to be able to read the Koran in the original and to stimulate a discussion between Muslims and Christians. He was convinced, however, that the debate
would show the superiority of the Christian faith and that the
Muslims would convert to it voluntarily. In a most unusual ges-
ture Henrique granted him a stipend which enabled him to continue his study of the Koran with the natives of Fez.[56] Once in
Africa Clenardus was not only on friendly terms with the Arabs,
but also with the Jews, many of whom were exiles from the Iberian Peninsula. The Portuguese consul in Fez reported Clenardus'
fraternization with Jews and Muslims back to Portugal, and Henrique withdrew his support. It is most likely that Henrique had
no choice in the matter because of the clergy's animosity
against the New Christians in the country.[57] Feelings against
the Arabs, Portugal's great antagonists, ran less high. In 1546
John III invited Guillaume Postel, the controversial humanist,
to teach Arabic at Coimbra.[58]

One may not find it easy to fully understand how scholars
and religious groups of various persuasions were tolerated by
the king at the same time. Although the Erasmians were small in
number, they exerted considerable influence. When the king
founded a Jesuit college in 1542, one may expect that this
marked the end of the liberal period. But such was not the

case. In 1546 a purged edition of Erasmus' *Colloquies* circulated in Portugal for a few years, although in many other countries it was already on the Index.[59] After Damião de Gois' return to his home country in 1545, Simão Rodrigues, the Jesuit leader in Portugal, denounced him several times before the Inquisition because of his former relations with the Protestants. But no action was taken against him. When in his old age Damião was imprisoned by the inquisitors he wrote long reports about his former associations. In one of them he mentioned the fact that on his visit to Portugal in 1533 "the king . . . and the princes, his brothers and other nobles of the realm had inquired with much interest about his travels. They had asked about Luther and Germany. . . ."[60] Damião told the truth. John III put him in charge of the national archives, and Henrique commissioned him to write the chronicle of the reign of Manuel I.

There is still more evidence of the king's broadmindedness in religious matters. In the middle twenties the king had endowed fifty scholarships for Portuguese students at the college of St. Barbe in Paris where Diogo de Gouveia, Sr., was principal.[61] He belonged to a Portuguese family famous for its many scholars who, however, disagreed as to the merit of humanism. Diogo Sr. was a conservative theologian and a great enemy of Erasmus. His nephew André, who also taught at St. Barbe, was a dedicated humanist and a liberal in religious matters. He was a friend of Nicolaus Cop who in a speech at the Sorbonne--Calvin may have had a hand in it--attacked the scholastics, for which he was accused of Protestant leanings.[62] The uproar that followed the address forced Cop and Calvin as well as André and some of his colleagues at St. Barbe to leave Paris. André became principal of the College of Guyenne in Bordeaux when Montaigne studied there. He took with him Diogo de Teive, João da Costa, and George Buchanan, who all taught at Guyenne.[63] It was a lively time at the college since the group from St. Barbe held open discussions on many controversial religious questions. They aroused the suspicion of the Parliament of Bordeaux.

John III's most ambitious project was to establish a College of the Arts at Coimbra which was to be fashioned after Busleiden College in Louvain. He thought of engaging the professors from Guyenne for this new institution. When the king asked Diogo de Gouveia, Sr., for advice in the matter, he warned him against the plan since he considered André and his colleagues to be Lutherans. But John III did not heed his advice.

In 1546 André de Gouveia, João da Costa, Diogo de Teive, and John Buchanan arrived in Coimbra to take up their positions at the College of the Arts.[64] André was appointed principal but

died only two years later. The other professors from Guyenne
soon faced serious trouble from their conservative colleagues.
The latter accused them of propagating unorthodox religious
views and denounced them before the Inquisition. The High Tribunal found them guilty of "heresy" and in 1550 imprisoned them.
From the trials an interesting picture of the religious conditions especially in France emerges.[65] When they were in Paris
and later in Bordeaux, the defendants admitted, it was their
custom to engage the students in debates on religious issues.
From the questions raised it is quite clear that Erasmus and the
reformers had made an impression on them. They argued, for example, the point whether an active life is preferable to a monastic one; or whether Christ is really or only symbolically in
the Eucharist.[66] Furthermore, they defended the view that in-
fants who die before they were baptised are saved; it is better,
they thought, to love than to fear God.[67] They did not deny
that they discussed the meaning of heaven, earth, and the soul
in philosophical and theological terms.[68] To make matters
worse, they had books in their respective libraries that were on
the Index. Teive thus owned Melanchthon's *Loci Communes* and
Calvin's *Institutes*. Costa possessed Melanchthon's *Rhetoric or
Dialectic* and Erasmus' *New Testament*.[69] As to their contacts
with heretics, Teive repeatedly denied ever to have met with
"atheists" like Etienne Dolet or Villanovus (Michael Servetus).[70]
John III it appears did not take the accusations very seriously.
After Teive was released from prison he appointed him principal
of the College of the Arts. It was more daring than prudent.
The animosity against the professor from Guyenne was quite intense; it caused an uproar at the college. The king, perhaps
utterly discouraged, turned the college over to the Jesuits.
One should, however, not draw the conclusion that he had changed
his mind. In 1556, one year after Teive's release from prison,
Queen Catherine wrote a letter to the Archbishop of Braga recom-
mending Teive for a church position "because of the good information she had received about his life and customs."[71]

Besides the Erasmians, some liberal Catholics and the Jesu-
its--humanist scholars with conservative religious leanings--oc-
cupied an important place in Portugal's intellectual landscape.
Two examples may suffice. Antonio Pinheiro, an alumnus of St.
Barbe, was frequently seen at the palace as teacher of the royal
princes. He showed his regard for the vernacular in translating
some ancient authors into Portuguese. Among other humanists
Erasmus, according to Damião de Gois, was in favor of rendering
classical writers into one's mother tongue. But Pinheiro differed from the Erasmians in that he believed the king's actions

not subject to moral judgment. He admonished the assembled estates to obey the ruler who was appointed by the will of God.[72]
Since the divine Being directed human affairs through his messengers, the angels, man's freedom was directly limited. Pinheiro's religious thoughts were shared by Jerónymo Osório, an
outstanding humanist scholar. In his *History of the Reign of
King Manuel I,* Osório expressed his admiration for Portugal's
overseas exploits but warned: "When they consider these things,
I say, let them ascribe the glory of such miraculous events not
to men, but to God, who has often manifested his presence in our
affairs."[73] In his scholarly tastes Osório, on the other hand,
was quite "modern": his favorite authors were the Church Fathers, St. Thomas, Plato, and Cicero. In contrast to Pinheiro,
Osório did not think that the king was above the law. Imbued
with a strong ethical sense, he attacked Machiavelli's concept
of a prince. As a student in Paris Osório was closely associated with the Jesuits; he later recommended the order to John
III. He was a dedicated bishop, who tried diligently to restore
morality among the clergy of his diocese. Osório was also a
militant Catholic and rejected any reconciliation with the Protestants. He despised Luther.[74]

To the colorful mosaic of humanists and writers who were
active during the period in question, other names could be added.
But from the short survey a picture already emerges that shows
Portugal's great contribution to Renaissance humanism as an European movement. Especially in the field of architectural design
Portugal takes her place side by side with the flowering of the
arts in other countries. The economic expansion, the luxuries
of many kinds, the progress in navigational sciences, and a certain experimental spirit are phenomena that characterize the new
era of the Western World. The growing national sensibility, the
support of the vernacular, and a plea for religious tolerance
are tendencies that can be observed in the rest of Europe. The
humanists everywhere speak of new human values without being
aware of the fact (except occasionally) that the discoveries
contradict the very same values. A new class of merchants opened
a social development of great importance for the future of Europe. Finally, centralization of political power in the hands of
the sovereign determined the history of Europe for several centuries.

The death of John III in 1557 signaled the end of a period.
Queen Catherine took over the regency for her grandson Sebastian
and continued her husband's liberal trend. But she grew tired
of the burden the regency imposed on her, and turned it over to
Cardinal Henrique in 1562. It was the year when the Council of

Trent convened for its last session. Henrique, for reasons of prudence or conviction, allied himself with the Jesuits. They were, after all, the instruments of the Counter-Reformation. During the last quarter of the sixteenth century the lines of confessionalism were fixed not only by the Roman Catholic Church but by the Protestant churches too. The previously open religious and intellectual horizon was closed. When Sebastian finally ascended to the throne in 1568, a new generation took over the reins of government. Sebastian, who was educated by the Jesuits, had no knowledge of the spirit that was alive under his grandfather. Nothing expresses the changed atmosphere better than the tragic fate of Damião de Gois. After a brilliant career as diplomat and humanist he was incarcerated by the Inquisition in 1572 because of his former relations with Wittenberg and Erasmus. In the streets of Lisbon many races and nationalities formerly mingled. Now foreigners were looked upon with suspicion. Moreover, the small country of a million people was exhausted by the conquests and the demands of a large empire for money and manpower. Unfortunately, Sebastian was a dreamer, far removed from the realities that faced the country. The king's ambition was to wrest Morocco from the Arabs. Against the advice from his counselors, the king went ahead with his plan. The result was disastrous. Without leaving any heir, Sebastian died on the battlefield in 1578. Two years later Philip II incorporated Portugal into his realm. It was a sad ending of a glorious century. A last and permanent ray of light was Luis de Camões' great epic poem celebrating the discoveries, for the *Lusiadas* appeared in 1572.[75]

Elisabeth Feist Hirsch

XIV.
THE REFORMATION AND ITS IMPACT ON SPANISH THOUGHT

The year 1492 is the symbolic "terminus a quo" for any account of Spanish intellectual history in the early modern period. In this year, the discovery of America by Columbus with Castilian ships and personnel determined a new course for Spanish history. In the same year the Catholic Kings captured Granada, thus putting an end to Moorish sovereignty in western Europe. Finally the expulsion of the Jews and the need to instruct the *conversos* in the Catholic faith placed new demands on the Church and the cultural institutions.

Chroniclers of the period and foreigners traveling through Castile at the time are unanimous in their praise for the Catholic Kings (Ferninánd and Isabella, 1474-1516). They are considered the ministers through whose agency God had lifted the punishment that began in 711 with the Moorish conquest of Spain.[1] The Catholic Kings' advent to the throne coincided roughly with the introduction of the printing press into Spain and the cultural revolution that it brought along. During their reign were founded a large number of colleges and universities, which would play a crucial role in the intellectual conflicts of the sixteenth century: "fuit per ea tempora divinus quidam in multis ad extruendas Academias per Hispaniam ardor."[2]

In order to understand the conflicts and decadence of Spanish thought in the sixteenth century, the first name that must be mentioned is Antonio de Nebrija (1441-1522). In 1460, at the age of nineteen, after studying at the University of Salamanca, he went to Italy, where he spent ten years in contact with Italian humanism. Although Nebrija could not meet Lorenzo Valla, who had died in 1457, he became imbued with Valla's method and ideas. Valla has been called "the most brilliant of humanists, and one of the keenest critics that Europe has ever produced."[3] Indeed, a study of his works confirms this judgement. Valla is the originator of the most salient features of modern European thought: critical reading, stylistic analysis, historical sense, aesthetic sense.

The scholastics thought in analogies. Instead of reading the Bible directly, they presented a thesis usually formulated in Aristotelian terms, and would then go to the Bible in order to seek proofs for that thesis. In *Exodus* 3.14, for example,

God gives his name to Moses: "I am who I am." For the majority of the scholastics, with the exception of Hugo de Sancto Victore and a few others, this name was the divine sanction for the Aristotelian concept of *Esse subsistens*.

> "Ego sum qui sum," in hebreo habetur "ero qui ero"; per utramque tamen literam idem significatur, scilicet, necessitas essendi et eternitas et immutabilitas per omnem modum, quae est conditio propria et singularis ipsius Dei. Omnia enim alia, eo ipso quod sunt, de nihilo habent principium sui esse, et sunt vertibilia in nihil.[4]

Another example of the confusion between Greek thought and the Bible to which the scholastic method was liable can be found in King Alfonso's *General e grande Estoria* (c.1270). Commenting on the activities of the children of Cain in *Genesis* 4, Alfonso attributes to them—the "bad guys"—the invention of the mechanic arts, while the children of Seth—the "good guys"—are credited with the invention of the liberal arts: "Segund la verdat de la estoria los pilares e la escriptura destos saberes fecho fue; e pudo ser que fizieron los de Caym lo suyo, e que fue de las artes que dizen mecanicas, e los de Seth de las artes liberales e de lo que a ellas pertenesçie."[5] Music, however, created a special problem, for the Bible says that it was first used by Jubal, a grandson of Cain. King Alfonso says that Jubal invented music by chance, hearing the noise that his brother made with metals (a mechanic art), and Nicolaus de Lyra would put the matter to rest by saying that Jubal used music for the adoration of the idols: "Hebrei dicunt quod canebat instrumentis musicis coram ydolis. . . . Soror vero Tubalcaym Noema, ista adinvenit lanificum ad faciendum vestes."[6] *Lanificum* was, of course, another mechanic art.

There are many other examples of distortion in the reading of the Bible brought about by the analogical method used by the scholastics: the division of all human history into fourteen ages, the correspondence of those ages with different septenaries such as the seven deadly sins, the seven virtues, seven sacraments, seven gifts of the Holy Spirit, etc. These examples indicate what the analogical method really is: an *a priori* enslavement of the mind within patterns founded upon symmetry and correspondence which prevent the direct investigation of the object. Using the terms of Levi-Strauss, analogical thinking is simply savage thought, and savage thought is nothing but analogical and symbolic thought.

Valla's revolution took place when he abandoned symmetries
and symbolism and proposed instead a direct reading of the Bible
according to the rules of grammar. That is, he proposed to look
into the meaning of words at the time when the text was written,
and to trace the changes of that meaning through time. He would
examine the translations in order to see whether or not they
rendered the original sense properly. In this way he would as-
certain the sense of the Bible from its own context, and not
from Greek cosmology. The analogical method of the scholastics
was replaced by the philological method. The significance of
this leap is immense. Erasmus and Luther were simply pupils of
Valla's school. Valla inaugurated historical semantics, thus
discovering what was called "historical sense" at the beginning
of our century. In his detailed analysis of words he practiced
what we call today stylistics and hermeneutics. The aesthetic
enjoyment that derives from this detailed concern with the text
must also be attributed to Valla. When these aspects of his
work are duly appreciated, he will occupy the central role he
deserves in the histories of European philosophy.

Armed with the new method, Nebrija returned to Spain and
immediately found himself at odds with Father Diego de Deza, a
Dominican who was a strict defender of the scholastic method.
The dispute between Nebrija and Deza foreshadows the cultural
drama of Spain in the sixteenth century, which is basically the
struggle for life between the scholastic and the philological
method. The inquisitorial trials against the *alumbrados* and the
followers of Erasmus, the *Index of Prohibited Books* (1559), the
trial of Father Luis de León (1572-75), the suspicion against
Saint Teresa and mysticism in general, the suspicion against the
conversos, and other social injustices are only variations of
the same struggle.

After Nebrija, Cardinal Jiménez de Cisneros (d.1517) must
be mentioned as a key figure in Spanish intellectual life of the
early sixteenth century. A devoted Franciscan, Cisneros became
the confessor of Queen Isabella in 1492. After the death of
Cardinal Mendoza, Archbishop of Toledo, in 1495, the queen wanted
to appoint a saintly nobleman to the post. The archbishop had
to be a nobleman because--once again on the basis of scholastic
convictions--the wealth of the diocese could not be trusted to a
man of poor extraction since the humble origin would make a person unfit for the administration and generous spending of such
revenues. The first choice for the Toledo chair was Father Juan
de la Puebla (1453-95), who had resigned the county of Benalcázar
and had founded the "Province of Los Angeles," a variety of ob-
servant Franciscans. However, Father Juan turned down the offer

and died later that year. His death paved the way for Cisneros'
appointment as Archbishop of Toledo.[8]

Being a Franciscan, Cisneros was less committed to the
preservation of the scholastic method than were the Dominicans.
The official *magister* of the Dominicans, Saint Thomas Aquinas
(1225-74), enjoyed undisputed authority not only within the Dominican order, but also in the whole Church. The Franciscans
had also their official *magister*, Duns Scotus, but they were not
as disciplined as the Thomists. Two dissident trends made it
impossible for the Franciscans to create a compact school: Ock-
ham's nominalism, and the mystical attitude, which in many cases
involved an anti-scholastic bias.[9]

Cisneros belonged primarily to the mystical tradition.
Alvar Gómez, his biographer, tells us that as a young priest
he was imprisoned by the Toledan archbishop, Acuña. While in
jail he had a vision that the castle of Uceda, where he was
being held, would one day be his when he eventually became Archbishop of Toledo. Upon the discovery of America, he ardently
wished to go to the New World as a missionary, but he was dis-
suaded by a visionary woman, who predicted greater tasks for him
in Spain. With mystical fervor, Cisneros became a reformer, administrator, counselor to the kings, and eventually regent of
Castile.

Our interest here focuses on his role in the introduction
of the philological method into Spain. Cisneros created the
University of Alcalá in 1508, and immediately called the greatest
philologists of the time, including Nebrija and Erasmus, for the
most ambitious philological achievement of the period--the Alcalá Polyglot Bible of 1517. Erasmus declined the invitation
and did not play an active role in the Polyglot. However, he
had a peripheral influence. In 1502, when Prince Philip of
Flanders, heir to the Castilian throne through his marraige to
Juana the daughter of the Catholic Kings, came to Toledo, several
humanists, friends of Erasmus, accompanied him. Curiously
enough, it is in this context that Alvar Gómez places the origin
of the Polyglot:

> Intentionem ad ea convertit (Cisneros) quae jamdiu
> animo meditabatur. Intelligebat sane vir prudens
> sacrorum voluminum lectionem, quae Biblia Graeco
> nomine passim appellantur, cunctis qui sacris ini-
> tiati sunt, sed praesertim theologis, maxime esse
> necessariam, nullibique magis eosdem illos rerum
> theologicarum studiosos dormitare, quam in ea versanda
> tractandaque; idque potissimum e trium linguarum

ignoratione provenire, Hebraicae, Grecae et Latinae,
quibus non solum quicquid scitu dignum est in omnibus
disciplinis profanis est proditum, sed sacra omnia
continentur. Divinabat vir prudentissimus, in tanta
hominum nostrorum inertia, divinas literas negligentium,
impios homines quamprimum exorituros qui, earum
lectione armati, et suos affectus detorquentes,
Christi Ecclesiam ausu quidem nefario et immani, a
nostra tamen imperitia profecto, impugnare et evertere
tentarent.[10]

To be sure, Alvar Gómez makes it clear that Cisneros had had the
idea of the Polyglot long before 1502, but it is more probable
that he foresaw the future thunderstorm of the Church in the
conversations with the Flemish humanists. In any case the prestige Erasmus enjoyed in Spain until around 1535 must be explained
on the basis of the philological work done for the Polyglot, in
the context of the nominalism of Salamanca and Alcalá, and in
the context of Valla's pre-Erasmian influence.

   If we ask for the core of Erasmus' message, he gave it to
us in the following words:

Ego studiis meis nihil aliud conatus sum quam ut
bonas literas poene sepultas apud nostrates excitarem,
deinde ut mundum plus satis tribuentem Judaicis
ceremoniis ad verae et Evangelicae pietatis studium
spergefacerem; postremo, ut studia theologiae scholas-
tica nimium prolapsa ad inanium quaestionumcularum
argutias, ad divinas Scripturae fontes revocarem.
Nihil unquam asseveravi, semperque fugi dogmatistae
personam.[11]

Erasmus' words reflect exactly Valla's doctrine and purpose. A
study of Luther's writings between 1516 and 1520, before he formally broke with the pope, shows the same obsession: direct
reading of the Bible without scholastic questions, and a clear
distinction between what is revealed in the Holy Scriptures and
the theological conclusions derived from scholastic disputes.
As a result of the simplification in theology, they envisaged a
simplification of the spiritual life of the community through
the elimination of unnecessary ceremonies.

   At stake in this struggle was not only a method of reading
texts, but also a whole range of issues--first and foremost,
the sense of the ecclesiastical tradition as a source of Divine
revelation together with the Bible. Since the Church had tra-

ditionally lived from the Vulgate version, a rejection of the
Vulgate in favor of the Hebrew and Greek texts implied addition-
ally a rejection of tradition. Although the bearers of the tradition are all the faithful under the guidance of the pope, the
teaching Church, the Fathers, and the scholastic theologians
were something like the brain of that tradition--the "ecclesia
docens." To reject the authority of this conscious part of the
Church was, again, to challenge tradition as a source of revelation. Once the authority of the scholastics was challenged, the
individual mind was granted more responsibility with regard to
its own spiritual development, and thus the layman was given an
active role in the Church. The scholastics were right in as-
serting that much more than grammar was involved in Valla's and
Erasmus' method. Valla and Erasmus might be personally sincere
Catholics, but their doctrine had unpredictable implications.
The accusations against Erasmus on the part of the Dominicans
must be interpreted in this context. Erasmus summarized those
accusations:

> Consulueris autem non ordini modo Praedicatorio,
> verum etiam universo theologico, si quorundam
> meledicentiam insulsissimam autoritate tua reprimas,
> qui passim in publicis aut privatis praelection-
> ibus . . . et, quod gravissimum est, in sacris ac
> publicis concionibus virulentissime deblaterant in
> linguarum peritiam, in politiores leteras. In harum
> invidiam antichristos, haereses et alias id genus
> tragoedias admiscentes, cum obscurum non sit quid
> Ecclesia debeat viris linguarum peritis, quid debeat
> eloquentibus.[12]

Luther's rebellion against the pope in 1520 and the wars of
religion in which Spain became so deeply involved gave a boost
to the anti-philological party. As we gather from Erasmus'
text, the Dominicans linked the study of languages to the origin
of Protestantism. This link was soon forgotten in the rest of
Europe. On the one hand Lutherans tempered their philological
studies with a certain degree of scholasticism, as is already
visible in Melanchthon, and on the other, the scholastics become
convinced of the need for philology. In Spain, however, the
struggle for life and death continued until 1575, ending in the
absolute predominance of scholasticism.

The issue was clearly stated at the trial of Maria Cazalla,
opening in 1532:

> Preguntada si ha llamado a Sto. Tomás aristotélico
> e a Escoto soñador e desvanitado, reprovando las
> cosas escolásticas, dixo que nunca tal ha dicho esta
> declarante. Preguntada si a dicho que Erasmo merecía
> ser canonizado, alabándole diziendo que tiene por
> evangelio todo lo que ha escrito, dixo que esta
> declarante muchas vezes a alabado las cosas de Erasmo
> e sus obras, e esta declarante a leído un Paternoster
> suyo en romance, el Ynquiridion e los Coloquios e
> los a tenido e tiene por buenas obras hasta que otra
> cosa esté determinado por la Yglesia.[13]

Father Francisco de Osuna (1492?-1541?), a great mystic,
improperly considered by scholars a master of Santa Teresa,
wrote in the midst of these polemics:

> La manera con que los filisteos alcançaron tanto
> dominio sobre Israel fue haziendo que no huviesse
> armero ninguno entre los israelitas e assi los
> hereges luego entran negando los doctores escolas-
> ticos, que con sus argumentos como con martillos
> apuradamente aclaran una verdad, que es arma de
> nuestro entendimiento. Comiençan tambien a negar
> las glosas de la Escriptura, pro que deçendamos a
> ellos y nos sirvamos de las suyas. Atrevense
> tambien al texto evangélico diziendo que assi assi
> avia de tresladar, porque como los israelitas,
> deçendamos y vamos a ellos, *usque ad stimulum corri-*
> *gendum,* hasta una palabra de la Escriptura que acaso
> por negligencia de los impresores se halla menos
> bien, querrian que fuessemos a la corregir con sus
> novedades para que assi nos pudiessen conformar
> con sus opiniones e subjectar a sus parecares y
> novedades que más de cierto son no-verdades. Porque,
> como diz Sant Buenaventura, quien busca en la
> Sagrada Escriptura otra cosa de lo que la Yglesia
> tiene, mentira busca y mentira fallara.[14]

In 1547, in a speech to the Council of Trent, the famous
theologian Domingo de Soto described the struggle bewteen Catholics and Protestants precisely as a conflict between scholasticism and philology:

> Theriacam philosophiam censete, circumspectissime
> senatus, quae earundem medetur viperarum morsibus,

ex quarum conficitur carnibus. Et quo semel finiam,
quinam linguas quam Germani excultius polivere? Qui
pluries sacram paginam revolverunt? Quid ergo restet
illius causae tam plurium errorum, quam quod theologiam
scholasticam neglexerint? Ex cujus ignorantia omnes
dimanasse, facile erit rem perpendenti conjicere.
Profecto simul, apud eosdemque coepere, et linguarum
cultura, et scholasticae rationis contemptus, et
haeresum turba.[15]

These words are the eulogy to the death of a culture; for Soto
is in effect documenting the cultural inferiority of Spain with
regard to Europe in 1547. He concedes that the Germans have
read the Bible and the Church Fathers, and have studied the
classical languages more and better than the Spaniards. When we
compare this statement with Nebrija's and Cisneros' passion for
philology, we must admit that Spain moved backward in the thirty
years between 1517 and 1547.

The connection between the study of languages and heresy
became popularized in treatises such as *Luz del alma cristiana,*
an anti-Erasmian book written by the Dominican Father Felipe de
Meneses and published in 1554. The intellectual struggle culminated in what I call the quadruple repression of 1559:
(1) the publication of the *Index of Prohibited Books,* in which
almost everything original written in Castilian was prohibited;
(2) the *autos de fe* of Valladolid and Seville; (3) the prohibition to Spaniards to study in European universities not controlled by the king of Spain; (4) the imprisonment of Archbishop
Carranza of Toledo because he had written a theological treatise
in Castilian *(Comentarios del Catecismo cristiano,* 1558). After
1559 anything that was mystical or philological in nature became
suspicious. The trial of Father Luis de León (1572-75) shows
that only the scholastic method was considered orthodox.

However, our view would be one-sided and exaggerated if we
presented the scholastics as obscurantists without intellectual
capacity or merit. Any unbiased outline of Spanish intellectual
life in the sixteenth century must emphasize the intellectual
power and contribution of at least four great scholastics:
Francisco de Vitoria (1492-1546), Melchor Cano (1509-60), Luis
de Molina (1535-1600), and Francisco Suárez (1548-1617). We
will single out Melchor Cano because of his direct participation
in the struggle we are describing.

Cano's principal book, *De locis theologicis,* was published
in 1563, three years after his death. He proposed to write it
in fourteen books, but left only twelve. In Kantian terms we

could call it a *Critique of Theological Reason,* for in it Cano
reflects upon the very foundations of theology, analyzing the
value of all sources of proof in this science. It is a theological treatise because Cano never questions the value of faith in
divine authority, but it is also a humanistic book because it
tries to give a rational foundation to faith. As a comprehen-
sive study of the nature and foundations of theology, Cano's
book is strictly a metatheology. Nothing similar can be found
in books with the same title such as Melanchthon's *De locis
theologicis* (last verison, 1544). Melanchthon writes theology;
he deals with God, sin, sacraments, virtues, freedom, and other
points of Christian faith, but he does not create, like Cano, a
theory of theological reasoning.

Like Erasmus, Cano criticizes harshly the practice of many
theologians who would not use the Bible in their discipline and
who ask superfluous speculative questions far removed from the
sources of revelation. Another target of his criticism is the
popular and uncritical belief in miracles and legends. At one
point Cano adds: "hujus generis sunt alia multa quae diligentis-
sime et rectissime Erasmus refutavit."[16]

However, this coincidence with Erasmus should not mislead
us. Cano was anti-Erasmian in all important points. For him
the ecclesiastical tradition was not only a source of authentic
revelation, it was also the primary source from which the written word of the Bible was derived. The life of the Church was
thus the ultimate criterion for the interpretation of the Scriptures. Concerning the Epistle to the Hebrews, for example, Cano
admitted that it was written by Saint Paul because it had been
traditionally attributed to Saint Paul. Yet this problem was
for him of secondary importance. Whoever the author might be,
the canonical character of the Epistle cannot be challenged.
Valla had demonstrated the falsification involved in the so-
called "donatio Constantini." For Cano that whole question was
a pseudo-problem; whether Constantine gave Rome to the popes or
not, the fact was that the popes now sat as sovereigns in Rome.
If not Constantine, somebody else had given Rome to the Church.

Concerning the role of laymen, Cano follows the traditional
doctrine of the *Ecclesia docens*--the clergy--and the *Ecclesia
discens*--the laymen:

> Inter haereticorum et Catholicorum traditiones maximum
> esse [est] discrimen. Haeretici enim mysteria sua
> mulierculis et idiotis homunculis produnt; at Catholici
> mysticas et sacras ecclesiae traditiones muliercularum
> Homuncionumque vulgo prodere, piaculi loco habent.[17]

Because of the role the Vulgate had played in the shaping of the western Church, Cano considered it to be the original Bible. It would be unthinkable that the great theologians over eleven centuries, although they did not know Hebrew or Greek, could have erred in their authoritative explanations of the Bible. Cano's commitment to the defense of ecclesiastical tradition was so deep that he believed that the Vulgate must be preferred wherever it differed from the original texts. Preference for the Vulgate did not mean complete rejection of the original languages. However, Cano did not consider such a study essential for the theologian. It was useful in order to fight heretics with their own tools. Cano's verdict in the struggle between scholastic method and philology coincided with those of Soto and Meneses: "connexae quippe sunt, ac fuere semper post natam scholam, scholae contemptio et haeresum pestes."[18]

The scholastics fought not only the philological method of reading the Bible; they were on guard against a third front that emerged as an historical force around 1500—mysticism. The origins of Spanish mysticism can be traced to the reformation of religious orders that took place in the second half of the fifteenth century and culminated with Cisneros. As literature, mysticism was just another aspect of the Italian influence in Spain during the fifteenth century. Through the spiritual writings of Saint Bonaventure (1221-74) and other Franciscans, the reformed friars and nuns were led to the texts of Saint Gregory, Saint Bernard, and above all, to "Saint Dionysius," whose writings determined with a few exceptions the language of mysticism in the western world.

The mystical process, according to Dionysius and Saint Bonaventure, is an ascension that reaches the union with God in three steps: (1) purification from external images and worldly concerns (purification from matter); (2) illumination in direct proportion to the degree of purification from matter; and (3) union with God, when all material and figurative elements have been left behind. The father of this doctrine was "Saint Dionysius," a supposed disciple of Saint Paul, member of the Athenian court (*Areopagos*), who converted to Christianity upon hearing the apostle. The writings of Dionysius, unknown before the sixth century, were metaphysical and neo-Platonic in nature. When Valla analyzed them and compared them to the language and intellectual horizon of Saint Paul, he declared it impossible that a disciple of the apostle could have written such a mixture of wine and water—i.e., religion and Greek metaphysics. However plausible Valla's thesis appeared on historical and philological grounds, the scholastics had so much invested in the au-

authority of those writings that they could not accept it.
Pseudo-Dionysius was an example of that very symbiosis of Greek
thought and Christianity which constituted the scholastic method;
yet that symbiosis seemed deplorable to Valla. As a result of
his discovery, Dionysius became an impostor for Valla and for
Erasmus a "Dionysius quidam." Yet for the Spanish scholastics
and mystics he continued to be Saint Dionysius, the disciple and
best interpreter of Saint Paul.

The first confrontation between scholastics and mystics
took place in 1525, when an edict was published in Toledo against
a spiritual movement called "the illuminati" (*los alumbrados*).
From their trials we gather that they intended to go beyond the
level of purification and to live in the level of illumination.
This ideal led them to intimate the need of mental prayer; as a
result, they showed a certain disdain for external ceremonies
and vocal prayer. The movement was just a variety of a Franciscan spiritualism that had traditionally scorned scholastic theology and worldly concerns. It coincided with the thought of
Luther and Erasmus in the disdain of ceremonies, but their aims
were absolutely different: they aspired to the mystical union
with God, while Erasmus considered mysticism something alien to
Christianity. Erasmus rejected Dionysius, the *alumbrados* followed him.[19] The *alumbrados* were as far removed from Erasmus
and Luther as one could be, and if it had not been for Luther
they probably would never have been disturbed. But what can be
allowed in peaceful times may be considered dangerous in times
of crisis. Frequently in the text of the trials of *alumbrados*
the inquisitors conceded that certain words might not be dangerous in general, but that "in these times" they were.

What made the *alumbrados* suspect of Lutheranism was that
they were laymen, and they dared to "teach," claiming a right
that was restricted to the clergy. As laymen they were supposed
to conduct a practical life, not a contemplative one. Chiding
the spiritual writings of Father Luis de Granada (1504-88),
Melchor Cano says:

> Aloisius iste contra prudentiam Pauli sapientiam
> inter imperfectos loquitur et parvulis solidum
> cibum dat, quem capere non possunt nedum concoquere.
> Item dum mulierculas et promiscuum vulgum atque
> universos demum homines ad contemplationem orationemque
> mentalem traducere nititur, otiosos reddit a labore
> et operis reipublicae necessariis avocat. . . .
> Quid quod Fr. Baptistam Cremensem, Seraphinum a
> Fermo, Henricum Herpp, Illuminatorum antesignanos

nimis laudibus effert?[20]

Cano condemned Father Luis de Granada because he opened the way
of perfection to laymen who, according to Saint Paul--in Melchor
Cano's interpretation--must be given only soft foods, like children. The spirituality of the layman could only be active, in
imitation of Martha, contemplation being for those who took the
three vows of chastity, poverty, obedience. Those vows, according to the scholastics, placed the individual in an objective
state of perfection which could not be attained by those who
were neither monks nor nuns. To be sure, a layman or a married
person might be more perfect than a monk or a nun, but the layman was never in the objective state of perfection. Erasmus
ridiculed the theology of the vows, and Luther rejected them as
sources of immorality. Thus when the *alumbrados* talked of perfection and union with God as laymen, they became the targets of
suspicion and persecution.

What was at stake in the struggle between the scholastics
and the *alumbrados* was the future of the vernacular languages as
vehicles of religious and theological expression. The scholastics had encapsuled their doctrine in stereotyped Latin formu-
las. For example, they claimed to be in "exemplary participation" with God's Being. They could not be in "formal participation" because then they would share the same nature with God,
which would be pantheism. When the *alumbrados, mulierculae,* and
homunculi, who did not know Latin, spoke of becoming one with
God, or of God inhabiting their soul, they were unable to talk
with the precision required by the scholastics. The vernacular
language became their mousetrap, and the end result was the
Index of Prohibited Books of 1559, which included all preceding
mystical writing. The early mysticism springing from the metaphysical tradition died that year in Spain. When those books
were prohibited, Saint Teresa (1515-82) was afflicted because
she was accustomed to read them. Christ appeared to her and
said: "I will be your teacher." As a result of this teaching,
she escaped the difficulties of the *alumbrados* by not making any
abstract statement or becoming involved with theologians. She
simply wrote an autobiography--pure facts and pure experience--
and gave it to two disciples of Melchor Cano who were full of
suspicion--Bartolomé de Medina and Domingo Báñez. Both were
overcome by the sublimity of Saint Teresa. She effected the
reconciliation between mysticism and theology.

The humanistic tradition never recovered. The intellectual
struggle between scholastics and philologists began as a lively
exchange conducted with learning and rigor, but soon one of the

sides resorted to devious means. Soto and Melchor Cano became
advisors to the Grand Inquisitor Fernando de Valdés, and they
were the forces behind the destructive repression of 1559.
Spain became a mousetrap of suspicion, espionage, and fear. A
good way to avoid danger was not to have any ideas, and the best
way of all was to be illiterate.

Yet if it is true that God makes good out of every evil,
the Spanish inquisition had an effect of lasting value: *Hamlet*,
for the source of its scenes of espionage and intrigue and of
several characters such as Rosenkrantz and Guildenstern, drew
from *The Arts of the Spanish Inquisition* by Reginaldus Gonsalvius
Montanus published in London in 1568. That poor Reynaldo, sent
to Paris to make inquiry about Laertes and other Danskers, was
called Montano in the "bad quarto" of 1603. He is the poor
Sevillan monk who fled the holocaust of 1559, and first published
his book on the Inquisition in Heidelberg. *Measure for Measure*
is yet another parody of the Spanish institution. And in *The
Comedy of Errors*, the characters are not referring to spices
when they say:

> Antipholus (S): Where Spain?
> Dormio (S): Faith, I saw it not; but I felt it
>   hot in her breath (III.ii.132-33)

Ciricao Morón Arroyo

Cornell University

NOTES

CHAPTER I

Research for this study was made possible by the grant of a Senior Fellowship from the Folger Shakespeare Library, a grant-in-aid from the American Association of Learned Societies, and a research grant from Westfield State College. Citations in parentheses following royal edicts are the catalogue numbers of Robert O. Lindsay and John Neu, *French Political Pamphlets, 1547-1648: A Catalog of Major Collections in American Libraries* (Madison, 1969). Peculiarities of accenting and spelling have been retained from the original text.

[1]Roger Doucet, "La mort de François Ier," *Revue historique*, 113 (1913), 306-16, esp. p. 315. The characterization of Henry II: Lucien Romier, *Jacques d'Albon de Saint-André* (Paris, 1909), p. 15.

[2]The manuscript journal of the sire de Gouberville for the years 1553-62 was discovered by the abbé de Tollemer in 1867. In 1880 he published a précis of the journal with copious extracts and a commentary which is valuable because Tollemer did have access to the then extant archives of the Norman countryside. It is impossible now to take seriously his pronounced views on heresy and cowardice. Tollemer's work has been reissued with a valuable introduction, particularly in its reconstruction of the agricultural and commercial life of the Cotentin, by Emanual LeRoy Ladurie, Abbé de Tollemer, *Un sire de Gouberville: Gentilhomme campagnard du Cotentin* (Paris, 1972). LeRoy Ladurie mentions a study of the journal as a whole currently being prepared by Nicole Bernageau. Four more years of the journal (1549-52) were discovered after the death of Tollemer. Two popular commentaries, with excerpts, have been published. Katharine Fedden, *Manor Life in Old France* (New York, 1934), and Claude Blanguernon, *Gilles de Gouberville: Gentilhomme du Cotentin, 1522-1578* (Coutances, 1969). Both journals were printed in their entirety by the Société des antiquaires de Normandie. These editions form the basis of this article. *Le journal du Sire de Gouberville, publié sur la copie du manuscrit original faite par M. l'abbé de Tollemer*, intro. Eugène de Robillard de Beaurepaire (Caen, 1892). To be cited as I. *Journal de Gilles de Gouberville pour les années 1549, 1550, 1551,*

1552, introd. A. de Blanguy. To be cited as II. Citations from the journals will be given by date, volume, and page.

[3]Lettres patentes dv Roy svr la defense et prohibition des traictes & transports des bleds & grains hors son Royaume, July 8, Paris: R. Estienne, 1565 (434). Claude de Seyssel felt that there were more officials in France than there were in the rest of Christendom. *La grãdmonarchie de France, composee par messire Claude de Seyssel* (Paris: Denys Ianot, 1541), fols. 18[v]-19[r]. Certainly contemporaries agreed with him. See the complaints registered in the cahiers of the Estates of Orleans in *Des États Généraux et autres assemblées nationales,* ed. C. J. Mayer (The Hague and Paris, 1789), XI, 58-59, 80, 88-89, 152, 195, 256, 347. That the proliferation of offices was apt to be due to royal financial exigency and hence to venality was recognized and deplored: for example, Ordonnances dv Roy Charles Neufiesme à present regnant, faictes en son conseil, sur les Plainctes, Doleances, & Remonstrances de deputez des trois Estatz, tenuez en la ville d'Orléans, Paris: I. Dailler, 1561 (240).

[4]Seyssel, *Grãdmonarchie,* is indispensable for a contemporary and sophisticated view of the monarchy at the beginning of the reign of Francis I. Cf. chaps. viii-xix, fols. 10[v]-22[r]. Cf. also Antoine Fontanon, *Les Edicts et Ordonnances des Roys de France* (Paris: Iacques du Puys, 1580), 4 vols. Nicolas de La mare, *Traité de la police* (Paris: Jean & Pierre Cot, 1705-38), 4 vols, which includes innumerable documents, is a mine of information. Norman customary law, 1552 edition, was very much out of date. Cf. *Le Covstumier du pays, & duche de Normendie* (Rouen: M. le Mesgissier, 1552), and the *lettres patentes* issued at Rouen, November 15, 1567, cited in C. A. Bourdot de Richebourg, *Nouveau Coutumier Général* (Paris: Claude Robuster, 1724), IV, 111.

[5]"François par la Grace de Dieu roy de France . . . Scavoir faisons, comme nous desirans toutes choses tant grandes que petites, concernans le bien de noz suiets estre reglées & mesurées par raison, & en prevoyant les inconveniens, qui dependent des erreurs, y obvier & pourvoir, arrestant de longue main & à temps de cours d'iceux erreurs, "Fontainbleau, May 22, 1539, in Fontanon, *Edicts,* I, 706. Crane Brinton notes the medieval antecedents of Jacobin legislation, *A Decade of Revolution, 1789-1799* (New York and London, 1934), p. 134. The crown made a constant effort to reform sloppy procedures. For example: Edict du Roy nostre sire, sur la nouvelle creation & reiglement des tresoriers generaulx de ses finances, Paris: G. Corrozet, 1552 (41), and Edict du Roy concernant le povvoir et ivrisdiction des Preuosts des Mareschaux, Vibaillifs & Viseneschaux, Paris: R. Estienne,

1567, (520).

[6]Pigs: La Mare, *Traité de la police,* II, 1311; butter, ibid., I, 576; meat: ibid., I, 571; fish: ibid., I, 576, III, 62. Sanitation: Ordonnance du Roy concernant le faict des sailles, des quais, paue, boués & immondices de la ville & faulxbourges de Paris (Paris: R. Estienne, 1563).

[7]June 15, 1561, Gouberville's illegitimate brother and servant, Noel, was set upon by one Robert Heu. "Le mercredi XVIIIe . . . Sanson assembla chez Gastemo, Lescures, Lefresne, Monceaulx, advocats, pour scavoir si je seroys prenable du faict de mes serviteurs, quand pour l'intérest cyvil," I, 683-84. From the battles over inheritances between contentious mothers and greedy children "s'ensuit la desolation des bonnes familes, & consequemment diminution de la force de l'estat publique." Edict du Roy, deffendant à tous et toutes venans à secondes nopces de n'auancer leurs secondes parties, ou leurs enfans l'vn plus que l'autre, ny les enfans de leurs enfans, Paris: Dallier & Sertenas, 1560 (190).

[8]Cf. Ordonnances . . . d'Orléans, fol. 38; La Mare, *Traité de la police,* I, 493; and Arrest du Parlement de Paris, qui ordonne aux Propriétaires & Principaux Locataires des Maisons de ceste Ville, de s'informer exactement des vies, moeurs, & Religion de ceux qui y demeurent, pour en rendre compte aux Commissaires & aux Quarteniers, September 6, 1559, in *Memoires de Condé, servant a l'éclaircissement et de preuves à l'Histoire de M. de Thou* (London, 1743), I, 308-09. Innkeepers were to disarm the guest; Ordonnance et arrest de la Court, suyvant l'expres mandement du Roy, sur les defences à toutes personnes, fussent ilz gentilzhommes, de porter pistoles, pistoletz, n'autres bastons à feu, sur peine de la vie, Paris: G. Nuyerd, 1560 (178).

[9]Ordonnances . . . Orleans, fols. 26v-27r. See the complaints of 1560: there were townspeople "si peu curieux du repos public, & si peu charitables, que, voyant deux hommes s'entrebattre ou avoir querele ensemble, qu'ils, s'enfermeront plutôt en leurs maisons pour n'en voir rien, que s'efforcer d'appaiser les noises & séparer ceux qui s'entrebattent," Mayer, ed., *Des États Généraux,* XI, 393.

[10]Francis I to Joachim de Matignon, Amiens, September 29, 1545, in L. H. Labande, ed., *Correspondance de Joachim de Matignon Lieutenant Général du Roi en Normandie (1516-1548)* (Monaco, 1914), p. 142.

[11]Lettres patentes dv Roy, contenãs reiteratiues defenses à toutes personnes, de quelque estat, qualité & condition qu'ilz soyent (sans nulz excepter) de porter hacquebutes, Paris: I. Dallier, 1559 (151). See also Ordinnances faites par le Roy a

Moulins, av mois de Feurier, MDLXVI (Lyon: B. Rigaud, 1566),
pp. 19, 74. Exceptions to the prohibitions were recognized:
Declaration dv Roy de cevlx à qui il est permis de porter har-
quebuzes & pistoletz à feu, Paris: A. le Clerc, 1559 (140);
Lettres patentes dv Roy contenantes les deffences de porter har-
quebuzes, pistolles, pistolletz à feu, ny Arbalestres, sur peyne
de confiscation de corps & de biens, Rouen: M. le Mesgissier,
1571. Cf. also the arguments of the nobility: Mayer, ed., *Des
États Généraux*, XI, 104-05, 131, 208-09, 238-39, and of the merchants, who knew that gun legislation would only put the lives
of the innocent in jeopardy. Ibid., XI, 473-74.

[12]Contemporary, albeit brief, descriptions of the Cotentin
may be found in La Mare, *Traité de la police*, II, 298, 1088,
1097-98, 1100, 1133, 1143, 1374, 1448-52; III, 36, 412-13, 765;
IV, 496; Robert Dallington, *The View of Fraunce, 1604*, introd.
W.P. Barrett (London, 1936); [Andre Duchesne], *Les Antiqvitez et
Recherches des Villes, Chasteaux, et places plvs remarquables de
toute la France*, 2nd ed. (Paris: I. Petit Pas, 1614), pp. 937-
98; J. Eliot, *The Svrvay or Topographical Description of France*
(London: I. Wolfe, 1592), pp. 34-42; *Les plans et profilz de
toutes les principalles Villes et lieux considerables de
France...Faictes par Le S*[r] *Tassin Geogra*[e] *Ordinaire de sa Mat*[e]
(n.p., n.d.; privilege granted, Château Thierry, November 15,
1631), p. 30. Maps: H. A. Moll, *A New and exact Map of France*,
I (London, 1701), and Richard Mount, *The Sea-Coasts of France
from Calais to Bayone* (London, 1701). Roads: Moll, *New and exact Map*, and Charles Estienne, *Le guide des chemins de France de
1553*, ed. J. Bonnerot (Paris, 1936), pp. 128-38. An overview is
given in *Histoire de la Normandie publiée sous la direction de
Michel de Boüard* (Toulouse, 1970). One volume of the definitive
historical geography of Normandy being prepared under the direction of the Centre de recherches d'histoire quantitative at the
University of Caen has appeared. Its starting point is 1631.
Cf. P. Gouhier, A. Vallez, and J. M. Vallez, *Atlas historique de
Normandie* (Caen, 1967). The current Michelin road map of Normandy, which shows Mesnil-au-Val, Gouberville, Russy, and Sorteval, is extemely useful.

[13]The division of the inheritance at Russy was a complicated
performance. His uncle died September 11, 1560, five days after
Gouberville had made him a present of some venison. I, 589-90,
and I, 590-710, *passim*, on the inventories.

[14]Cf. Généalogie des sires de Russy, de Gouberville, et du
Mesnil-au-Val, I. The family surname was Picot.

[15]For example: in 1549, 1551, 1552, 1554, 1555, 1557. II,
204, 250; I, 95, 178, 243, 345, 411, and see above, p. 7.

[16]November 26-28, 1555, I, 231-32. In 1561 Gouberville was elected deputy for the nobility of the Cotentin to the Estates at St. Lo. May 7, 22-June 2, 1561, I, 669, 674-78.

[17]Généalogie, I.

[18]As *lieutenant des eaux et forêts*, Gouberville was responsible for the forest of Brix; his specific duties are discussed in Michel Devèze, *La vie de la forêt française au XVIe siecle* (Paris, 1961), I, 157-60. On the confirmation of his office under Francis II, April 18, 1560, I, 559. The forest of Brix was cleared in 1789 to make way for a housing development. André Plaisse, "La forêt de Brix au XVe siècle" *Annales de Normandie*, 14th year, no. 4, December 1964, pp. 411-43.

[19]November 18, 1557, I, 386; October 1, 1560, I, 594-95.

[20]On the relations between François Picot, sire de Sorteval, and his wife, Marie de La Fontaine, for example: February 26, 1556 o.s., I, 334; November 8, 1557, I, 383; December 7-8, 1557, I, 390; April 27, 1558, I, 423; December 31, 1560, I, 624-25. There were two other legitimate brothers: Guillaume, who died in Paris sometime before 1555, and Louis, who vanishes from the Journal in 1557. Tassine Picot was not amenable to fraternal criticism of her life-style. February 23, 1560 o.s., I, 645. The other illegitimate brothers were Ernoulf, Jacques, Noel, and Jean, II, 7, n. 1. Noel is the most frequently mentioned, and was clearly in the position of servant.

[21]There are innumerable references to *corvées* and dues: cf. August 4, 1562, I, 699; October 5, 1552, II, 278.

[22]April 9, 1954, I, 84. Trips to Rouen were ordinarily referred to as "voyages"; cf. June 12, 1550, II, 101; January 20-February 19, 1555 o.s., I, 247-49: the famous trip to Blois.

[23]Henry II: July 17, 1559, I, 505; March 19, 1560 o.s., I, 653; Vassy: March 27, 1562, I, 764; Pantagruel: June 4, 1552, II, 251.

[24]Apprentices: July 4, 1552, II, 258; pigs: November 17, 1556, I, 312, and La Mare, *Traité de la police*, II, 1310; sheep: September 18, 1552, II, 275.

[25]Tusks; I, 107; blacks: I, 289.

[26]Street fight: June 18, 1551, II, 188; suffocation: July 26, 1554, I, 110; woman: June 26, 1556, I, 227.

[27]This was particularly true in August and September, the harvest months.

[28]On special preparations: May 29-31, 1549, I, 15; January 18-29, 1559 o.s., I, 547. Gouberville was regularly included at weddings and christenings at Bricbeque and Tocqueville: cf. February 11, 1553 o.s., I, 72-73; February 20, 1557 o.s., I, 409. He lost at cards to Adrienne d'Estouteville, July 8, 1552,

II, 258-59. Cf. January 12, 1559 o.s., I, 544: "Je fus quérir Thomas Drouet à sa maison pour me tenir compagnie à desieuner."

[29]For a sample of daily life: June 21, 1553, I, 18 (trees); January 31, 1554 o.s., I, 154-55 (millstones); September 29, 1554, I, 125 (stags); December 28, 1551, II, 214 (horses); November 6, 1556, I, 309 (mad dogs); July 31, 1561, I, 698 (lightning); April 9, 1561, I, 757 (wolves); February 27, 1560 o.s., I, 646 (colic); April 15, 1561, I, 662 (gout); July 7, 1552, II, 258 (rash); July 5, 1561, I, 688 (poverty); January 1, 25, 1553, I, 69-70 (over-indulgence). There are references to an unspecified "peste": cf. February 19, 1551 o.s., II, 227; September 12, 1552, II, 273; November 9, 1561, I, 722. Gouberville always refers to "maladeries" as directional landmarks. Cf. June 11, 1551, II, 165. Leprosy does seem to have disappeared: cf. Pierre Goubert, *Beauvais et le Beauvaisis de 1660 à 1730* (Paris, 1960), I, 70, and André Fouré, "Lépreux et léproseries dans le diocése de Rouen," *Revue des Sociétés savantes de Haute Normandie*, no. 31, 3rd trimestre, 1963, pp. 7-16.

[30]Advice: March 27, 1562, I, 764. Legal aid: June 30, 1549, II, 22. The instances of medical care are legion: for example, the case of Jacquet Le Barbenchon, December 7, 1555, I, 234-35. Loans were also constant: cf. June 16, 1549, II, 18. See Elizabeth S. Teall, "The Seigneur of Renaissance France: Advocate or Oppressor?" *Journal of Modern History*, 37 (1965), 131-50.

[31]Diagnosis: September 21-22, 1551, II, 189; woman: July 15, 1562, I, 801; widow: January 9, 14, 1553 o.s., I, 65-66; drunk: October 18, 1551, II, 195.

[32]Child: December 12, 1557, I, 391; loans: cf. August 3, 6, 24, I, 112-16.

[33]On three occasions he failed to have a party: in 1559, when he thought he was dying, I, 515, and in 1561 and 1562, see above, p. 7. Babies, etc.: March 13, 1549 o.s., II, 81; February 19, 1551 o.s., II, 227, to give but two examples.

[34]None of the commentary is very flattering. Cf. Duchesne, *Antiqvitez*, p. 995; Eliot, *Svrvay*, p. 41; Jean de Marcouville, *La Maniere de bien policer la Respublique Chrestienne* (Paris: I. Dallier, 1562), fol. 91r; *Les plans et profilz...par le Sr Tassin*, p. 30.

[35]From a multitude of examples: December 8, 1553, I, 57; January 28, 1553 o.s., I, 70; February 15, 1553 o.s., I, 74; October 16, 1554, I, 130 (Mesnage); February 1, 12, 1558 o.s., I, 474; March 8, 1558, I, 480-81 (Dufour); October 27, 1559, I, 527; January 14, 1561 o.s., I, 746 (Berger).

[36]Cf. April 28, 1549, II, 7; November 13, 1549, II, 55; May

3, 1550, II, 92-93; April 9, 1553, I, 4; July 27, 1553, I, 25; February 19, 1553 o.s., I, 76; June 21, 1561, I, 684-85; November 1, 1561, I, 719-20; February 26, 1561 o.s., I, 756.

[37]Apprehension, witnesses, recovery of property: cf. October 6, 1549, II, 47; November 2, 1549, II, 53; December 6, 1549, II, 61; February 4, 1549 o.s., II, 73; March 7, 1549 o.s., II, 79-80; April 3, 1550, II, 86; November 15-27, 1552, II, 286-89; October 10-11, 1555, I, 218-19; September 11-12, 1556, I, 295-96; August 3, 1557, I, 366.

[38]Seigneurial activity did not discount the law: cf. the cases of Symon DuBosc, September 9-13, 1550, II, 109, and of one Labellec, March 6, 1558 o.s., I, 480. Cf. also Edict du Roy par leqvel il confirme tovs ivgemens donnez sur les compromis des parties, pour auoir telle force & vertu, que les sentences données par les Iuges Royaulx . . . mil cinq cens soixante & un, Rouen: M. le Mesgissier, 1569 (661).

[39]On the career of Nicolas Quentin: September 3, 1550-December 31, 1551, II, 108-210, *passim;* April 30-September 25, 1553, I, 8-38, *passim;* June 8-10, 1554, I, 100-01; July 14, 1556, I, 281; November 16, 1556, I, 312; January 2, 1557 o.s., I, 397-98.

[40]The LeParmentiers enjoyed an unpleasant reputation: cf. June 5, 1553, I, 15; July 31, 1553, I, 26. The attack on the curé: February 13, 1553 o.s., I, 74.

[41]August 20-26, 1558, I, 443-44.

[42]September 6, 1558-July 13, 1561, I, 446-691, *passim.*

[43]November 8, 1560, I, 605.

[44]Anne Chandeleur was a constant dinner guest. Cf. January 12, 1559 o.s., January 11, 1562 o.s., I, 544-858 *passim.* "Avant que fusse levé, la femme de feu Chandeleur estoyt venue pour sçavoyr comme je me portoys," January 24, 1561 o.s., I, 748.

[45]On the apprehension of murderers, Mayer, ed., *Des États Généraux,* XI, 390, and Ordonnances . . . Orléans, fols. 28[v]-29[r]. Norman custom in 1552 still officially recognized the archaic procedures of challenge by the kin and trial by battle. Ch. lxviij, "De suyte de meurdre," *Covstumier du pays & duche de Normandie,* fols. liii[v]-liiiiij[v]. In 1583, article 68 and others equally old-fashioned "ont esté declarez abrogez comme inutils: d'autant que ce qui en usage a esté employé audit cayer de Coustumes reformée sanz aultres tiltres & articles, au bien y a esté pourveu par les ordonnances," Procés Verbal des Coustumes de Normandie, in Bourdot de Richebourg, *Nouveau Coutumier Général,* IV, 122.

[46]Cf. particularly the battles with the vicomte de Valognes:

December 3, 10-14, 1555, I, 233, 235. Cf. also on the forest
administration, July 27, 1549, II, 30; August 3, 1549, II, 33-
34; March 4, 1549 o.s., II, 79, and July 28, 1551, II, 175.

[47]Quentin: May 29, 1549, II, 14; June 2, 1549, II, 15;
January 23, 1551 o.s., II, 221-22, DuBosc: December 11, 1553,
I, 58. Symonnet: December 7, 1561, II, 734. Coins: June 24,
1554, I, 104; May 1, 1557, I, 347.

[48]October 14, 25, 1549, II, 49, 51; October 23, 1550, II,
118; January 17, 1557 o.s., I, 401; June 13, 1551, II, 165;
October 25, 1552, II, 282; March 19, 1554 o.s., I, 168; March
26, 1555, I, 170. Business was normally conducted at the conclusion of mass, cf. September 15, 1555, I, 213, a practice to
which the clergy protested in 1560, Mayer, ed., Des États Généraux, XI, 81, but cf. Edict de reiglement sur le faict des
Criees & Decretz, Fontainebleau, September 3, 1551, bound with
Ordonnances . . . Moulins.

[49]Fortifications: May 6-August 30, 1549, II, 26-40; May 5-
June 10, 1550, II, 98-100. The crown's interest in the fortifications of the Cotentin is attested in Labande, ed., Correspondance de . . . Matignon, passim. The problem of provisioning was annual: cf. 1550: II, 132-33; 1551, II, 223; 1552, II,
265-66; 1553: I, 8, 24-25, 55, 75; 1554: I, 110, 120, 151;
1555: I, 198-200, 209-14, 218, 227; 1556, I, 302; 1557, I, 374;
1558, I, 432. Quartering: October 3, 1558, I, 452.

[50]August 13, 1551, II, 179; June 4, 1552, II, 251; April
10, 1555, I, 174. In 1560 the clergy asked that gypsies be banished; the crown agreed, Mayer ed., Des États Généraux, XI, 55,
79. Ordonnances . . . Orléans, sig. 39r-v.

[51]Jully 11, 1556, I, 280. It was a famous summer. Cf.
François de Belleforest, Les Chroniqves et Annales de France
(Paris: N. du Chemin, 1573), fol. 489v; and Emanuel LeRoy
Ladurie, Les paysans de Languedoc (Paris, 1966), I, 37-38.

[52]July 16-27, 1556, I, 280-83. Cf. also the problem of the
flood at Gattemare, March 9-19, 1561 o.s., I, 759-61.

[53]The choule is usually mentioned in connection with grievous injury: for example, December 25, 1555, I, 239.

[54]For example: September 8, 1552, II, 272-73; March 25,
1558, I, 417.

[55]For example: April 8, 13, 1561, I, 661. Maîtres des
eaux et forêts had to approve commissions to track wolves: June
6, 1555, I, 190. The ordonnance of 1583 is quoted by Tollemer,
Un sire de Gouberville, pp. 202-03.

[56]For example: November 18, 1550, II, 122; November 30,
1551, II, 208; July 14, 1556, I, 281; October 11, 17, 1557, I,
378-79; August 9, 1560, I, 585.

⁵⁷For example: January 4, 1551 o.s., II, 151; April 18, 1552, II, 241; November 27, 1552, II, 289; February 19, 1553 o.s., II, 76; October 13-16, 1555, I, 220-21; October 11, 1556, I, 303; December 29, 1560, I, 623.

⁵⁸May 29, June 2, 1549, II, 14-15; April 3, 1551, II, 237-38; January 23, 1551 o.s., II, 221-22; August 15, 1553, I, 29; March 31, 1554, I, 84; cf. particularly the occasion of a rumored English descent upon Cherbourg, June 10, 15-19, July 4, 1557, I, 355-60. See the protest of 1604 in Articles de Remonstrances Faictes en la Convention des Trois Estats de Normandie, tenue a Rouen le cinquiesme iour de Nouembre, et autres iours ensuyuans, mil six cens quatre, Rouen: M. le Mesgissier, 1605. There is a contemporary testimonial to the effectiveness of citizen military organization: [Martin Liberge], *Ample discours de ce qui c'est faict et passe au siege de Poictiers: ecrit durant iceluy, par home qui estoit dedans* (Paris: N. Chesneau, 1569).

⁵⁹Roads: March 21, 1560, I, 654; November 18, 1561, I, 725. Guides were often a necessity: July 23, 1549, II, 29; September 27, 1552, II, 276; December 23, 1555, I, 238; February 17, 1557 o.s., I, 408. Weather: August 8, 1549, II, 34; April 15, 1555, I, 176. Russell Major's speculations on the real proportion of bureaucracy to subject belie the complaints of the delegates to the Estates of Orleans. See "The French Renaissance Monarchy as Seen through the Estates General," *Studies in the Renaissance,* 9 (1962), 117-19. An edict of 1553 is explicit on the problems of distance and procedure: "Edict dv roy de la creation en offices des tresoreries & receptes alternatiues du payement des gens de cheual estans au seruice dudict Seigneur," Paris: V. Sertenas, I. Dallier, 1553 (47).

⁶⁰Cf. August 13, 1562, I, 701; January 18, 1562 o.s., I, 861.

⁶¹I, 775. There was one earlier indication of religious trouble, the desecration of the shrine of St. Maur, December 25, 1554, I, 145.

⁶²I, 782, 788. The tocsin had sounded earlier at Valognes, "et pour ce que nous debvions coucher, nous ne peusmes sçavoyr l'occasion," May 18, 1562, I, 783. Under any circumstances, a curious reaction.

⁶³June 7-12, 1562, I, 789-90. On the rising at Valognes, see Jaques-August de Thou, *Histoire universelle* (Basle, 1747), III, 179-80. More trouble was rumored at Valognes, March 9, 1562 o.s., I, 873.

⁶⁴June 10, 1562, I, 790. Symonnet was sent to the manor of Gouberville with strongboxes, but apparently was distracted by the opportunity to see action, June 13-14, 1562, I, 791. June

13, the *receveur des tailles* at Valognes sent his small children out of the town; June 15, the sire de Saulsemesnil fled.

[65]I, 792. Material in the Fonds Matignon, Archives du Palais de Monaco (41, 42, 118, 121, 137-38) make clear the significance that local commanders and officials attached to the uprising; "a faulte de secours la perte de ceste place en ire en consequence de la ruine du reste," De Cossé to Matignon, Coutances, June 3, 1562. Robert de La Marck to Matignon, Caen, July 19, 1562: "s'ils ne sont promptement secourez ne peut advenir sinon l'entiere et totalle ruine de leur ville. . . ." I have not yet had an opportunity fully to examine the archival material in Monaco. I owe the references to the Fonds Matignon to the extreme kindness of the archivists, Franck Bianchieri and Stephan Vilarem, and to Anne Christine Fannin.

[66]His first reaction was disbelief. He was convinced by the arrival of a fourth messenger. June 18-21, 1562, I, 792-93.

[67]June 24-30, 1562, I, 794-95.

[68]The chasse Hellequin, April 14, 1553, I, 5. On this singularly Norman phenomenon, see the late Marthe Moricet, "Traditions populaires de la Normandie: La 'Chasse Hellequin'," *Annales de Normandie*, II, No. 2 (May 1952), 169-74. Fairies: February 17, 1553 o.s., I, 75; September 30, 1554, I, 125. St. Hubert: November 6, 17, 1556, I, 309, 311. Cf. Andre Dubuc, "Traditions populaires de Normandie: Le culte de Saint Hubert en Normandie," *Annales de Normandie*, IV, No. 1 (1954), 67-70.

[69]The rain of blood (and vile weather generally) was a portent, as was the deformed child: for example, Jean de Marcouville, *Receuil memorable d'avcvns cas merueilleux aduenuz de noz ans* (Paris: I. Dallier, 1564), fols. 7ʳ-8ʳ, 34ᵛ-74ʳ; and Pierre Boaistuau, *Histoires prodigieuses* (Paris: I. de Bordeaux, 1571), fols. 224ᵛ-225ᵛ. On the other hand, natural calamities were also considered the wages of sin. Cf. *Histoire memorable et tres-veritable, contenant le vain effort des Huguenots au Prieuré de S. Philbert en Normandie* (1562) (Paris: I. Noyau, 1587), rpt. in *Archives curieuses de l'histoire de France*, ed. L. Cimber and F. Danjou, 1st series (Paris, 1835), Vol. 53; and *Discovrs svr l'espovvantable et merueilleux desbordement du Rosne* (Lyon: B. Rigaud, 1570; rpt. in *ibid.*, 1st series, VI, 400-02. Despite apparent contemporary attachment to the notion of werewolves--cf. Marthe Moricet, "Traditions populaires de Normandie: Le 'Varou'," *Annales de Normandie*, II, No. 1, pp. 73-82, and Robert Mandrou, *Magistrats et Sorciers en France au XVIIᵉ siècle* (n.p., 1968), pp. 118-26--Gouberville does not mention them. Marcouville, *Receuil memorable*, fol. 78ᵛ., be it said, was skeptical.

70Cf. July 12, 1549, II, 26; January 23, 1551 o.s., II, 221-22; November 14, 1555, I, 228; June 15, 1557, I, 356-57; May 23, 1558, I, 429.

71Artillery: July 1-8, 1562, I, 796; Aumale: July 10, 13, 1562, I, 799-800; July 19, 1562, I, 802; flotillas: August 24, 1562, I, 811; September 5, 1562, I, 815.

72Colombieres: August 21, 1562, I, 810. Fairs: August 30, 1562, I, 812-13; September 16, 1562, I, 819. Forest: October 22-28, 1562, I, 831-34.

73Original responsibility was laid at the door of Francois Dauge. Thomas Drouet saved the baptismal font, August 13, 1562, I, 808. The attack: September 4, 1562, I, 815. The DuBoscs had a long and dishonorable record: April 11-12, 1554, I, 88; June 9-13, 1554, I, 99-102; July 13, 1554, I, 107; July 30, 1554, I, 111; August 8, 1554, I, 114; August 30-September 3, 1554, I, 118-19; June 21, 1556, I, 276; October 19, 1556, I, 305.

74August 18, 1562, Ypolite Hue, brother of the Robert Hue who had earlier fought with Noel (see above, note 6) attempted to murder one of Gouberville's retainers in broad daylight. I, 809-10.

75January 22-23, 1562 o.s., I, 862. On February 12, Gouberville asked that the company of Captain Lesmottes not pass through the parish of Gouberville, I, 866. That the problems of quartering, supplies and payment were serious is attested not only by Gouberville, cf. November 6, 20, 1562, I, 837, 842, and March 24, 1562 o.s., I, 877, but also by the correspondence in the Fonds Matignon: Minute d'un mandement envoyé a Vallognes [par Matignon] pour les parroisses de led. viconte pour eviter aux pilleryes que les soldats y pourvienne faire, 1562, and the letters of August 9, 24, 27, letters to and from Matignon, September 5, 8, 13, 15, 19, October 1-2, 9 all deal with the lack of money for provisions, powder and fortifications. Cf. also Le Memoire envoyé par le sieur de Matignon, 28 septembre 1562, and Lettres de M. de Rabodanges à M. de Matignon, 22 septembre 1562, in Cimber and Danjou, eds., *Archives curieuses*, 1st series, V, 57-63.

76Particularly with François and Symonnet, who vanished and resurfaced, always under suspicious circumstances, cf. July 21-22, 1562, I, 802-03; August 6, 1562, I, 806-07; August 19, 24, 1562, I, 810-11; September 3, 1562, I, 814.

77September 30-October 1, 1562, I, 823-24.

78Challenge: October 13, 1562, I, 828-29; November 20, 1562, I, 842-43; review: August 29-September 4, 1562, I, 812-14.

[79]October 31, November 1, 3, 10, 1562, I, 834-38.

[80]Provisioning: September 12, October 11, February 18-23, March 7, 1562 o.s., I, 818, 827, 868, 873; help: September 20, 1562, I, 819-20.

[81]He was at Russy, I, 813. Curé: September 9, 1562, I, 816-17. Mass: February 14, 1562 o.s., I, 867.

[82]September 7, 1562, I, 816.

[83]"'Unus est Deus ab eterno et eternus.' Nour ne pourrions fère des dieulx, puys que nous ne sommes que hommes," August 4, 1562, I, 806.

[84]Of Francis II, "Ce Regne est court, mais memorable," Ian de Serres, *Inventaire general de l'histoire de France* (Paris, 1600), III, 1205; "ce roiaume est sur le point de sa dernière ruine," Prosper de Sainte-Croix to Cardinal Borromée, Poissy, January 17, 1562 o.s., Lettres anecdotes écrites au Cardinal Borromée par Prosper de Sainte-Croix, in Cimber and Danou, eds., *Archives curieuses*, 1st series, VI, 16-17. Cf. François de Belleforest, *Histoire des Nevf Roys Charles de France* (Paris, 1568), p. 622, and the official view: Edict du Roy, svr le faicte de la Police de son Royaume, Rouen: M. le Mesgissier, 1572 (734). In this chorus of misery, Fernand Braudel may sound the still, small voice of calm: *The Mediterranean and the Mediterranean World in the Age of Philip II*, trans. Sian Reynolds (New York, 1972), I, 221-22.

[85]In "Bureaucracy," *From Max Weber: Essays in Sociology*, trans. and ed. H. H. Gerth and C. Wright Mills (New York, 1946), pp. 204-09.

[86]For example: "ET pourautant que nous desirons signulieremãt que toutes les occasions de ces troubles, tumultes, & seditions cessent, . . . Auons ordonné & ordonnons, entendons, voulons, & nous plaist, Que toutes iniures & offenses qui l'iniquité du temps, & les occasiõs qui en sõt suruenues . . . demourerõt esteinctes, comme mortes, enseuelies & non aduenues," Edict et Declaration faicte par le Roy Charles IX de ce nom sur la pacification des troubles de ce Royaume: le xix iour de Mars, mil cinq cens soixante deux, Paris: R. Estienne, 1562 (332). Cf. December 27, 1562: "Symonnet revinst de Toqueville . . . et m'apporta lettres comme le roy avoyt pardonné à tous ceulx qui avoyent prins les armes contre son vouloyr," I, 855.

[87]Executions: "c'a este vn spectacle si terrible & de si grande vtillite, pour le seruice de Dieu & reputatio de sa maieste, que par aduanture il ne s'en est iamais oy vn semblable," Executiõ de la sentence et ivgement donnez, contre les Comtes d'Aiguement & de horne, & autres seigneurs declarez

seditieux" (n.p., 1568). See Samuel Y. Egerton, Jr., "Maniera and the Mannaia: Decorum and Decapitation in the Sixteenth Century," in *The Meaning of Mannerism,* ed. F. W. Robinson and S. G. Nichols, Jr. (Hanover, N.H., 1972), pp. 67-103. One doubts that Gouberville got the message: cf. April 17, 1554, I, 89; April 14, 155, I, 261; May 2, 1556, I, 264; December 10, 1558, I, 465. Associations: Lettres Patentes et Mandement dv Roy, alencõtre des couenticules & assemblées des Hereticques, Auec l'exemption & don aux denonciateurs desdictz conuenticules & assemblees, Paris: G. Nyuerd, 1559 (132).

88On Catherine's many problems, see the impressive study of N. M. Sutherland, *The Massacre of St. Bartholomew and the European Conflict, 1559-1572* (New York, 1572).

89The language of a noble petition of 1586 echoes Francis I: "Ce sõt les trois choses q̃ les Roys doiṽet desirer, d'avoir la religiõ c'est à dire la metteté de leurs cõsciõses, la Noblesse pour sa defence par les armes & la iustice pour la cõservatiõ de leurs subiects tellemẽt que si ensemblement nour y employons chacun selõ sa vocatiõ, à laquelle Dieu l'appellé," La Harangue faicte au Roy par la noblesse de France, sur les Estats de son Royaume, Lyon: Prins sur la coppie imprime à Paris pour Antoine Salé, 1586. The sire de Gouberville should have the last word: August 30, 1562: "Led. jour, apprès soupper, nous nous pourmenasmes . . . , en devisant des troubles et malheur qui est de présent entre les gouverneurs de ce royaulme et les subjectz," I, 812-13.

CHAPTER II

1*Ander Teil des Adelspiegels. Was Adel mache . . . ein schoener Regenten-Spiegel Allen in der Obrigkeit, in allen loeblichen Tugenden aus Gottes Wort fuergestellet* (Smalcald: Michael Schmück, 1594), fol. 341ʳ. The first volume is entitled *AdelsSpiegel. Historischer Ausfuerlicher Bericht: Was Adel sey vnd heisse . . . Dem gentzen Deutschen Adel zu besondern Ehren, aus etlich hundert Authorn mit grosser muehe vnd auffs fleissigste beschrieben* (Smalcald: Michael Schmück, 1591).

2See Wilhelm Maurer, *Der junge Melanchthon zwischen Humanismus und Reformation, 1. Der Humanist* (Göttingen: Vandenhoeck & Ruprecht, 1967), pp. 99-128.

3On the basic differences between the Gnesio-Lutherans and the Philippists, see my "Dynamics of Party Conflict in the Saxon Late Reformation, Gnesio-Lutherans vs. Philippists," *Journal of Modern History* 49 (1977), 1289-1305.

4On Flacius' position and the related controversies, see

Wilhelm Preger, *Matthias Flacius Illyricus und seine Zeit*, II
(1861; rpt. Hildesheim: Olms, and Nieuwkoop: De Graaf, 1964),
310-412, and Hans Kropatscheck, "Das Problem theologischer An-
thropologie auf dem Weimarer Gespräch von 1560 zwischen Matthias
Flacius Illyricus und Viktorin Strigel" (dissertation, University of Göttingen, 1943).

[5]No biography of Spangenberg has been written in the modern
era; the best overview of his life is that by Gustav Kawerau in
Realencyklopädie für protestantische Theologie und Kirche, 3rd
ed. (Leipzig: Hinrich, 1906), XVIII, 567-72. Early in his career Spangenberg began writing history, e.g., his *Ursach und
Handelung des Sechsischen Krieges bey dem Welphesholz* (Wittenberg: Georg Rhau, 1555), and his *Historia. Vom Leben, Lere und
Tode Hieronymi Savanarole* (Wittenberg: Peter Seitz's heirs,
1556). His major chronicles include the *Mansfeldische Chronica*
(Eisleben: Adam Petri, 1572), the *Saechssische Chronica* (Frankfurt am Main: Sigmund Feyerabend, 1585), and the *Hennebergische
Chronica* (Strassburg: ·Bernhard Jobin's heirs, 1599).

[6]*Chronica Zeitbuch unnd Geschichtbibel* (Strassburg: Balthasar Beck, 1531).

[7]*Adelspiegel*, I, [ij^r-]iiij^r.

[8]His published correspondence reflects his contacts with
the counts of Mansfeld and other princes, most notably Duke
Johann Albrecht of Mecklenburg; see Heinrich Rembe, *Der Briefwechsel des M. Cyriacus Spangenberg* (Dresden: Naumann, 1887-88),
pp. 3-4, 9-10, 12-13, 24-27, 33-36, 39-55, 64-65, 69, 71-78,
81-86, 113-14.

[9]*Der Jagtteüffel. Bestendiger vnnd Wolgegründter bericht,
wie fern die Jagten rechtmessig, vnd zugelassen. Vnd widerumb
worinnen sie jetziger zeyt des meherer theils Gottlos, gewalt-
sam, vnrecht, vnd verdammlich sein, Vnd derhalben billich vnter-
lassen, oder doch geendert werden solten* (n.p., 1560).

[10]*Adelspiegel*, I, [vj^v-][ij^v; II,][ij^r,][iij^v. Against
Franck and others, see I,] ij^v, II, 9-11, 480-85.

[11]Ibid., II, 484^v. On Luther's concept of the two king-
doms, see Gustaf Wingren, *Luther on Vocation*, trans. Carl C.
Rasmussen (Philadelphia: Muhlenberg, 1957), esp. pp. 1-37; Paul
Althaus, *The Ethics of Martin Luther*, trans. Robert C. Schultz
(Philadelphia: Fortress, 1972), esp. pp. 43-82; and George W.
Forell, *Faith Active in Love* (Minneapolis: Augsburg, 1954).

[12]*Ehespiegel, Das ist, Alles was von dem heyligen Ehe-
stande, nutzliches, noetiges, vnnd troestliches mag gesagt werden* (Strassburg: Rihel, 1570), sigs. I, II; cf. his *Die Christ-
liche Haustafel, Wie sich ein jeglich Gottselig Mensch in seinem
stande vnd beruff, nach Gottes willen rechtschaffen halten solle*

(Wittenberg: Lorentz Schwenck, 1558), sigs. Di^v-E^v.

[13]*Adelspiegel*, I, 1^r-4^v; cf. fol. 257^v.

[14]*Ibid.*, II, 2^v-3^r, 6-7, 17^v-21^r.

[15]In this point Spangenberg showed the influence of Melanchthon, who put greater faith in laws than did Luther, who preferred decisions made by the wisdom of the prince. See his *Von weltlicher Oberkeit, wie weit man ihr Gehorsam schuldig sei* (1523), *D. Martin Luthers Werke* (Weimar: Böhlau, 1883-), XI, 271-72. On Melanchthon's attitude toward law, see Guido Kisch, *Melanchthons Rechts-und Soziallehre* (Berlin: De Gruyter, 1967), pp. 80-140.

[16]*Adelspiegel*, II, 147^v-148.

[17]Ibid., II, 147^v-148^r; cf. fol. 407.

[18]Ibid., II, 408^r; cf. fol. 17^v.

[19]Ibid., II, 150^r, 408, 403^v-404^r, 408^v-409.

[20]Luther wrote his *Ermahnung zum Frieden auf die zwölf Artikel der Bauernschaft in Schwaben* (1525), *D. Martin Luthers Werke*, XVIII, 291-334, not only to warn against peasant violence but also to criticize the oppression of the lords. Most famous of the articles which expressed peasant grievances were the so-called Twelve Articles, the text of which is printed in Günter Franz, *Quellen zur Geschichte des Bauernkrieges* (Munich: Oldenbourg, 1963), pp. 113-27. The sixth and eleventh articles protested against unfair taxes and the increase of customary obligations. On the reaction of other followers of Luther to the Peasants Revolt at the time of the Revolt, see Robert Kolb, "The Theologians and the Peasants, Conservative Evangelical Reactions to the German Peasants Revolt," *Archiv für Reformationsgeschichte* 69 (1978).

[21]*Adelspiegel*, I, 137^r, II, 47^v-78.

[22]Ibid., on the education of their own children, see I, 56^r, 203^v-204^r; II, 13^v, 100^v, 137^v-140, and a special chapter on learned nobles of the past, II, 174-276; on general education, see II, 74^v-75.

[23]Ibid., I, 359^r.

[24]Ibid., II, 22-32^r; cf. 396^v-400^r.

[25]Ibid., II, 44-73^r, esp. fols. 58^r, 62-63, 69^v-70.

[26]Ibid., II, 32^v-43.

[27]Ibid., II, 146^v-147^r, 387^v:

[28]Ibid., II, 388^r, 73^v.

[29]Ibid., II, 119^v-127. On Magdeberg resistance theory, see Oliver K. Olson, "Theology of Revolution: Magdeburg, 1550-1551," *The Sixteenth Century Journal*, 3(1972), 56-79.

[30]See point 3 in "Dynamics of Party Conflict," *The Journal of Modern History*, 50(1978), 1299-1302.

[31]For several thirteenth century treatments of the nobility, see Mary Paul Goetz, *The Concept of Nobility in German Didactic Literature of the Thirteenth Century* (Washington: Catholic University of America, 1935).

[32]Desiderius Erasmus, *Opera Omnia*, IV, 1 (Amsterdam: North-Holland, 1974), 95-219.

[33]*D. Martin Luthers Werke*, XLIV, 404-07, 431-37, 487-88, contain presentations of Luther's two kingdoms concept as it relates to secular authority; comments on taxation are found on pp. 416 and 652, and criticism of princes for mistreatment of clergy is recorded on pp. 178, 347, 350-51, 624-26, 670-72.

[34]See the development of this point in Robert Kolb, *Andreae and the Formula of Concord, Six Sermons on the Way to Lutheran Unity* (St. Louis: Concordia, 1977), pp. 47-54.

CHAPTER IV

Abbreviations
CDHFSH   *Coleccion de documentos historicos de la formacion social de hispano-America*. 6 vols. Madrid, 1953.
JGSWGLA *Jahrbuch für Geschichte von Staat Wissenschaft und Gesellschaft Latein-Amerikas*.

[1]Sigmund Diamond has developed these ideas for Virginia and New France. See Sigmund Diamond, ed., *The Creation of Society in the New World* (Chicago, 1963).

[2]Helen Nader, "The Nobility as Borrowers and Lenders: A New Look at the Censos," unpublished paper presented at the American Historical Association (December 1976).

[3]The classic but preliminary analysis is Richard Konetzke, "Entrepreneurial Activities of Spanish and Portuguese Noblemen in Medieval Times," *Explorations in Entrepreneurial History*, 6 (1953-54), 115-20. The quotation from Mercado is taken from Ruth Pike, *Aristocrats and Traders. Sevillian Society in the Sixteenth Century* (Ithaca, 1972), p. 22. See also Hans Pohl, "Zur Geschichte des adligen Unternehmers im Spanischen Amerika," *JGSWGLA*, 2 (1965), 218-44.

[4]Virginia Rau, "Fortunas ultramarinos e a nobreza no século XVII," *Revista Portuguesa da Historia*, 8 (1959), 1-25.

[5]Maria de los Angeles de la Campa, "La nobleza en la administracion," *Hidalguia*, 114 (September-October 1972), 591-612.

[6]Luis Cabrera de Córdoba, *Relaciones de las cosas sucedidas en la Corte de Espana desde 1599 hasta 1614* (Madrid, 1857), p. 124. Such hopes may have been ephemeral as well since Cabrera reported in 1606 that the Viceroy of Peru, the Count of Monter-

rey, had died so poor that a collection had to be made to pay for his funeral. See Cabrera de Córdoba, *Relaciones*, p. 286. Despite this statement, Antonio Dominguez Ortiz, *Las clases privilegiadas en la Espana del Antiguo Regimen* (Madrid, 1973), argues that the American viceroyalties were sought as money-making offices (pp. 108-09).

[7]Diogo Botelho to Conde de Linhares (Recife, probably 1603), ANTT, Cartorio dos Jesuitas, maco 8, doc. 129.

[8]I have discussed this conflict and the literature in some detail in Stuart B. Schwartz, *Sovereignty and Society in Colonial Brazil* (Berkeley, 1973).

[9]*Capitulos do Stado da Nobreza e as respostas que a elles mandei dar* (Lisbon, 1582), chapt. xi.

[10]Schwartz, *Sovereignty and Society*, especially Chapters VIII and XII.

[11]Rufina Blanco-Fombona, *El conquistador español del siglo xvi* (Madrid, 1921); Angel Rosenblat, "Base del español de América: Nivel social y cultural de los conquistadores y pobladores," *Revista de Indias*, 31, 125-26 (1971), 13-75.

[12]The works of Peter Boyd-Bowman are fundamental in this context and the percentile citations are drawn from them. They are ably reviewed and synthesized in Magnus Morner, "Spanish Migration to the New World Prior to 1810: A Report on the State of Research," and the accompanying appendix, "A Bibliography of Spanish Migration," in Fredi Chiappelli, ed., *First Images of America* (Berkeley, 1976), II, 737-82, 797-806. See especially Peter Boyd-Bowman, *Patterns of Spanish Emigration to the New World* (1493-1580) (Buffalo, 1973). See also Juan Friede, "Los estamentos sociales en Espana y su contribuicion a la emigracion a America,""*Revista de Indias*, 103-104 (January-June 1966), 13-30.

[13]Cited in Lohmann Villena, *Los americanos*, p. xiv.

[14]Ibid., p. xxii.

[15]James Lockhart, *The Men of Cajamarca* (Austin, 1972), pp. 44-59.

[16]Real cedula que sean hidalgos los que fueron a las Indias con Don Francisco Pizarro, Konetzke, *CDHFSH*, I, 126-27.

[17]Ibid.

[18]J. Merino Inchaustegui, ed., *Reales cedulas y correspondencia de gobernadores de Santo Domingo* (Madird, 1958-59), I, 94-96.

[19]"Relacion de los oidores Licenciado Espinosa y Licenciado Zuazo al Consejo de Indias (30 March 1528)," Inchaustegui, *Reales cedulas*, I, 200-12.

[20]Konetzke, *CDHFSH*, I, 120-26.

[21]"Ordenanza sobre la población de la Isla Española (9 July 1560)," Konetzke, *CDHFSH*, I, 378-84; "Ordenazas para los nuevos descubrimientos conquistas, pacificaciones (13 July 1573)," Konetzke, *CDHSFH*, I, 471-78.

[22]Richard Konetzke, "La formacion de la nobleza en Indias," *Estudios Americanos*, 3, 10 (July 1951), 329-60.

[23]Ibid., pp. 337-44. Lohmann Villena, *Los Americanos*, p. xx, points out opposition even in the 1630's from the Viceroy of Peru, Count of Chinchon.

[24]Lohmann Villena, *Los Americanos*, p. xxxv. See the discussion in John Lynch, *Spain Under the Habsburgs* (New York, 1963-69), II, 132.

[25]Luis Arraz Marquez, "La nobleza colombina y sus relaciones con la castellana," *Revista de Indias*, 139-42 (June-December 1975), 83-123. On the Duke of Veragua see R. D. Carles, *220 Años del Período Colonial en Panamá*, 2nd ed. (Panama, 1959); C.A. Castillero, *Estructuras sociales y económicas de Veragua desde sus orígenes históricos* (Panama, 1967). On the Cortes title see Bernardo García Martínez, *El Marquesado del Valle* (Mexico, 1969); Michel G. Riley, *Cortes and the Marquesa do del Valle*, p, 197.

[26]Doris M. Ladd, *The Mexican Nobility at Independence 1780-1826* (Austin, 1977), pp. 14-17; José Bravo Ugarte, "Títulos Nobiliarios hispanoamericanos," *Memorias de la Academia Mexicana de la Historia*, 15, 3 (July-September 1956), 258-63.

[27]Luis de Izcue, *La nobleza titulada en el Perú Colonial* (Lima, 1929); Alberto Marquez Abanto, "Los títulos nobiliarios en el Perú 1737-1764," *Revista del Archivo Nacional del Perú*, 22 (1958), 476-89; 23 (1959), 92-118, 362-84. Rúben Vargas Ugarte, "Títulos Nobiliarios en el Perú," *Revista Historica* (Lima), 15 (1942), 272-308.

[28]L. P. Wright, "The Military Orders in Sixteenth and Seventeenth Century Spanish Society. The Institutional Embodiment of a Historical Tradition," *Past and Present*, 43 (May 1969), 34-70.

[29]Lockhart, *Men of Cajamarca*.

[30]Keniston, *Francisco de los Cobos*, p. 106.

[31]D. Luis Velasco to Crown (1553), in James Lockhart and Enrique Otte, eds., *Letters and People of the Spanish Indies* (Cambridge, 1976), p. 189. Luis de Velasco rewarded colonists with a liberal hand and was severely criticized by the royal investigator, Jeronimo Valderrama. See "Relacion de algunas estancias e caballerias que el Virrey D. Luis de Velasco dio a sus paniaguados, 1551-1563," in *Cartas del Licenciado Jeronimo Valderrama y otros documentos sobre su visita al gobiernode*

Nueva España, 1563-1565 (Mexico, 1961).

[32]Lohmann Villena, *Los Americanos.*

[33]Even when the inflation of honors in the seventeenth and eighteenth centuries are taken into account, the numbers are still not large. In Chile, for example, only sixty-five caballeros of the military orders born in Chile can be identified and only fifty others who served in Chile but were born elsewhere. Fewer than 25 percent of these knights also held noble titles. See Gonzalo Vial Correa, "La nobleza chilena a fines del periodo indiano. Esquema para su estudio jurídico, teórico y práctico," *Actas y Estudios III Congreso de Instituto Internacional de Historia del Derecho Indiano* (Madrid, 1973), pp. 757-78.

[34]Magnus Moener, "La hacienda hispanoamericana: Examen de las investigaciones y debates recientes," in Enrique Florescano, ed., *Haciendas Latifundios y plantaciones* (Mexico, 1975), pp. 28-29.

[35]Guillermo Fernández de Recas, *Mayorazgos de la Nueva España* (Mexico, 1965); Domingo Amunátegui Solar, *Mayorazgos y titulos de Castilla*, 3 vols. (Santiago de Chile, 1901).

[36]Domenico Sindico, "El mayorazgo en la legislación española durante el período colonial," *Cathedra* (Nuevo León), 3 (1975), 73-88. See also the important monograph by Bartolomé Clavero, *Mayorazgo. Propriedad feudal en Castilla (1369-1836)* (Madrid, 1974).

[37]Juan de Olazaga H., "Mayorazgo de Hernán Cortés," *Hidalguia*, 5 (April-June 1954), 237-48. Promises to establish entails for those founding towns and settling new areas are found in the Ordinances for the Population of Hispaniola (1560) and the Ordinance for New Discoveries and Conquests (1573).

[38]Keniston, *Francisco de los Cobos*, p. 115. For other examples of Mayorazgo grants and deeds, see Amunátegui Solar, *Mayorazgos y titulos de Castilla.*

[39]L. P. Wright, "The Military Orders," pp. 53-55.

[40]Gunter Kahle, "Die Encomienda als Militarische Institution in Kolonialen Hispanoamerika," *JGSWGLA*, 2 (1965), 88-105.

[41]Mario Góngora, *Studies in the Colonial History of Spanish America* (Cambridge, 1975), p. 108.

[42]King to Viceroy Enrique (13 November 1581), in Konetzke, *CDHFSH*, I, 541-42. See also Antonio Domínguez Ortiz, *Las clases privilegiadas en la España del Antiguo Régimen* (Madrid, 1973), pp. 87-145.

[43]The interrelationship is discussed in Clavero, *Mayorazgo*, pp. 181-210.

[44]Gonzalo Gomez de Cervantes, *La vida económica y Social de Nueva España al finalizar del Siglo XVI (1599)*, ed. Alberto

María Carreno (Mexico, 1944), p. 124. Francisco Nuñez de Piñeda y Bascuñán, *Caufiverio feliz y razón individual de las guerras dilatadas del reino de Chile* (Santiago, 1863).

[45]Real Decreto al Presidente de Indias (Madrid; 23 June 1621), Konetzke, *CDHFSH*, II, Pt. 1, 260-62. See also Juan Friede, "Proceso de formación de la propiedad territorial en la América intertropical," *JGSWGLA*, 2 (1965), 75-87, emphasizes the *de facto* control of land by the conquerors and their similarity to the peninsular nobility.

[46]"Consulta del Consejo de las Indias (Madrid; 19 July 1875)"; Konetzke, *CDHFSH*, II, Pt. 2, 616-19.

[47]Ibid., II, Pt. 2, 735-38. See also Silvio Zavala, *Las instituciones jurídicas en la conquista de América*, 2nd ed. (Mexico, 1971), p. 200.

[48]Cited in Vial Correa, p. 768.

[49]On this aspect see the suggestive essays of Nestor Meza Villalobos, *Estudios sobre la conquista de América* (Santiago de Chile, 1971), and also his *La conciencia política chilena durante la monarquía* (Santiago de Chile, 1958), pp. 55-99.

[50]Irving Leonard, *Books of the Brave* (Ann Arbor, 1949); see also Juan Pérez de Tudela Buesco, "Razgos semblante espiritual de Gonzalo Fernández de Oviedo: La hidalguía caballeresca ante el Nuevo Mundo," *Revista de Indias*, 69-70 (July-December 1957), 391-444; Mario Hernández y Sánchez Barba, "La influencia de los libros de caballería sobre el conquistador," *Estudios Americanos*, 19, 112 (May-June 1960), 235-56.

[51]Statement made in 1544, cited by Lohmann Villena, *Los Americanos*, p. xiv.

[52]Fr. Buenaventura de Salinas, *Memorial de las historias del Nuevo Mundo* (Lima, 1631), cited in Lohmann Villena, *Los Americanos*, p. xv.

[53]Thomas Gage, *The New Society of the West Indies, 1648*, ed. A. P. Newton (New York, 1929), pp. 152, 158.

[54]Konetzke, *CDHFSH*, II, Pt. 2, 617; Consulta del Consejo de las Indias sobre una proposición de que se beneficien en las Indias ciento y cincuenta titulos de Castilla (19 July 1675).

[55]Clements R. Markham, ed. and trans., *The Life and Acts of Don Alonzo Enriquez de Guzman* (London, 1862), pp. 78, 84-85, 94-98.

[56]James Lockhart, *Spanish Peru 1532-1560* (Madison, 1968), pp. 35-39, 225.

[57]Vial Correa, "La nobleza chilena," p. 768.

[58]See Lawrence Stone, *The Crisis of the Aristocracy, 1558-1641*, abridged ed. (Oxford, 1967), p. 61.

CHAPTER V

[1]Maurice Dobb, *Studies in the Development of Capitalism,* rev. ed. (1947; rpt. New York, 1963), pp. 120-21. There, too, the Marx quotation above.

[2]Karl Czok, "Zur Stellung der Stadt in der deutschen Geschichte," *Jahrbuch für Regionalgeschichte,* 3 (1968), 17.

[3]Brigitte Berthold, Evamaria Engel, and Adolf Laube, "Die Stellung des Bürgertums in der deutschen Feudalgesellschaft bis zur Mitte des 16. Jahrhunderts," *Zeitschrift für Geschichtswissenschaft,* 21 (1973), 199-200.

[4]Czok, "Zur Stellung der Stadt in der deutschen Geschichte," p. 16; *idem,* "Die Bürgerkämpfe in Süd- und Westdeutschland im 14. Jahrhundert," *Jahrbuch für Geschichte der oberdeutschen Reichstädte,* 12/13 (1966/67), 40-72, reprinted in *Die Stadt des Mittelalters,* ed. Carl Haase, Wirtschaft und Gesellschaft (Darmstadt, 1973), III, 303-44.

[5]Leo Kofler, *Zur Geschichte der bürgerlichen Gesellschaft. Versuch einer verstehenden Deutung der Neuzeit,* 5th ed. (Darmstadt-Neuwied, 1974), p. 119.

[6]Fernand Braudel, *La méditerranée et le monde méditerranéen à l'epoque de Philippe II,* 2nd ed. (Paris, 1966), II, 68, and in detail pp. 72-75. For particular examples, see Gene A. Brucker, *Florentine Politics and Society, 1343-1378* (Princeton, 1962), pp. 28-29 (Florence); A. Ventura, *Nobiltà e popolo nella società Veneta del'400 e '500* (Bari, 1964), pp. 275-79 (Venezia); J. M. Roberts, "Lombardy," *The European Nobility in the Eighteenth Century: Studies of the Nobilities of the Major European States in the Pre-reform Era,* ed. Albert Goodwin (1953; rpt. New York, 1967), pp. 60-82, here at pp. 61-65 (Lombardy); J. Russell Major, "The Crown and the Aristocracy in Renaissance France," in *Lordship and Community in Medieval Europe,* ed. Frederic Cheyette (New York, 1968), pp. 241-43 (France), reprinted from the *American Historical Review,* 69 (1964), 631-45; Sylvia Thrupp, *The Merchant Class of Medieval London* (Ann Arbor, 1948), pp. 286-87 (England). In Genoa, however, the two aristocratic fractions did not merge. See Jacques Heers, *Genes au XVe siècle, activité économique et problèmes sociaux* (Paris, 1961), pp. 557-62.

[7]Czok, "Zur Stellung der Stadt in der deutschen Geschichte," pp. 16-17. In his paper appearing in this volume, Christopher Friedrichs objects to my acceptance of Czok's scheme, because classical forms of urban revolt did not cease with the Reformation. This is true enough, but these later revolts seem to have simply continued late medieval patterns with-

out holding much significance for German society as a whole--
something which cannot be said of medieval urban revolts. Besides, Czok's scheme fits the *medieval* German city well enough.

[8]Several acknowledgements by non-socialist scholars of the
validity of the socialist interpretation of the Reformation,
from Friedrich Engels to Max Steinmetz, appeared among the literature which celebrated the 450th anniversary of the Peasants'
War in 1975. See Heiko A. Oberman, "The Gospel of Social Unrest: 450 Years after the so-called 'German Peasants' War' of
1525," *Harvard Theological Review*, 69 (1976); and Martin Brecht,
"Die Bedeutung des Bauernkrieges in Südwestdeutschland," *Schwä-
bische Heimat. - Zeitschrift zur Pflege von Landschaft, Volkstum,
Kultur*, 26 (1975), 297-301, esp. p. 297.

[9]Rolf Kiessling, *Bürgerliche Gesellschaft und Kirche in
Augsburg im Spätmittelalter*, Abhandlungen zur Geschichte der
Stadt Augsburg, 19 (Augsburg, 1971); Friedrich Blendinger, "Die
wirtschaftlichen Führungsschichten in Augsburg 1430-1740," in
*Führungskräfte der Wirtschaft in Mittelalter und Neuzeit 1350-
1850*, Part I, ed. Herbert Helbig, Deutsche Führungsschichten in
der Neuzeit, 6 (Limburg/Lahn, 1973), pp. 51-86.

[10]Gottfried Geiger, *Die Reichsstadt Ulm vor der Reformation. Städtisches und Kirchliches Leben am Ausgang des Mittelalters*, Forschungen zur Geschichte der Stadt Ulm, 11 (Ulm,
1971).

[11]Hans-Christoph Rublack, *Die Einführung der Reformation in
Konstanz von den Anfängen bis zum Abschluss 1531*, Quellen und
Forschungen zur Reformationsgeschichte, 40 = Veröffentlichungen
des Vereins für Kirchengeschichte in der evang. Landeskirche in
Baden, 27 (Gütersloh-Karlsruhe, 1971).

[12]Peter Eitel, *Die oberschwäbischen Reichsstädte im Zeitalter der Zunftherrschaft. Untersuchungen zu ihrer politischen
und sozialen Struktur unter besonderer Berücksichtigung der
Städte Lindau, Memmingen, Ravensburg und Überlingen*, Schriften
zur südwestdeutschen Landeskunde, 8 (Stuttgart, 1970); Raimund
Eirich, *Memmingens Wirtschaft und Patriziat von 1347 bis 1551.
Eine wirtschafts- und sozialgeschichtliche Untersuchung über das
Memminger Patriziat während der Zunftverfassung* (Weissenhorn,
1971); Albrecht Rieber, "Das Patriziat von Ulm, Augsburg, Ravensburg, Memmingen, Biberach," *Deutsches Patriziat 1430-1740*,
ed. Hellmuth Rössler, Schriften zur Problematik der deutshcen
Führungsschichten in der Neuzeit, 3 (Limburg/Lahn, 1968), pp.
299-352.

[13]Gerd Wunder, "Der Adel der Reichsstadt Hall im späten
Mittelatler," *Deutsches Patriziat 1430-1740*, pp. 277-98; *idem*,
"Die Sozialstruktur der Reichsstadt Schwäbisch Hall in späten

Mittelalter," *Untersuchungen zur gesellschaftlichen Struktur der mittelalterlichen Städte in Europa. Reichenau-Vorträge 1963-64, Vorträge und Forschungen,* 11 (Constance-Stuttgart, 1966), pp. 15-52.

[14]Alfred Graf Kageneck, "Das Patriziat im Elsass unter Berücksichtigung der Schweizer Verhältnisse," *Deutsches Patriziat 1430-1740,* pp. 377-94; Thomas A. Brady, Jr., *Ruling Class, Regime, and Reformation at Strasbourg, 1520-1555,* Studies in Medieval and Reformation Thought, 23 (Leiden, 1977).

[15]Hanns Hubert Hofmann, "Nobiles Norimbergenses, Beobachtungen zur Struktur der reichsstädtischen Oberschicht," *Untersuchungen zur gesellschaftlichen Struktur der mittelalterlichen Städte in Europa,* pp. 53-92; Wolfgang von Stromer, "Reichtum und Ratswürde. Die wirtschaftliche Führungsschicht der Reichsstadt Nürnberg 1348-1648," *Führungskräfte der Wirtschaft in Mittelalter und Neuzeit 1350-1850,* Part I, pp. 1-50.

[16]Pierre Jeannin, *Merchants of the 16th Century,* trans. Paul Fittinghoff (New York, 1972), p.55.

[17]See the discussion of definitions by Philippe Dollinger, "Patriciat noble et patriciat bourgeois à Strasbourg au XIVe siècle," *Revue d'Alsace,* 90 (1950-51), 52-82, here at p. 52n, whose definition is here adopted. On the history of the term and the concept, see Ingrid Bátori, "Das Patriziat der deutschen Stadt. Zu den Forschungsergebnissen über das Patriziat besonders der süddeutschen Städte," *Zeitschrift für Stadtgeschichte, Stadtsoziologie und Denkmalpflege,* 2 (1975), 1-30.

[18]See Henry Kamen, *The Iron Century; Social Change in Europe, 1550-1650* (London and New York, 1972), pp. 129-31.

[19]Henri Dubled, L'écuyer en Alsace au moyen âge," *Revue d'Alsace,* 92 (1953), 47-56; Bernhard Theil, introduction to *Das älteste Lehnbuch der Markgrafen von Baden (1381),* Veröffentlichungen der Kommission für geschichtliche Landeskunde in Baden-Württemberg, ser. A, vol. 25 (Stuttgart, 1974), pp. 131-35.

[20]Brady, *Ruling Class,* pp. 67-68, 124-25.

[21]Hofmann, "Nobiles Norimbergenses," pp. 66-74; Gerhard Hirschmann, "Das Nürnberger Patriziat," *Deutsches Patriziat 1430-1740,* pp. 261-62.

[22]Jakob Strieder, *Zur Genesis des modernen Kapitalismus. Forschungen zur Entstehung der grossen bürgerlichen Kapitalvermögen am Ausgange des Mittelalters und zu Beginn der Neuzeit, zunächst in Augsburg,* 2nd ed. rev. (Munich-Leipzig, 1935), pp. 75-134.

[23]Wunder, "Die Sozialstruktur der Reichsstadt Schwäbisch Hall," pp. 34-35; *idem,* "Der Adel der Reichsstadt Hall im späten Mittelalter," p. 287. See Rieber, "Das Patriziat von Ulm, Augs-

burg, Ravensburg, Memmingen, Biberach," pp. 314-18, 305-06. On Memmingen, see Eirich, *Memmingen*, pp. 115ff.

[24]Brady, *Ruling Class*, p. 124.

[25]See Heers, *Genès au XVe siècle*, pp. 557-62; David Herlihy, *Medieval and Renaissance Pistoia: The Social History of an Italian Town, 1200-1430* (New Haven, 1967), pp. 194-96; Lauro Martines, *The Social World of the Florentine Humanists, 1390-1460* (Princeton, 1963), pp. 34-37.

[26]Brady, *Ruling Class*, Chapt. V; Kiessling, *Bürgerliche Gesellschaft und Kirche in Augsburg*, pp. 197-201.

[27]The patterns in Lower Alsace are relatively well known. See Jean Vogt, "A propos de la propriété bourgeoise en Alsace (XVIe-XVIIIe siècles)," *Revue d'Alsace*, 100 (1961), 48-66; F.-J. Fuchs, "Bourgeois de Strasbourg propriétaires ruraux au XVIIe siècle," *Paysans d'Alsace*, Publications de la Société Savante d'Alsace et des Régions de l'Est, 7 (Strasbourg, 1969), pp. 99-120; and, for the example of Hans Baldung Grien (1484/85-1545), the painter who was also a land speculator and usurer, Thomas A. Brady, Jr., "The Social Place of a German Renaissance Artist: Hans Baldung Grien (1484/85-1545) at Strasbourg," *Central European History*, 8 (1975), 295-315, here at pp. 299-303.

[28]Fritz Rörig, *The Medieval Town* (Berkeley and Los Angeles, 1967), pp. 126-27; Fritz Blaich, *Die Reichsmonopolgesetzgebung im Zeitalter Karls V. Ihre ordnungspolitische Problematik*, Schriften zum Vergleich von Wirtschaftsordnungen, 8 (Stuttgart, 1967), pp. 10-81.

[29]For an excellent regional study of the effects of the economic crisis on noble family fortunes, see Hans-Pater Sattler, "Die Ritterschaft der Ortenau in der spätmittelalterlichen Wirtschaftskrise. Eine Untersuchung ritterlicher Vermögensverhältnisse im 14. Jahrhundert," *Die Ortenau*, 42 (1962), 220-58; 44 (1964), 22-39; 45 (1965), 32-57; 46 (1966), 32-58. See in general Wilhelm Abel, "Landwirtschaft 1350-1500," in *Handbuch der deutschen Wirtschafts-und Sozialgeschichte*, ed. Hermann Aubin and Wolfgang Zorn, I (1971), 300-34, here at pp. 323ff.

[30]Hofmann, "Nobiles Norimbergenses," pp. 74-76; and, in general, Hermann Mitgau, "Geschlossene Heiratskreise sozialer Inzucht," *Deutsches Patriziat 1430-1740*, pp. 1-26. On the *Turnierfähigkeit* of Strasbourg patricians, see Brady, *Ruling Class*, 82-83.

[31]I have argued the case for Strasbourg in *Ruling Class*, Chapt. IV. On Schwäbisch Hall, see Wunder, "Die Sozialstruktur der Reichsstadt Schwäbisch Hall," pp. 31-33.

[32]Brady, *Ruling Class*, pp. 84-85.

[33]G. Benecke, "Ennoblement and Privilege in Early Modern

Germany," *History*, n.s. 56 (1971), 360-70; Erwin Riedenauer, "Kaiserliche Standeserhebungen für reichsstädtische Bürger 1519-1740," *Deutsches Patriziat 1430-1740*, pp. 27-98.

[34]See the references in note 6 above.

[35]Karl Theodor von Eheberg, ed., *Verfassungs-, Verwaltungs- und Wirtschaftsgeschichte der Stadt Strassburg bis 1681*, I (Strasbourg, 1899), 453, No. 216.

[36]Based on Eirich, *Memmingen*, pp, 24-27.

[37]Brady, *Ruling Class*, pp. 287-88.

[38]Rieber, "Das Patriziat von Ulm," p. 313. Thirty-eight new families entered the patriciate, most from the ranks of the "Mehrer der Gesselschaft."

[39]Brady, *Ruling Class*, pp. 61-63.

[40]Eitel, *Die oberschwäbischen Reichsstädte*, pp. 37-50.

[41]A vast subject which badly needs study. See the model investigation by Heinz Lieberich, "Die gelehrten Räte. Staat und Juristen in Baiern in der Frühzeit der Rezeption," *Zeitschrift für bayerische Landesgeschichte*, 27 (1964), 120-89.

[42]James H. Overfield, "Nobles and Paupers at German Universities to 1600," *Societas*, 4 (1974), 175-210.

[43]Rudolf Wackernagel, *Geschichte der Stadt Basel* (Basel, 1907-24), III, 84-86, 283-85.

[44]Eberhard Naujoks, *Obrigkeitsgedanke, Zunftverfassung und Reformation. Studien zur Verfassungsgeschichte von Ulm, Esslingen und Schwäb. Gmünd*, Veröffentlichungen der Kommission für geschichtliche Landeskunde in Baden-Württemberg, B 3 (Stuttgart, 1958), pp. 87-96.

[45]Paul Hecker, "Der Augsburger Bürgermeister Jakob Herbrot und der Sturz des zünftischen Regiments in Augsburg," *Zeitschrift des Historischen Vereins für Schwaben und Neuburg*, 1 (1874), 34-98.

[46]Philippe Dollinger, "Les villes allemandes au moyen âge: les groupements sociaux," in *La Ville*, 2 (Recueils de la Société Jean Boden, VII; Brussels, 1955), pp. 371-372.

[47]Stromer, "Reichtum und Ratswürde"; Eitel, *Die oberschwäbischen Reichsstädte*, pp. 156-60; Brady, *Ruling Class*, Chapt. V.

[48]Erich Maschke, "Verfassung und soziale Kräfte in der deutschen Stadt des späten Mittelalters, vornehmlich in Oberdeutschland," *Vierteljahrschrift für Sozial-und Wirtschaftsgeschichte*, 41 (1959), 289-349, 433-76, here at pp. 475-76.

[49]Ibid., pp. 284-96; Peter Eitel, "Die politische, soziale und wirtschaftliche Stellung des Zunftbürgertums in den oberdeutschen Reichsstädten am Ausgang des Mittelalters," *Städtische Mittelschichten*, ed. Erich Maschke and Jürgen Sydow, Veröffentlichungen der Kommission für geschichtliche Landeskunde in

Baden-Württemberg, B 69 (Stuttgart, 1972), pp. 78-93, here at pp. 88-89; Rublack, *Die Einführung der Reformation in Konstanz*, pp. 139-42; Brady, *Ruling Class*, pp. 173-78.

[50]Immanuel Wallerstein, *The Modern World System: Capitalist Agriculture and the Origins of the European World-Economy in the Sixteenth Century* (New York-London, 1974), p. 124.

CHAPTER VI

For advice and assistance in the preparation of this paper, I am particularly indebted to Janos M. Bak, Rhoda L. Friedrichs, and Rhiman A. Rotz.

[1]Bernd Moeller, *Reichsstadt und Reformation*, Schriften des Vereins für Reformationsgeschichte, 180 (Gütersloh, 1962); the English translation by H. C. Erik Midelfort and Mark U. Edwards, *Imperial Cities and the Reformation* (Philadelphia, 1972), will be cited here.

[2]According to Steven E. Ozment, *The Reformation in the Cities: The Appeal of Protestantism to Sixteenth-Century Germany and Switzerland* (New Haven, 1975), recent studies of the urban Reformation "look forward to the development of modern institutions" (p. 1), but in fact this is true neither of his own analysis, which ends with the Reformation period, nor of most other recent works. See, for example, the overviews of this subject provided by Basil Hall, "The Reformation City," *Bulletin of the John Rylands Library*, 54 (1971), 103-48, and by Winfried Becker in his *Reformation und Revolution* (Münster, 1974), pp. 82-104. The same applies to Marxist historians, e.g., Karl Czok, "Revolutionäre Volksbewegungen in mitteldeutschen Städten zur Zeit von Reformation und Bauernkrieg," in Leo Stern and Max Steinmetz, eds., *450 Jahre Reformation* (Berlin, 1967), pp. 128-45. In fact I know of only one recent study which emphasizes the relationship between urban attitudes and movements of the Reformation era and those of later centuries: Heinz Schilling, "Aufstandsbewegungen in der Stadtbürgerlichen Gesellschaft des Alten Reiches: Die Vorgeschichte des Münsteraner Täuferreichs, 1525-1534," in Hans-Ulrich Wehler, ed., *Der Deutsche Bauernkreig 1524-1526*, Geschichte und Gesellschaft, Sonderheft 1 (Göttingen, 1975), pp. 191-238.

[3]Moeller, p. 112.

[4]A. G. Dickens, *The German Nation and Martin Luther* (London, 1974) p. 119.

[5]Miriam U. Chrisman, "Urban Society and the Reformation," *The Forum Series*, FE 142 (1976), p. 13.

[6]See, for example, the paper by Thomas A. Brady, Jr.,

"Patricians, Nobles, Merchants: Internal Tensions and Solidarities in South German Urban Ruling Classes at the Close of the
Middle Ages," elsewhere in this volume, or the observations by
Wilfried Ehbrecht in "Hanse und spätmittelalterliche Bürgerkämpfe in Niedersachsen und Westfalen," *Niedersächsisches Jahrbuch für Landesgeschichte,* 48 (1976), 88.

[7]Moeller, pp. 113-14.

[8]Christian Burckstümmer, *Geschichte der Reformation und
Gegenreformation in der ehemaligen freien Reichsstadt Dinkelsbühl (1524-1648),* Schriften des Vereins für Reformationsgeschichte, 115-16 and 119-20 (Leipzig, 1914-15), I, 149-63; II,
passim.

[9]The following is based on Heinz Schilling, "Bürgerkämpfe
in Aachen zu Beginn des 17. Jahrhunderts: Konflikte im Rahmen
der alteuropäischen Stadtgesellschaft oder im Umkreis der früh-
bürgerlichen Revolution?" *Zeitschrift für historische For-
schung,* 1 (1974), 175-231.

[10]Werner Spiess, *Geschichte der Stadt Braunschweig im Nach-
mittelalter* (Braunschweig, 1966), I, 131-38.

[11]For a useful summary of these events, see Percy Ernst
Schramm, *Neun Generationen: Dreihundert Jahre deutscher Kultur-
geschichte im Lichte der Schicksale einer Hamburger Bürger-
familie (1648-1948)* (Göttingen, 1963), I, 95-98, 105-19.

[12]Franz Lau, "Der Bauernkrieg und das angebliche Ende der
lutherischen Reformation als spontaner Volksbewegung," *Luther-
Jahrbuch,* 26 (1959), 109-34. A partial translation is available
in Kyle C. Sessions, ed., *Reformation and Authority: The Meaning of the Peasants' Revolt* (Lexington, Mass., 1968), pp. 94-
101.

[13]The tone of this argument differs sharply from that advanced by Gerald Strauss, "Success and Failure in the German
Reformation," *Past and Present,* No. 67 (May 1975), 30-63. But
it should be noted that Strauss' conclusions are based almost
exclusively on rural evidence; his evidence for urban attitudes
(pp. 59-60) is inconclusive.

[14]Hans Mauersberg, *Wirtschafts-und Sozialgeschichte zen-
traleuropäischer Städte in neuerer Zeit, dargestellt an den
Beispielen von Basel, Frankfurt a.M., Hamburg, Hannover und
München* (Göttingen, 1960), p. 114.

[15]For Aachen and Brunswick, see the works by Schilling and
Spiess already cited. For the other cities mentioned, see Her-
bert Schwarzwälder, *Geschichte der freien Hansestadt Bremen,* I
(Bremen, 1975), 286-88; Friedrich Bothe, *Geschichte der Stadt
Frankfurt am Main* (Frankfurt/M., 1913), pp. 409-37; Jürgen Asch,
Rat und Bürgerschaft in Lübeck 1598-1669, Veröffentlichungen zur

Geschichte der Hansestadt Lübeck, 17 (Lübeck, 1961), pp. 56-93;
Herbert Langer, *Stralsund 1600-1630: Eine Hansestadt in der
Krise und im europäischen Konflikt*, Abhandlungen zur Handels- und
Sozialgeschichte, 9 (Weimar, 1970), pp. 161-221. Other cities
which experienced internal conflicts during this period included
Augsburg, Cologne, Danzig, Emden, Greifswald, Hamburg, Pader-
born, Stettin and Wismar; cf. Schilling, "Bürgerkämpfe in
Aachen," p. 176n, and Langer, p. 161.

[16]In Rothenburg ob der Tauber, for example, the Bürgermeister was physically assaulted in 1645 by a member of the politically insignificant outer council, who accused the magistrates of virtually stealing from the citizens; see Karl Rank,
*Die Finanzwirtschaft der Reichsstadt Rothenburg ob der Tauber
während des dreissigjährigen Krieges*, Erlanger Abhandlungen zur
mittleren und neueren Geschichte, N.F. 5 (Erlangen, 1940), pp.
126-27. In Bremen in the 1630's citizen opposition to heavy taxation took a more structured form; see Schwarzwälder, pp. 336-
37.

[17]See Gerald L. Soliday, *A Community in Conflict: Frankfurt Society in the 17th and Early 18th Centuries* (Hanover,
N.H., 1974). This is an excellent description of one urban conflict, but the author only notes briefly in passing (pp. 6-7)
that the conflict in Frankfurt was typical of a phenomenon that
affected many German cities.

[18]Gustav Mödl, "Weissenburg Contra Weissenburg: Ein
Beitrag zum Verhältnis zwischen Rat und Bürgerschaft," in *Uui-
zinburc/Weissenburg, 867-1967* (Weissenburg, 1967), pp. 105-10.

[19]Reinhard Hildebrandt, "Rat contra Bürgerschaft: Die
Verfassungskonflikte in den Reichsstädten des 17. und 18. Jahrhunderts," *Zeitschrift für Stadtgeschichte, Stadtsoziologie und
Denkmalpflege*, 1 (1974), 225. This article (pp. 221-41) provides a useful analysis of conflicts between citizens and councils in imperial cities, though almost exclusively for the period after 1648. A less reliable survey of urban conflicts between 1648 and 1789 is provided by the introductory chapter of
Helga Schultz, *Soziale und politische Auseinandersetzungen in
Rostock im 18. Jahrhundert*, Abhandlungen zur Handels-und Sozialgeschichte, 13 (Weimar, 1974), pp. 11-44. This interpretation
is flawed, for example, by an excessive concentration on those
cities in which opposition movements were led by artisans as
opposed to merchants.

[20]Spiess, pp. 165-66, 169-71.

[21]Asch, Chapts. 12 and 14; Soliday, Chapt. 7.

[22]Hildebrandt, pp. 230-31.

[23]Stadtarchiv Nördlingen: Lodweberakten: Lodenhandel

1696-1715, Danksagung 31 Oct. 1698; see also Christopher R. Friedrichs, "Early Capitalism and Its Enemies: The Wörner Family and the Weavers of Nördlingen," *Business History Review*, 50 (1976), 265-87.

[24]Stadtarchiv Nördlingen: Ordnungsbuch 1641-88, fols. 27v-28v (26 Dec. 1643). For a more general discussion of the Nördlingen council's attitude towards the citizenry, see Christopher R. Friedrichs, *Nördlingen, 1580-1700: Society, Government and the Impact of War* (Princeton University Ph.D. thesis, 1973), Chapt. 8.

[25]Otto Brunner, "Souveränitätsproblem und Sozialstruktur in den deutschen Reichsstädten der früheren Neuzeit," *Vierteljahrschrift für Sozial- und Wirtschaftsgeschichte*, 50 (1963), 329-60, esp. pp. 352ff. Hildebrandt also develops this theme, pp. 236-37.

[26]The vigorous political life of south German imperial cities in the eighteenth century is described by Otto Borst, "Zur Verfassung und Staatlichkeit oberdeurscher Reichsstädte am Ende des alten Reiches," *Esslinger Studien*, 10 (1964), 106-94.

[27]Cf. Hildebrandt, p. 229. In his rigorously Marxist analysis of events in Stralsund, Langer makes the same point but adds that the fear of a plebian uprising contributed to the eventual willingness of patricians and burgher leaders to reach a compromise (pp. 214-15 and *passim*).

[28]For a discussion of the social structure of early modern German cities, see Christopher R. Friedrichs, "Capitalism, Mobility and Class Formation in the Early Modern German City," *Past and Present*, No. 69 (Nov. 1975), 24-49.

[29]Hildebrandt, pp. 228-29.

[30]Bothe, pp. 425-26, describes these events.

[31]This was the case, for example, in Aachen during the disturbances of 1611 (see Schilling, "Bürgerkampfe in Aachen," esp. pp. 197-99), in Stralsund during the upheavals of 1612-16 (see Langer, pp. 199-211), and in Brunswick during the "Dohausensche Revolution" of 1613-15 (see Spiess, pp. 167-77)..

[32]This famous statement is cited by Moeller, p. 113. But Brunner (p. 345) places it more correctly in its historical context.

[33]Soliday, pp. 113.

[34]Moeller, pp. 112-14.

[35]Asch, Chapt. 18.

[36]Two influential interpretations of these conflicts, with an emphasis on south and west German cities, are by Erich Maschke, "Verfassung und soziale Kräfte in der deutschen Stadt des späten Mittelalters, vornehmlich in Oberdeutschland," *Vier-*

teljahrschrift für Sozial- und Wirtschaftsgeschichte, 46 (1959), 289-349, 433-76, and by Karl Czok, "Die Bürgerkämpfe in Süd- und Westdeutschland im 14. Jahrhundert," *Jahrbuch für Geschichte der oberdeutschen Reichsstädte (Esslinger Studien),* 12/13 (1966/67), pp. 40-72. North German uprisings are analyzed by Wilfried Ehbrecht, "Bürgertum und Obrigkeit in den hansischen Städten des Spätmittelalters," in Wilhelm Rausch, ed., *Die Stadt am Ausgang des Mittelalters,* Beiträge zur Geschichte der Städte Mitteleuropas, 3 (Linz, 1974), pp. 275-94. For a recent summary of findings on this topic, with some fresh evidence, see Rhiman A. Rotz, "Investigating Urban Uprisings with Examples from Hanseatic Towns, 1374-1416," in William C. Jordan, Bruce McNab, and Teofilo F. Ruiz, eds., *Order and Innovation in the Middle Ages: Essays in Honor of Joseph R. Strayer* (Princeton, N.J., 1976), Chapt. 16.

[37]Cf. Brunner, p. 349; Langer, pp. 186, 201.

[38]Asch, p. 112; Mödl, p. 106, Cf. Langer's comment, p. 165.

[39]Moeller, p. 65.

[40]See, for example, the two volumes edited by Rainer Wohlfeil, *Reformation oder frühbürgerliche Revolution?* Nymphenburger Texte zur Wissenschaft, 5 (Munich, 1972) and *Der Bauernkrieg 1524-26: Bauernkrieg und Reformation,* Nymphenburger Texte, 21 (Munich, 1975).

[41]See, for example, Heinz Schilling, "Aufstandsbewegungen," cited above, and, in the same volume, Otthein Rammstedt, "Stadtunruhen 1525"; also Hans-Christoph Rublack, "Die Stadt Würzburg im Bauernkrieg," and Lawrence P. Buck, "Civil Insurrection in a Reformation City: *The Versicherungsbrief* of Windsheim, March 1525," both in the *Archiv für Reformationsgeschichte,* 67 (1976). Professor Buck's paper on "Demands for Reform by Urban Dissidents During the German Peasants' Revolt" is to appear in the 1977 *Beiheft* of the *Archiv für Reformationsgeschichte.*

[42]Rudolf Endres, "Zünfte und Unterschichten als Elemente der Instabilität in den Städten," in Peter Blicke, ed., *Revolte und Revolutionen in Europa,* Historische Zeitschrift, Beiheft 4 (Munich, 1975), pp. 151-70. See also Erich Maschke, "'Obrigkeit' im spätmittelalterlichen Speyer und in anderen Städten," *Archiv für Reformationsgeschichte,* 57 (1966), 7-22.

[43]Dickens, Chapt. 8, provides a useful description of the burgher movements of the Reformation era in a number of North German cities. For a more detailed treatment of three such cities, see Johannes Schildhauer, *Soziale, politische und religiöse Auseinandersetzungen in den Hansastädten Stralsund, Rostock und Wismar im ersten Drittel des 16. Jahrhunderts,* Ab-

handlungen zur Handels- und Sozialgeschichte, 11 (Weimar, 1959).

[44]Bothe, pp. 301-05.

[45]Friedrich Bothe, *Geschichte der Stadt Frankfurt am Main,* 2., umbearbeitete Auflage (Frankfurt/M., 1923), p. 131.

[46]Soliday, p. 15.

[47]To say this is not to deny that the governments of early modern German cities were oligarchical, but only to express a doubt that they were necessarily *more* oligarchical in, say, the eighteenth century than they had been in the fourteenth. Magistrates in both periods had to face the possibility of citizen opposition if their rule became too harsh or arbitrary. By the same token, membership in the urban patriciate was not necessarily more "closed" in the later period than it had been in the earlier one. In every city the patriciate suffered from constant attrition which could only be compensated for by the recruitment of new members—although, of course, the attrition of old families and thus the absorption of new ones could take place more slowly in large cities than in smaller ones. Cf. Ingrid Bátori, "Das Patriziat der deutschen Stadt: Zu den Forschungsergebnissen über das Patriziat besonders der süddeutschen Städte," *Zeitschrift für Stadtgeschichte, Stadtsoziologie und Denkmalpflege,* 2 (1975), 1-30.

[48]Mack Walker, *German Home Towns: Community, State and General Estate, 1648-1871* (Ithaca, N.Y., 1971), suggests that "'Smothering' is a good word for the way the home town coped with internal differences" (p. 55). Yet in fact Walker himself provides (pp. 59-72) a vivid description of the way in which recurrent conflicts between magistrates and citizens emerged and were resolved in the small towns of Germany during the last 150 years of the Empire. Walker is primarily concerned, however, with territorial towns.

CHAPTER VII

[1]Erich Maschke und Jürgen Sydor, *Gesellschaftliche Unterschichten in den südwestdeutschen Städten,* Veröffentlichung der Kommission für Geschichtliche Landeskunde in Baden-Württemberg, Reihe B., Forschungen, V, 41 (Stuttgart, 1967), p. 6.

[2]Ibid., p. 59.

[3]Maschke states that two-thirds of the population of Augsburg in 1475 fall within these categories. Ibid., p. 18.

[4]Jean Pierre Kintz, "Topographie et démographie," Colloque International, *Strasbourg au Coeur Religieux de XVIe siècle,* 25-29 mai 1975. Full statistics will be available in Kintz's doctoral thesis: *Strasbourg du milieu du XVIe siècle au milieu du*

XVIIe siècle, Essai d'histoire demographique et sociale, Université de Strasbourg.

[5]Francois Joseph Fuchs, "L'Immigration Artisanale L'Strasbourg de 1544 à 1565," *Artisans et Ouvriers d'Alsace* (Strasbourg: Librairie Istra, 1965), p. 187.

[6]*Fragments de diverses vieilles Chroniques,* Fragments des Anciennes Chroniques d'Alsace, Recueillis par l'abbe l'Dacheux, Strasbourg (Strasbourgeoise, 1901), p. 16.

[7]*Les Collectanées de Daniel Specklin,* Rod. Reuss, ed., Bulletin de la Societé pour la Conservation des Monuments Historiques d'Alsace (Strasbourg, 1889), XIV, 328.

[8]Ibid., p. 347.

[9]Ibid., p. 351.

[10]*Les Chroniques Strasbourgeoises de Jacques Trausch et de Jean Wencker,* Fragments des Anciennes Chroniques d'Alsace, III, Fragments Receuillis par l'Abbe L. Dacheux (Strasbourg, 1892), p. 158.

[11]Otto Winckelmann, *Das Fürsorgewesen der Stadt Strassburg,* Quellen und Forschungen zur Reformationsgeschichte (Leipzig, 1922), II, no. 3.

[12]Ibid., II, no. 38.

[13]Ibid., II, no. 40.

[14]Manfred Krebs and Hans Georg Rott, *Elsass I, Stadt Strassburg 1522-1532,* Quellen zur Geschichte der Täufer, 7 (Gütersloh: Verlaghaus Gerd Mohn, 1959), No. 252, p. 334.

[15]The major portions of Hackfurt's *Tagebuch* are available in print in Otto Winckelmann's *Das Fürsorgewesen der Stadt Strassburg,* Vol. II., Urkunden und Akten. I will refer to these sources which are more readily available. The complete *Tagebuch* is in the Strasbourg Municipal Archives.

[16]Windkelmann, II, 1527, No. 71, pp. 115-17.

[17]Ibid., II, 1530, No. 94, pp. 134-35.

[18]Ibid., II, 1530, No. 95, pp. 135-36.

[19]Ibid., II, c.1526-30, No. 102, pp. 138-40.

[20]Ibid., II, 1531, No. 108, p. 146.

[21]Ibid.

[22]Ibid., II, 1530, No. 93, p. 133.

[23]Ibid.

[24]Ibid., II, 1532, No. 113, pp. 157-58.

[25]Ibid., p. 151.

[26]Ibid., p. 162.

[27]Ibid., II, 1527, No. 71, p. 115.

[28]Ibid., II, 1529, No. 76, p. 119.

[29]Ibid., II, 1531, No. 108, p. 147.

[30]Ibid.

[31]*Müntzordnung wider Lothringische müntz*, 1515 (Arch. Mun. R3, 54), 1517 (Arch. Mun. R5, 159), 1589 (Arch. Mun. R5, 159). *Müntzordnung wider Niderlandische Thaler*, 1578 (Arch. Mun. R5, 111).

[32]*Müntzordnung*, 1580 (Arch. Mun. R5, 123).

[33]*Weinordnanz*, 1518 (Ritter 3, 1681), 1580 (Arch. Mun. R5, 121), 1588 (Arch. Mun. R5, 150), 1591 (Arch. Mun. R5, 177). *Kauffsordnanz*, 1529 (Arch. Mun. R30, 160), 1531 (Arch. Mun. R30, 199), 1532 (Arch. Mun. R30, 203), 1533 (Arch. Mun. R3, 223), 1539 (Ritter 3, 1703), 1546 (Ritter 3, 1714), 1552 (Arch. Mun. R5, 28), 1594 (Arch. Mun. R5, 192).

[34]*Niemand zu kauffen sonder was sie für die woche bedürfen*, 1573 (Arch. Mun. R5, 87).

[35]*Beherbergen von Frembden Volck*, 1554 (Arch. Mun. R5, 38), 1575 (Arch. Mun. R5, 103).

[36]*Wider die Häuser zusammen brechen*, 1552 (Arch. Mun. R5, 32), 1582 (Arch. Mun. R5, 134b).

[37]Winckelmann, *op. cit.*, II, 1532, no. 113, p. 150.

[38]*Ordnanz der Barchantandel*, 1594 (Arch. Mun. R5, 194).

[39]For the system of in-house relief, see Winckelmann, II, 1524, 43, p. 98. For the supervision of bakers see ibid., 1529, 78, pp. 122-23.

[40]Winckelmann, *op. cit.*, II, 1531, No. 108, p. 147.

[41]Ibid., II, 1529, No. 76, p. 120.

[42]Ibid., 1529, No. 77, pp. 120-21.

[43]Ibid., p. 121.

[44]Ibid., II, 1531, No. 108, p. 148.

[45]Ibid., II, 1532, No. 113, p. 160.

CHAPTER VIII

[1]Jacques Le Goff, "La conception française de l'université à l'époque de la Renaissance," in Colloque International à l'occasion du VIe centenaire de l'université Jagellonne de Cracovie, 1964, *Les universités européennes du XIVe au XVIIIe siècle. Aspects et problèmes* (Geneva: Droz, 1967), pp. 94-100.

[2]Jacques Verger, "The University of Paris at the End of the Hundred Years' War," in John Baldwin and Richard Goldthwaite, ed., *Universities and Politics* (Baltimore and London: Johns Hopkins Press), pp. 69-74.

[3]Franco Simone, *The French Renaissance: Medieval Tradition and Italian Influence in Shaping the Renaissance in France*, trans. H. Gaston Hall (London: Macmillan, 1969), pp. 168-69.

[4]See my Ph.D. dissertation, "The Faculty of Theology of Paris, 1500-1536: Institution, Personnel, and Activity in Early

Sixteenth-Century France," 2 vols., Universtiy of Toronto, 1976. Vol. 2, "Biographical Register of Paris Doctors of Theology, 1500-1536," will be published by the Pontifical Institute of Medieval Studies, Toronto, in the series *Subsidia Medievalia*, in 1978.

[5]Charles Du Plessis d'Argentré, *Collectio judiciorum de novis erroribus qui ab initio duodecimi saeculi . . . usque ad annum 1632 in ecclesia proscripti sunt et notati* (Paris: Cailleau, 1725-1736), I, Pt. 2, 344.

[6]Johan Huizinga, *The Waning of the Middle Ages* (London: Arnold, 1924), p. 55.

[7]P. S. Allen, ed., *Opus epistolarum Desiderii Erasmi Roterodami* (Oxford: Clarendon, 1906-47), VI, Ep. 1581, lines 20-23. See also Leon-E. Halkin, "Erasme docteur," in *Religion et politique: Mélanges offerts à M. le doyen André Latreille*, Collection du Centre d'histoire du catholicisme, Université de Lyon, II, No. 10 (Lyon, 1972), pp. 39-47.

[8]Jules-Alexandre Clerval, ed., *Registre des procès-verbaux de la faculté de théologie* (Paris: Lecoffre and Gabalda, 1917), p. 154.

[9]This is similar to the case, cited at the Kalamazoo conference in 1977 by Prof. Heiko Oberman, of Jakob Fugger's consultation of the theologians of Tübingen on this same matter.

[10]See J. S. Brewer, ed., *Calendar of Letters and Papers, Foreign and Domestic, of the Reign of Henry VIII* (London, 1876), IV, Pt. 3, *passim*.

[11]Clerval, *Registre des procès-verbaux de la faculté de théologie*, p. 39.

[12]See my thesis, "The Faculty of Theology of Paris, 1500-1536," pp. 192-94.

[13]Ibid., pp. 327-31.

[14]Ibid., pp. 322-27.

[15]Paris, Archives Nationales, MM 248, fols. 18v-19r; Bibliothèque Nationale, MS. Lat. 15445, p. 662.

[16]See my thesis, "The Faculty of Theology of Paris, 1500-1536," p. 335.

[17]Paris, Archives Nationales, MM 249, fol. 14r-v (16 June 1559).

[18]d'Argentré, *Collectio*, I, Pt. 2, 344; César-Egasse Du Boulay, *Historia universitatis parisiensis* (Paris: P. de Bresche and F. Noël, 1665-73; rpt. Frankfurt am Main: Minerva, 1966), VI, 179.

[19]Clerval, ed., *Registre*, p. 154; Du Boulay, *Historia universitatis parisiensis*, VI, 181.

[20]Paris, Bibliothèque Nationale, MS. Nouvelle Acquisition

Latine 1782, fol. 260^v.

[21]Clerval, *Registre des procès-verbaux*, p. 369.

[22]Ibid., p. 362.

[23]The 1529 financial report of the Faculty contained an entry for 53 écus d'or au soleil "pro arresto contra Berquinum." Paris, Bibliothèque Nationale, MS. Lat. 13884, fol. 64^r.

[24]Quoted in Romain Rolland, "Le dernier procès de Louis de Berquin," Ecole française de Rome, *Mélanges d'archéologie et d'histoire*, XII (1892), 314-15, 320, 322.

[25]Brewer, ed., *Calendar*, IV, Pt. 3, No. 6459.

[26]d'Argentré, *Collectio judiciorum de novis erroribus*, II, Pt. 1, 325.

[27]Ibid., II, Pt. 1, 325.

[28]Ibid., II, Pt. 1, 317-22, 329-31.

[29]Elizabeth Armstrong, *Robert Estienne, Royal Printer: An Historical Study of the Elder Stephanus* (Cambridge: University Press, 1954).

[30]Roger Doucet, *Les institutions de la France au XVIe siècle* (Paris: Picard, 1948), II,' 797.

[31]Armstrong, *Robert Estienne, Royal Printer*, p. 198.

CHAPTER IX

[1]For the Reformation of the University of Tübingen, see the author's 1975 Vanderbilt University Ph.D. dissertation: "The Reformation of the Theological Faculty of the University of Tübingen, 1534-1555" (Ann Arbor: University Microfilms). See also August Friedrich Bok, *Geschichte der Herzoglich Württembergischen Eberhard Carls Universität zu Tübingen im Grundrisse* (Tübingen: Johann Georg Cotta, 1975); H. F. Eisenbach, *Beschreibung und Geschichte der Stadt und Universität Tübingen* (Tübingen: C. F. Osiander, 1822); Johannes Haller, *Die Anfänge der Universität Tübingen, 1477-1537*, 2 vols. (Stuttgart: W. Kohlhammer, 1927); Heinrich Hermelink, *Die Theologische Fakultät in Tübingen vor der Reformation 1477-1534* (Tübingen: J. C. B. Mohr, 1906); Karl August Klüpfel, *Geschichte und Beschreibung der Universität Tübingen* (Tübingen: L. F. Fues, 1849); K. V. von Riecke and Julius Hartmann, *Statistik der Universität Tübingen* (Stuttgart: H. Lindemann, 1877); Rudolph von Roth, *Urkunden zur Geschichte der Universität Tübingen aus den Jahren 1476 bis 1550* (Tübingen: H. Laupp, 1877); Karl Heinrich von Weizsäcker, *Lehrer und Unterricht an der evangelischen Facultät der Universität Tübingen von der Reformation bis zur Gegenwart* (Tübingen: L. F. Fues, 1877).

[2]For the background of the restitution of Ulrich to his

Württembergian duchy, see J. Wille, *Philipp der Grossmütige und die Restitution Ulrichs v. Wirtemberg 1526-1535* (Tübingen: H. Laupp, 1882).

[3]Gustav Bossert, "Ökolampad als Seelsorger des Herzogs Ulrich von Württemberg nach seinen Predigten über Psalm 137 im Herbst 1526," *Blätter für Württembergische Kirchengeschichte,* 36 (1932), pp. 208-29.

[4]Theodor Pressel, *Ambrosius Blaurer; Nach handschriftlichen und gleichzeitigen Quellen* (Elberfeld: R. L. Friedrichs, 1861), p. 353. The best single collection of Blarer material is *Briefwechsel der Brüder Ambrosius und Thomas Blaurer 1509-1567,* edited by Traugott Schiess, 3 vols. (Freiburg im Breisgau: Friedrich Ernst Gehsenfeld, 1908-12)--hereafter referred to as Schiess, followed by the number of the letter to which the reader is directed.

[5]Roth, *Urkunden,* p. 177; Schiess, No. 506.

[6]Heinrich Hermelink, editor, *Die Matrikeln der Universität Tübingen,* I (Stuttgart: W. Kohlhammer, 1906), 251-319.

[7]Chr. Fr. Schnurrer, *Erläuterungen der Württembergischen Kirchen-Reformations-und Gelehrten-Geschichte* (Tübingen: Cotta, 1978), pp. 344-45. "Gymnasium nostrum mirifice crescit, advenientibus quotidie magistris et scholaribus ab oppido Tübingen, Luteranum perfidiam, quae illic coepit introduce, detestantibus." Ulrich Zasius, *Epistolae ad viros aetatis,* ed. Johannes Ant. Rieggerus (Ulm: Aug. Lebrecht Stettinum, 1774), p. 222. For student enrollments in German universities during this period, see Franz Eulenburg, "Die Frequenz der deutschen Universitäten von ihrer Gründung bis zur Gegenwart," *Abhandlungen der philosophischen-historischen Klasse der königlichen sächsischen Gesellschaft der Wissenschaften,* XXIV, (1904), 55, 102-03; and also by Eulenburg, "Ueber die Frequenz der deutschen Universitäten in früherer Zeit," *Jahrbücher für Nationalökonomie und Statistik,* 3rd ser., 13 (1897), 543, as referred to by Denys Hay, "Schools and Universities," *The New Cambridge Modern History,* II, *The Reformation 1520-1559,* ed. G. R. Elton (Cambridge: Cambridge Univ. Press, 1958), p. 432. Eulenburg shows that there was a general and substantial rise in university enrollments in Germany in the 1530's and 1540's.

[8]Hastings Rashdall, *The Universities of Europe in the Middle Ages,* ed. F. M. Powicke and A. B. Emden (Oxford: Oxford University Press, 1936), II, 279.

[9]Ibid., pp. 76-78; also, Georg Kaufmann, *Die Geschichte der deutschen Universitäten,* II (Stuttgart: I. G. Cotta'sche Buchhandlung, 1888-96), 125-55, has a discussion of the chancellorship in this period.

[10]Haller, *Anfänge*, pp. 76-77.

[11]University of Tübingen Archives (hereafter referred to as UTA), Acta Senatus, 2/1a, fols. 115^r, 116^v, 117^r, 120^r, 122^v, 126^r, 126^v, 135^r, 142^v, 154^r, 154^v; UTA, Cancellariat et Probstei, 5/11, folios 66-71, 73-75^v.

[12]Schnurrer, *Erläuterungen*, pp. 380-83, 415-16.

[13]Julius Rauscher, *Württembergische Reformationsgeschichte*, No. 3, of *Württembergische Kirchengeschichte* (Stuttgart: Calwer Vereinsbuchhandlung, 1934), pp. 142-43.

[14]E. Hochstetter, "Geistliche, Professoren der Theologie, Missionäre aus der evangelischen Kirche Württembergs nach ihren Todestagen zusammengestellt," *Blätter für Württembergische Kirchengeschichte*, 5 (1890), 92-93; Pressel, *Blarer*, p. 354.

[15]Weizsäcker, *Lehrer und Unterricht*, p. 6; Roth, *Urkunden*, pp. 183-84.

[16]Roth, *Urkunden*, pp. 183-84.

[17]Melanchthon kept himself informed of the progress of the Reformation at Tübingen, especially through correspondence with his good friend Joachim Camerarius who joined the liberal arts faculty as a Professor of Greek and classical literature in 1535. See, for example, *Corpus Reformatorum: Philippi Melanchthonis Opera quae supersunt omnia*, ed. C. G. Bretschneider and H. E. Bindseil, Vol. II (Halle: Gustav Schwetschke, 1834), No. 1281, in which Melanchthon bemoans the partisan strife at Tübingen.

[18]*Corpus Reformatorum*, 3, Nos. 1473-75.

[19]Roth, *Urkunden*, p. 177.

[20]Martin Leube, *Geschichte des Tübinger Stifts*, 3 vols. (Stuttgart: Chr. Scheufele, 1921-54), remains the standart history of the Stift.

[21]Heinrich Hermelink, "Die Universität Marburg von 1527-1645," in *Die Philipps-Universität zu Marburg, 1527-1927* (Marburg: Elwert, 1927), pp. 1-126.

[22]Martin Brecht, "Geht das Tübinger Stift auf ein Strassburger Vorbild züruck?" *Zeitschrift für Württembergische Landesgeschichte*, 23 (1964), 228-29.

[23]Leube, *Geschichte des Tübinger Stifts*, pp. 8-13.

[24]Ibid., and Julius Hartmann, *Das Tübinger Stift; ein Beitrag zur Geschichte des deutschen Geisteslebens* (Stuttgart: Strecker u. Schroder, 1918), pp. 4-18.

[25]This was a part of the second general ordinances for the university issued by Ulrich, this set of statutes coming on the heels of his consultation with Melanchthon. Roth, *Urkunden*, pp. 186ff.

[26]Leube, *Geschichte der Tübinger Stifts*, p. 9.

[27]Ibid., p. 10.

[28]Ibid., p. 11.

[29]Jacob Andreä, one of the primary authors of the Formula of Concord, was a *Stipendiat* as a student, and later in his career had strong ties to the *Stift* when he served as Chancellor of the university.

[30]Roth, *Urkunden*, pp. 270-73.

[31]Melchior Adam, *Vitae Germanorum Theologorum, qui Superiori Seculo Ecclesiam Christi Voce Scriptis que Propagarunt et Propugnarunt, Congestae et ad Annum Usque (I) IC XVIII* (Frankfurt: J. Rosae viduae, 1653), pp. 97-98.

[32]UTA, Acta Senatus, 2/1b. folio 11b; Weizsacker, *Lehrer und Unterricht*, pp. 12-13.

[33]Julius Hartmann, *Erh. Schnepff, der Reformator in Schwaben, Nassau, Hessen, und Thuringen* (Heilbronn: Scheurlen, 1872), p. 68; Charles V to Rector, Doctors and regents of the University of Tübingen, 18 May 1548, Hauptstaatsarchiv Stuttgart, A274, Bu. 21.

[34]Theodor Schnepff, *Oratio Funebris de pia vita, et lugubri obitu Reverendi, eximii, et Clarissmi Theologi, Dn. D. Iacobi Beurlini Dornstettensis*(Tübingen: Theodorici Werlini, 1613), pp. 18-19; see also Weizsäcker, *Lehrer und Unterricht*, p. 6; and also Schiess, No. 562.

[35]Gustav Bossert, *Das Interim in Württemberg*, Schriften des Vereins für Reformationsgeschichte, No. 46/47 (Halle: Max Niemeyer, 1895), p. 64.

[36]Ibid., pp. 88-89, 99-100, 110, 113-14.

[37]Ulrich died November 6, 1550, and was buried in the chancel of the *Stiftskirche* in Tübingen. See Karl Brandi, *The Emperor Charles V: The Growth and Destiny of a Man and a World Empire*, trans. C. V. Wedgwood (1939; rpt. London: Jonathan Cape, 1965), p. 599.

[38]Hochstetter, "Geistliche," p. 69; Weizsäcker, *Lehrer und Unterricht*, p. 16.

[39]Hochstetter, "Geistliche," p. 69; Gustav Bossert, "Jakob Beurlin," *Realencyklopädie für protestantische Theologie und Kirche*, 3rd ed., ed. Albert Hauck (Leipzig: J. C. Hinrichs'sche Buchhandlung, 1896-1913), II, 672.

[40]Hermelink, *Die Matrikeln*, p. 275. Beurlin received his B.A. in September of 1537, his M.A. on January 28, 1541, and his Th.D. in April of 1551; Hochstetter, "Geistliche," p. 77.

[41]On August 10, 1556, the Academic Senate discussed the replacement of Käuffelin, and turned the matter over to the theological faculty (Beurlin and Frecht, although Frecht was already out of Tübingen, seeking a "cure" at a resort), which was to

consider the matter and bring back a recommendation to the Senate. UTA, Acta Senatus, 2/1b. fol. 212^V.

[42]Schnurrer, *Erläuterung*, p. 412. Dietrich received his B.A. June 15, 1541, at the age of fifteen and a half, his M.A. in August of 1544, and his Th.D. in 1554, after having served as a teacher of Greek in the *Stift*. He had also served in one pastoral position. He was to remain in Tübingen for the rest of his life, serving as rector on six occasions. Hermelink, *Matrikeln*, p. 298; Hochstetter, "Geistliche," p. 86.

[43]Heerbrand and Schnepff were named to the faculty of theology during a meeting of the University Senate on November 5, 1556, with both appointments to take effect the following February. UTA, Acta Senatus, 2/1b, fol. 218^V.

[44]Hochstetter, "Geistliche," pp. 38-39. Heerbrand served a parish in Herrenberg, just south of Tübingen, after he lost his position as Deacon in Tübingen due to his oppostion to the Interim. He also participated in the Württembergian delegation to the Council of Trent in 1552, and in 1556 he joined with Jacob Andreä in the reformation of several areas, including the Markgrafschaft Baden. According to Hochstetter, "Geistliche," pp. 38-39, he received his doctoral degree from Tübingen about 1550. The rather thorough notes of Hermelink in his edition of the *Matrikeln* (p. 413) do not indicate this, although he was matriculated at Tübingen on October 17, 1543. From that time to his appointment to the university faculty, he lived and worked in and around Tübingen. The University Senate, in its minutes, refers to Heerbrand as "Doctor Herrbrand," which probably means that Hochstetter is correct, at least insofar as to say that Heerbrand had earned a doctorate. UTA, Acta Senatus, 2/1b, fol. 218^V.

CHAPTER X

[1]André Mercier, ed., *Der Flüchtling in der Weltgeschichte*, Ein ungelöstes Problem der Menschheit, Universität Bern, Kulturhistorische Vorlesungen, 1973-74 (Bern: Herbert Lang, 1974).

[2]Ovidius, *Tristia*, III, 3, 53. Cum patriam amisi, tunc me perisse putabo: et prior et gravior mors fuit illa mihi.

[3]Augustinus, *De Civitate Dei*, XIX, 17.

[4]O. Noordmans, *Augustinus* (Haarlem, 1933), pp. 51ff, 252ff.

[5]G. W. Locher, "Bullinger und Calvin--Probleme des Vergleichs ihrer Theologien," in U. Gäbler und E. Herkenrath, ed., *Heinrich Bullinger 1504-1575*, Gesammelte Aufsätze zum 400 (Zürich 1975), II, 1-33; Leonhard von Muralt, ed., *Zwingliana*, 10, No. 3 (1955).

[6]Heinryche Bullingeri, *Epistola ad ecclesias Hungaricas . . .* scripta MDLI, ed. and trans. Barnabas Nagy (Budapest 1968). Cf. Joachim Staedtke, *Heinrich-Bullinger-Bibliographie,* I (Zürich 1972), Nos. 383-85.

[7]Cf. ibid., Nos. 575-81.

[8]Martin Schmidt, *RGG*[3] 2, 1010f.

[9]L. von Muralt und W. Schmidt, ed., *Quellen zur Geschichte der Täufer in der Schweiz,* I (Zürich, 1952), No. 202. For philological reasons I disagree with the editors and accept the poem as genuine; the prose version (No. 201) is an eighteenth century paraphrase.

[10]G. W. Locher, "Staat und Politik in der Lehre der Reformatoren," *Reformatio,* 1 (1952) 202-13; H. H. Schrey, ed., *Reich Gottes und Welt,* Die Lehre Luthers von den Zwei Reichen, WdF, CVII (Darmstadt, 1969)(with bibliography). The fact that in the discussion of the doctrine of the two kingdoms banishment is never mentioned cannot be ignored.

[11]Alfred Schultze, *Stadtgemeinde und Reformation* (Tübingen, 1918); Leonhard von Muralt, *Stadtgemeinde und Reformation in der Schweiz,* ZSG, X, No. 3 (Zürich, 1930); Bernd Moeller, *Reichsstadt und Reformation,* SVRG, No. 180 (Gütersloh, 1962); Bernd Moeller, "Die Kirche in den evangelischen freien Städten Oberdeutschlands im Zeitalter der Reformation," *ZtsGesch des Oberrheins,* 112 (1964), 148-62; Bernd Moeller, "Zwinglis Disputationen," Studien zu den Anfängen der Kirchenbildung und des Synodalwesens im Protestantismus," *ZsRG, Kan. Abt.,* 17 (1970), 275-324, and 91 (1974), 213-364; Bernd Moeller, "Die Ursprünge der reformierten Kirche," *ThLZ,* 100 (1975), 641-53; Gerhard Pfeiffer, "Das Verhältnis von politischer und kirchlicher Gemeinde in den deutschen Reichsstädten," in W. P. Fuchs, ed., *Staat und Kirche im Wandel der Jahrhunderte* (Stuttgart, 1966), 79-99; Guy E. Swanson, *Religion and Regime: A Sociological Account of the Reformation* (Ann Arbor, 1967); Steven E. Ozment, *The Reformation in the Cities* (New Haven and London: Yale Univ. Press, 1975).

[12]Martin Haas, "Täufertum und Revolution," in *Festschrift für Leonhard von Muralt* (Zürich, 1970), pp. 286-95; Martin Haas, "Der Weg der Täufer in die Absonderung," in H. J. Goertz, ed., *Umstrittenes Täufertum 1525-1975* (Göttingen, 1975), 50-78.

[13]E. Stähelin, *Johannes Calvin,* 2 vols. (Elberfeld, 1863); Carl Pestalozzi, *Heinrich Bullinger* (Elberfeld, 1858); Friedrich Brandes, *John Knox,* (Elberfeld, 1858); P. Hume Brown, *John Knox,* 2 vols. (London, 1895); Joseph Chambon, *Der Puritanismus* (Zollikon, 1944).

[14]Hans Scholl, *Reformation und Politik. Politische Ethik*

bei Luther, Calvin und den Frühhugenotten, (Stuttgart, 1976); E. Riesser, *Calvin-Franzose, Genfer oder Fremdling?* (Zürich, 1968); cf. Calvin, *CO,* VI, 576, 606; *CO Letters,* No. 508, 509, 689, 1084, 1756, 1958, 2082, 2107, 2380, 2829, 3047, 3485. I am grateful to Hans Scholl for drawing my attention to a number of these references.

[15]Carl Bernhard Hundeshagen, *Calvinismus und staatsbürger-liche Freiheit,* ed. L. Wyss (Zollikon, 1946); Heinz Schilling, *Niederländische Exulanten im 16. Jahrhundert,* SVRG, No. 187 (Gütersloh, 1972).

[16]Perry Miller, *The New England Mind* (1954); William Haller, *Liberty and Reformation in the Puritan Revolution* (New York, 1955); Kai T. Erikson, *Wayward Puritans: A Study in the Sociology of Deviance* (New York, 1966).

[17]Martin Schmidt, *RGG*[3], V, 384,

[18]Joseph Chambon, *Der Puritanismus: Sein Weg von der Reformation bis zum Ende der Stuarts* (Zürich, 1944); William Haller, *The Rise of Puritanism* (New York, 1957); Haller, *Liberty and Reformation in the Puritan Revolution.*

[19]G. W. Locher, "Zwinglis Einfluss in England und Schottland--Daten und Probleme," *Zwingliana, 14, No. 4* (1975), 165-209.

[20]Staedtke, *Heinrich-Bullinger-Bibliographie,* I, Nos. 327-56, especially Nos. 355-56.

[21]Letter of Prof. George Yule in Melbourne, April 1977. In the seventeenth century, the theology of the last Bishop of the Bohemian Brotherhood, Johann Amos Comenius, offers a perfect example of the kindling of apocalyptic expectations as a result of suffering the fate of a refugee.

[22]Letter of G. Yule, April 1977.

[23]W. S. Hudson, *John Ponet (1516?-1556): Advocate of Limited Monarchy* (Chicago, 1942); Ch. Garret, *The Marian Exiles: A Study in the Origins of Elizabethan Puritanism* (Cambridge, 1966), pp. 253-58; W. Nijenhuis, *John Ponet (c.1514-1556) als revolutinair pamflettist* (Assen and Amsterdam, 1976).

[24]Chr. Goodman, *How superior powers ought to be obeyed* (Geneva, 1558); John Knox, *The first blast of the trumpet against the monstrous regiment of women* (Geneva, 1558).

[25]Jürgen Dennert, ed., *Beza, Brutus, Hotman, Calvinistische Monarchomachen,* trans. H. Klinghöfer, introduced by J. Dennert, Klassiker der Politik, 8 (Köln, 1968); Theodor Beza, *De iure magistratuum, Vom Recht der Regierungen gegenüber ihren Mitbürgern,* trans. W. Klingenhaben, Polis, 43 (Zürich, 1971).

[26]C. W. Bard, *A History of the Huguenot emigration to America,* 2 Vols. (New York, 1884); Samuel Smiles, *The Hugue-*

nots . . . in England and Ireland (London, 1889); F. de Schick-
ler, Les églises du refuge en Angleterre, 3 vols. (1892); Helmut
Erbe, Die Hugenotten in Deutschland (Essen, 1937)(with bibliography); Joseph Chambon, Der französische Protestantismus, Sein
Weg bis zur französischen Revolution (München, 1937); Kurt Gal-
ling, "Hugenotten," RGG[3], III (1959), 469-74; Hans Scholl, Reformation und Politik, Politische Ethik bei Luther, Calvin und
den Frühhugenotten (Stuttgart, 1976).

[27]Epistola ad Diognetum, 5, 5, in Patrum apostolicorum
Opera, ed. V. de Gebhardt, Th. Zahn, A. Harnack, Editio minor
(Leipzig, 1877), p. 81.

CHAPTER XI

[1]Charles Martin, Les Protestants Anglais réfugiés à Genève
au temps de Calvin 1555-1560 (Geneva: A. Jullien, 1915), p. 2.
  [2]Ibid., p. 4.
  [3]Ibid., p. 21.
  [4]Ibid., pp. 23-24. See also Horatio B. Hackett, "Church-
Book of the Puritans at Geneva, from 1555 to 1560," Bibliotheca
Sacra (July 1862), pp. 469ff; Th. Heyer, "Notice sur la Colonie
Anglais, Etablié à Genève de 1555 à 1560," Memoires et Doc-
ments, publies par la Societie d'archeologie de Genève, IX
(1855), pp. 337-68.
  [5]Nicholas Dorcastor, The Humble and Unfained Confession of
the Belief of Certain Poor Banished Men (Wittenburg, 14 May
1554). sigs. Ci[v], Cii[r]. There has been considerable discussion
regarding the authorship and origin of this curious little document. A beginning point would be to compare the views of Chris-
tina H. Garrett in The Marian Exiles (Cambridge: Cambridge
Univ. Press, 1938) and Winthrop Hudson in John Ponet (Chicago:
Univ. of Chicago Press, 1942).
  [6]Ibid., sigs. Di[v]-Dii[r].
  [7]Ibid., sigs. Eii[r].
  [8]Ibid., sig. Eiii[v].
  [9]Patrick Collinson has shown quite conclusively, I believe,
that Whittingham was not the author and that Thomas Wood was the
likely candidate. See Patrick Collinson, "The Authorship of A
Brieff Discours off the Troubles Begonne at Franckford," Journal
of Ecclesiastical History, 9 (1958), 188-208.
  [10]William Whittingham, A Brief Discourse of the Troubles
at Frankfort, 1554-1558 A.D. (London: Elliot Stock, 1575), pp.
23ff.
  [11]A. F. Mitchell, ed., Livre des Anglais (n.d.). This document, which contains a number of valuable records of the En-

glish exiles while they were in Geneva, has been made available by J. Southernden Burn, published at London in 1831, and later inserted into his *History of Parish Registers*. See also Hackett, pp. 469ff, and Heyer, pp. 337-68, as well as Martin, pp. 43ff.

[12]Ibid.

[13]Ibid.

[14]Ibid.

[15]See my "Anthony Gilby: Puritan in Exile--A Biographical Approach," *Church History*, 40 (1971), 412-22, and also my unpublished dissertation, University of Iowa, 1969: *The Theology of the Geneva Bible of 1560: A Study in English Protestantism*; Richard L. Greaves, "Traditionalism and the Seeds of Revolution in the Social Principles of the Geneva Bible," *Sixteenth Century Journal*, 7 (1976), 94-109.

[16]W. D. Maxwell, *John Knox's Genevan Service Book, 1556* (Edinburgh and London, 1931), p. 17.

[17]*The forme of prayers and ministration of the Sacraments, &c. used in the Englishe Congregation at Geneva: and approued, by the famous and godly learned man, John Caluyn* (Geneva, 1556), sigs. Aii[v]-Bi[v].

[18]Ibid., sigs. Ciii[v]-Ci[v].

[19]Ibid., sig. Cvii.

[20]James C. Spalding, "Restitution as a Normative Factor for Puritan Dissent," *Journal of the American Academy of Religion*, 44 (1976), 47-63.

[21]*The forme of prayers...*, sig. Cviii[r].

[22]*Ibid.*, sigs. Fv[r]-vii[r].

[23]Ronald J. Vander Molen, "Anglican Against Puritan: Ideological Origins during the Marian Exile," *Church History*, 42 (1973), 45-57.

[24]Richard L. Greaves, "John Knox and the Covenant Tradition," *Journal of Ecclesiastical History*, 24 (1973), 23-32. See also my article on Christopher Goodman and the English Protestant tradition of civil disobedience forthcoming in *Sixteenth Century Journal*.

[25]John Milton, *Of Reformation in England and the causes that hitherto have hindered it*, Book I, in *Complete Prose Works of John Milton*, Vol. I (New Haven: Yale Univ. Press, 1953), pp. 524f.

CHAPTER XII

[1]The nature of, and factors contributing to this sense of paranoia are well dealt with by Joshua Trachtenberg, *The Devil*

*and the Jews: The Medieval Conception of the Jew and Its Rela-
tion to Modern Antisemitism* (New Haven, 1943; rpt. Meridian
Books and the Jewish Publication Society, 1961).

[2]See the following works: Y. Baer, *A History of the Jews
in Spain*, 2 vols. (Philadelphia, 1961); A. A. Neuman, *The Jews
in Spain*, 2 vols. (Philadelphia, 1942; rpt. New York: Octagon
Books, 1969). Concerning the Spanish Inquisition, see H. C.
Lea, *A History of the Spanish Inquisition*, 4 vols. (New York,
1906-07); H. Kamen, *The Spanish Inquisition* (New York, 1965); C.
Roth, *The Spanish Inquisition* (London, 1937).

[3]Concerning these Spanish Jews, see M. Kayserling, *Geschichte der Juden in Portugal* (Leipzig, 1867); M. Kayserling,
Sephardim (Leipzig, 1859); L. Zunz, *Zur Geschichte und Literatur*
(Berlin, 1845); R. D. Barnett, *The Sephardi Heritage* (New York,
1971).

[4]See C. Roth, *A History of the Marranos*, 4th ed. (New York,
1974); A. D. Ortiz, *Las Judeo Conversos in España y America* (Madrid, 1971).

[5]Concerning the alienation of conversos from the Christian
community due to the 'pure blood laws,' see Albert A. Sciroff,
*Les Controverses des Statuts de 'purité de sang' en España du
XVe au XVIIe Siècle* (Paris, 1960); Ortiz, Chapt. 5: "Los esta-
tutos de limpieza de sangre"; C. Roth, *Marranos and Racial Antisemitism* (London, 1940). Concerning the alienation of conversos
from the Jewish community, see B. N. Netanyahu, *The Marranos of
Spain from the Late 14th to the Early 16th Century* (New York,
1966); H. J. Zimmels, *Die Marranen in der Rabbinischen Literatur*
(Berlin, 1932).

[6]Jehiel ben Samuel, *Minhat Kanaot* (Berlin 1898), pp. 2-3.

[7]Concerning Jewish Messianic speculation, see A. H. Silver,
A History of Messianic Speculation in Israel (New York, 1927;
rpt. Boston, 1959); Joseph Klausner, *The Messianic Idea in Is-
rael from its Beginning to the Completion of the Mishna* (New
York, 1955); G. Scholem, *The Messianic Idea in Judaism* (New
York, 1971); Joseph Sarachek, *The Messianic Ideal in Medieval
Jewish Literature* (New York, 1932); M. Zobel, *Der Messias und
die Messianische Zeit in Talmud und Midrasch* (Berlin, 1938).

[8]Concerning Jewish Cabbalistic systems, the reader might
consult any of the excellent works by Gershom Scholem, especially *Major Trends in Jewish Mysticism* (New York, 1946), *Kabbalah*
(New York, 1974), *On the Kabbalah and its Symbolism* (New York,
1965).

[9]Cited in Abraham Azulai, *Or haHammah*, I (Przemysl, 1896),
Introduction.

[10]For a list of cities in Germany expelling Jews at the end

of the fifteenth century and later during the sixteenth century, see Salo W. Baron, *A Social and Religious History of the Jews* (New York, 1969), XI, 275-77, and XIII, 255. Professor Philip Bebb of Ohio University has prepared a list of cities expelling Jews during the fifteenth and sixteenth centuries as part of a paper presented at the Sixteenth Century Studies Conference, St. Louis, Oct. 1976, entitled: "Jewish Policy in 16th Century Nürnberg."

[11]Isaac Abarbanel, *Ma'ayanei Ha'yeshua* (Amsterdam, 1647), fol. 91[v].

[12]Ibid., fol. 12[v].

[13]Abraham Halevi, *Mashre Kitrin* (Constantinople, 1508), fol. 18[v]. Halevi believed the messiah would appear in 1530.

[14]Azariah dei Rossi, *Me'or Aiynayim* (Wilna, 1865), Chapt. XLIII.

[15]Daniel ben Perachiah, *She'erit Yoseph* (Salonica, 1568), p. 8.

[16]Eliezer Ashkenazi ven Eli Rote, *Ma'aseh Adonai* (Venice, 1583), fol. 181[v].

[17]Gedaliah ibn Yahya, *Sefer Shalshelet HaKabbalah* (Amsterdam, 1697), fol. 36[v].

[18]See H. Graetz, *History of the Jews* (1894; rpt. Philadelphia, 1956), IV, 482-83. Also see Silver, pp. 143-45.

[19]David Ganz, *Tzemach David* (Warsaw, 1859), fol. 29[v].

[20]Joseph HaCohen, *Emek Habacha* and *Divrei Hayamim,* cited in Silver, p. 144.

[21]Tobias Cohen, *Ma'aseh Tuvia* (Venice, 1707), fol. 26[v].

[22]See Graetz, IV, 509-11, and in Index, p. 736; also, Silver, p. 145-47.

[23]Cited in Silver, p. 147.

[24]See Scholem, *Major Trends,* Chapt. VII: "Isaac Luria and his School," and *The Messianic Idea,* pp. 37-48.

[25]Chaim Vital, *Sefer HaLiqqutim* (Jerusalem, 1913), fol. 89[v].

[26]See footnote 24, above.

[27]Y. Baer, *Toledot haYehudim B'Sefarad haNotzrit* (Tel-Aviv, 1959), pp. 365, 464.

[28]See B. Netanyahu, *The Marranos of Spain,* pp. 1-4, and *Don Isaac Abravanel* (Philadelphia, 1953), p. 275.

[29]Diego de Simancas (Pseudo: Didaco Velasquez), *Defensio Statuti Toletani* (Antwerp, 1575), fol. 70[v].

[30]Samuel ben Abraham Aboab, *Debar Shmuel* (Venice, 1702), No. 45. Another famous Marrano, Isaac Orobio de Castro, also maintained this position; see Philip van Limborch, *De Veritate religionis Christianae Amica collatio cum eruditio Judaeo*

(Gouda, 1687), p. 178.

[31]Abraham Cardozo, *Sefer Inyanei Shabtai Zevi* (Berlin, 1913), p. 88.

[32]Concerning Menasseh ben Israel, see Lucien Wolf, *Menassah ben Israel's Mission to Oliver Cromwell* (London, 1901); C. Roth, *A Life of Menasseh ben Israel* (Philadelphia, 1934).

[33]The first person to relate the expulsion of Jews from Spain and the discovery of America was Columbus himself, who noted: "After the Spanish monarchs had expelled all the Jews from their kingdom and lands in January, in that same month they commissioned me to undertake the voyage to India with a properly equipped fleet." Cited by J. Prinz, *The Secret Jews* (New York, 1973), p. 56.

The Marranos sailing with Columbus were, among others: Dr. Marco, ship's surgeon; Dr. Merta Bernal, physician; Luis de Torres, interpreter (baptised under Columbus' sponsorship just one day before setting sail); and Rodrigo de Triana, navigator. Two historians who have advanced the notion that Columbus was of Marrano origins are Salvador de Madariaga, *Christopher Columbus* (New York, 1940), and M. David, *Who Was Columbus?* (New York, 1933). Concerning Marrano participation in the voyages to the New World, see M. Kayserling, *Christopher Columbus and the Participation of Jews in the Spanish and Portuguese Discoveries* (Leipzig, 1894).

[34]The best account by far of Zvi's tumultous career is G. Scholem's *Sabbatai Sevi, The Mystical Messiah,* trans. R. J. Zwi Werblowsky (Princeton, 1973).

[35]See Scholem, *The Messianic Idea,* pp. 70-142.

[36]"Catholics who Celebrate Passover," *Time Magazine,* 11 April 1977, p. 66.

[37]Concerning the Doenmeh, see G. Scholem, *Die Kryptojüdische Sekte der Doenmeh in der Türkei* (Leiden, 1931), and his *Doenmeh's Prayer Service* (New York, 1942).

CHAPTER XIII

[1]*Renaissance Quarterly,* 29 (1976), 688.

[2]See Joaquim de Carvalho, "Estudos sobre a Cultura Portuguesa do Seculo XVI," in *Acta Universitatis Conimbrigensia* (1948), pp. 25-27.

[3]António José Saraiva, *História da Cultura em Portugal,* Vol. II in collaboration with Oscar Lopes and Luis Albuquerque (Lisbon: Jornal Do Fôro, 1955), p. 531.

[4]See Elisabeth Feist Hirsch, "Damião de Gois: The Life and Thought of a Portuguese Humanist 1502-1574," *International Ar-*

chives of the History of Ideas, 19 (1967), 103.

[5]See Vitorino Nemésio, "Vida e Obra do Infante D. Henrique," in *Colecção Henriquina* (Lisbon, 1959), p. 61. The reasons Zurara ascribed to Henry's adventures can be found in his *Chronicle of Guinea,* Chapt. 5. Las Casas in his *História de las Indias* quotes Zurara on several occasions. He stressed the latter's report of the terror the Portuguese had of Cape Bojador. See Léon Bourdon and Robert Richard, Gomes Eanes de Zurara "Chronique de Guinée," in *Mémoires de l'Institut Français d'Afrique Noire* (Ifan-Dakar, 1960), Introduction, p. 17 and note 2. For an English translation of Zurara's work see *The Chronicle of the Discovery and Conquest of Guinea,* trans. and ed. Sir Raymond Beazley and Edgar Prestage, 2 vols. (London: Hakluyt Society, 1896-99).

[6]See António José Saraiva, *História,* p. 383. Chapt. IV, "As Navegacões e a Mentalidade Cientifica," pp. 396-507, contains a wealth of information on the science of navigation.

[7]Ibid., pp. 383ff, 406. Lullus' book *Liber acquisitione terrae sanctae* was published in 1288.

[8]See C. Raymond Beazley, *Prince Henry the Navigator: The Hero of Portugal and of Modern Discovery 1394-1460* (London, New York: G. P. Putnam's Sons, 1931), Chapt. IX, "Henry's Settlement at Sagres and First Discoveries," pp. 160-67.

[9]See Francis M. Rogers, *The Travels of the Infante Dom Pedro of Portugal* (Cambridge: Harvard Univ. Press, 1961), p. 260.

[10]See João de Barros, *Decadas,* ed. Hernani Cidade with notes by Manuel Murias (Lisbon, 1945), *passim,* and Damião de Gois, *Chronica do Felissimo Rei Dom Emanuel,* 4 vols. (Coimbra: Univ. Press, 1943-55), *passim.*

[11]The *Lusiadas* were translated in English by Sir Richard Fanshawe in 1655. The University of Illinois Press has reprinted this edition.

[12]It is the *Colóquios dos simples e drogas e cousas medicinais de India e assi de algumas frutas achadas nela* (Goa, 1563; rpt. Lisbon, 1963). In 1567 Carolus Clusius, the Dutch botanist, translated d'Orta's book into Latin. A new edition appeared in 1963.

[13]See António José de Saraiva, *História,* pp. 458-63.

[14]Ibid., pp. 463ff.

[15]See Francis M. Rogers, *The Quest for Eastern Christians* (Minneapolis: Univ. of Minnesota Press, 1962). Also see U. Slessarey, *Prester John, the Letter and the Legend* (1959).

[16]It is the "Fides, Religio, Moresque Aethiopum sub Imperio Preciosi Joannis," in *Aliquot Opuscula* (1544), p. 262: "Sed

multo consultius erit huiusmodi christianos homines, sive
Graecos, sive Armenios, sive Aethiopes, sive ex quavis septem
Christianorum Ecclesiarum in charitate et Christi amplexibus
sustinere, et eos sine contumeliis permittere inter alios
fratres christianos vivere aut versari; quoniam omnes filii bap-
tismi sumus et de vera fide unanimiter sentimus."

[17]See Antonio Rotondò, "Studi E Ricerche Di Storia Ereti-
cale Italiana Del Cinquecento," *Pubblicazioni Dell'Istituto Di
Science Politiche Dell'Universita Di Terino* (1974), Appendix I:
"Due Scritti Inediti Di Guillaume Postel" (p. 483).

[18]See Robert Oliver & J. D. Fage, *A Short History of Africa*
(Baltimore: Penquin, 1963), Chapt. 11.

[19]See Beazley, *Prince Henry the Navigator*, p. 215.

[20]See the letter of Erasmus to Damião de Gois in Allen-
Garrod, No. 2846.

[21]On Las Casas' defense of the Indians, see Lewis Hanke,
*All Mankind is One: A Study of the Disputation between Bartol-
omé de las Casas and Juan Ginés de Sepúlveda in 1550 on the Intellectual and Religious Capacity of the American Indians* (De
Kalb: Northern Illinois University Press, 1974).

[22]Gilberto Freyre, *The Masters and the Slaves*, trans.
Samuel Putnam (New York: Knopf, 1964), p. 185.

[23]See Américo da Costa Ramalho, *Estudios Sobre A Época Do
Renascimento* (Coimbra, 1969). On Cataldo, Chapts. III-V.

[24]See Joachim de Carvalho, *Estudos*, p. 36; he calls John
III's character enigmatic. A. H. Oliveira Marques, *History of
Portugal*, I (New York: Columbia Univ. Press, 1972), 215, sees
in John III a change from "the tolerant Renaissance prince" to
a "fanatic, narrow-minded ruler." Marcel Bataillon, *Etudes sur
le Portugal au temps de l'humanisme* (Coimbra: Univ. Press,
1952) speaks in connection with the circulation of the purged
edition of Erasmus's *Colloquies* from 1545-47 of a "manifestation
extrême et tardive du libéralisme méconnu" (p. 227).

[25]Vicente's letter to the king is printed in his *Collected
Works* (Porto, 1965). The letter is discussed by Reis Brasil,
"As Determinantes do Humanismo na obra de Gil Vicente," in *Mis-
celânea de Estudos à Joaquim de Carvalho* (Figueira da Foz,
1960), pp. 499-502.

[26]Reis Brasil, p. 500.

[27]Ibid., p. 501.

[28]Ibid., "E parece mais justa virtude aos servos de Deus e
seus pregadores animarsa estes, e confessa-los, e provoca-los
que scandaliza-los, e correlos, por contentar a desvairada
opinião do vulgo."

[29]For Vicente's social criticism the *Auto Das Barcas* is

most characteristic. See I. S. Révah, *Recherches sur les Oeuvres de Gil Vicente,* Vol. I, Edition critique du premier "Auto das Barcas" (Lisbon, 1951).

[30]See I. S. Révah, "Antiquité et christianisme"; "Anciens et Modernes" dans l'oeuvre de João de Barros in *Revue Philosophique de la France et de l'Étranger* (Vendôme: Presses Universitaires de France, 1966), pp. 165-85.

[31]See Manuel Cardozo, "The Idea of History in the Portuguese Chroniclers of the Age of Discovery," *The Catholic Historical Review,* 49 (1963), 8.

[32]The Greek title the author has chosen is *Ropica Pefma* which Barros suggested could be translated into Portuguese as *Mercadoria Espiritual.* This corresponds to the English translation *Spiritual Wares.*

[33]I. S. Révah has published a new edition of the *Spiritual Wares* in Lisbon, 1932; the first edition appeared in 1532.

[34]P. 5, "Não lhe parea que o digo por os de Erasmo que estes já são velhos, mas por alguns novos portugueses que vós e eu temos ouvido. . . ."

[35]See the intricate study of the *Spiritual Wares* by António José Saraiva, *História,* pp. 564-606.

[36]Ibid., p. 584.

[37]See I. S. Révah, "Antiquité et christianisme," p. 172. Révah reminds us that Erasmus had a particularly high opinion of certain ancient authors in spite of the fact that Christian ethics were superior to pagan morality.

[38]António José Saraiva, *História,* p. 574.

[39]Ibid., pp. 580, 583.

[40]*Spiritual Wares,* p. 5.

[41]António José Saraiva, *História,* p. 597.

[42]Ibid.

[43]See Alphonse Roersch, "La correspondence de Nicolas Clénard," ed. *Académie Royale de Belgique* (Brussels, 1940-41), No. 63.

[44]"Nao sabes que toda súbita mudança se faz com tormento do ânimo? Leixa estas cousas em meu poder porque assi como eu som cousa do muito amor, assi ensino sofrer a apartamento das que se muito amam" (p. 151).

[45]This was at the time when Portugal was united with Spain.

[46]See Hirsch, p. 68.

[47]Ibid., p. 70.

[48]Ibid., p. 33.

[49]See Marcel Bataillon, "Les Portugais contre Erasme à l'Assemblée Théologique de Valladolid (1527)," *Études sur le Portugal au temps de l'humanisme* (Coimbra: Univ. Press 1952),

pp. 9-48.

[50]See Odette Sauvage, "L'Itinéraire Érasmien d'André de Resende," in *Série Histórica & Literária, IX* (Paris: Fundação Calouste Gulbenkian, 1971), "Desiderii Erasmi Roteradami Encomium," Latin text and trans. into French with many helpful notes.

[51]See André de Resende, *Oração de Sapiência,* facsimile, Latin text, and trans. into Portuguese by Miguel Pinto de Meneses; introd. and notes by A. Moreira de Sá (Lisbon: Institutio de Alta Cultura, 1956).

[52]"Haec ubi perdidiscerit noster adolescens magnam disciplinarum omnium sibi fenestram aperuit. Hinc ad divinam poesin facilior excursus hic primus ad ortoriam gradus, modo adsit dialectices cognitio sine qua frustra in quovis eloquentiam quaeres" (p. 40).

[53]See Hirsch, p. 170. Resende said in the poem: "Woe to me. Silent is the voice that was heard throughout the world."

[54]Ibid., p. 166.

[55]See M. Gonçalves Cerejeira, *Clenardo* (Coimbra, 1926), Chapt. III.

[56]Hirsch, p. 179.

[57]See above, p. 126.

[58]See S. Stahlmann, "Die Stellung Guillaume Postel's in der religiösen Propaganda," in *Aspect de la Propagande Religieuse* (Geneva: Droz, 1975), p. 301.

[59]See Marcel Bataillon, *Études sur le Portugal,* "L'édition scolaire coimbroise des Colloques," pp. 219-56.

[60]Hirsch, pp. 219-20.

[61]See the magisterial study by Mário Brandão, *A Inquisição e os Professores do Colégio das Artes* (Coimbra: Univ. Press, 1948), Chapt. I.

[62]On André, Chapt. II; on Cop, p. 180.

[63]Ibid.

[64]Ibid., p. 517f.

[65]The trials of Diogo de Teive and João da Costa were published by Mário Brandão, *O Processo na Inquisição de Diogo de Teive* (Coimbra, 1943) and *O Processo na Inquisição de João da Costa* (Coimbra, 1944).

[66]Teive, Trial, p. 56, and Costa, Trial, pp. 68, 76.

[67]Teive, Trial, p. 47, and Costa, Trial, p. 68.

[68]Teive, Trial, p. 12.

[69]Teive, Trial, pp. 9, 16, and Costa, Trial, pp. 29, 35.

[70]Trial, *passim.*

[71]This letter is published in the trial of Costa, p. 269.

[72]See Hirsch, pp. 181-82.

[73]See Manuel Cardozo, *Portuguese Chroniclers*, p. 4.

[74]Hirsch, p. 183. A study of Osório's life and thought was written by Aubrey F. Bell, "The Humanist Jerónymo Osório," *Revue Hispanique*, 73 (1928), 525-56. This has been translated into Portuguese by A. A. Dória, *O Humanista Dom Jerónymo Osório* (Coimbra, 1943).

[75]For a study of the *Lusiadas*, see Hernani Cidade, *Luis de Camões*, Vol. II, *O Épico* (Lisbon, 1953).

CHAPTER XIV

[1]Ricardo G. Villoslada, y Bernardino Llorca, *Historia de la Iglesia Católica*, 2nd ed., II (Madrid: BAC, 1967), p. 606; R. B. Tate, Introd. to Fernando del Pulgar, *Claros varones de Castilla* (Oxford: Clarendon Press, 1971), p. xxx.

[2]Alvar Gómez de Castro, *De rebus gestis a Francisco Ximenio Cisneros* (1569), ed. Andreas Schotus, *Hispania illustrata* (Frankfurt/M, 1607), I, 933.

[3]Preserved Smith, *Reformation in Europe* (New York: Collier, 1962), p. 47.

[4]Nicolaus de Lyra, *Postilla super totam Bibliam* (Strassburg, 1492; facs. rpt. Frankfurt/M: Minerva, 1971), LIII. See Cornelius a La pide, *In Exodum*, in J. Migne, ed., *Scripturae Sacrae Cursus Completus*, -V (Paris, 1840), 919-25; and F. Prat, "Jéhova," in F. Vigouroux, ed., *Dictionnaire de la Bible*, III (Paris, 1903), 1231-32.

[5]Alfonso X, *General e grande estoria*, ed. by Antonio Ga. Solalinde (Madrid, 1930), p. 14.

[6]Lyra, sig. Dvi^v.

[7]See Alois Dempf, *Die Einheit in der Wissenschaft* (Stuttgart: Kohlhammer, 1955), p. 23. Hans Baron mentions a generation of young humanists around 1400 who in their passion for philology attacked Dante, Petrarch, and Boccaccio as men of another epoch. See *The Crisis of the Early Italian Renaissance* (Princeton: Princeton Univ. Press, 1966), pp. 292ff.

[8]"Regina, ut Ximenius postea referebat, Joannem Belalcazarem ex Astuniga familia, qui non ita pridem Belalcazario principatu relicto, Ranciscano ordini se addixerat, designare voluit, Rex certe pro filio Alfonso Aragonio, Caesaraugustano antistite, vehementer laborabat" (Alvar Gómez, *op. cit.*, p. 939).

[9]One of the most illustrious reformers of the Franciscans, Fr. Pedro de Villacreces (d.1428) used to say: "Rescebi en Salamanca grado de maestro que no merezco; empero, mas aprendi en la cella lorando en tiniebra, que en Salamanca o en Tolosa o

en Paris estudiando a la candela . . . mas quisiera ser una vejezuela simple con caridad de amor de Dios e del proximo, que saber la teologia de San Agustin o del doctor Sutil Escoto" (Lope de Salinas, *Satisfacciones* (1457?), ed. *Archivo Iberoamericano*; Special Issue: *Introducción a los orígenes de la observancia en España*, 17 (1957), 862-63.

[10]Alvar Gómez, p. 965.

[11]Erasmus, Epistola 1183, ad Artebum of Boskowitz (Louvain, 1/28/1521), in P. S. Allen, *Opus epistolarum Des. Erasmi* (Oxford: Clarendon Press, 1906-58), IV, 439,

[12]Erasmus, Ad Jacobum Hochstrat, Antwerp, 8/2/1519 (Allen, IV, 51).

[13]Proceso of Maria Cazalla, ed. Milagros Ortega, Doctoral Diss., Univ. of Massachusetts, Amherst (1974), p. 148.

[14]Francisco de Osuna, *Abecedario espiritual*, 5a. parte (1542), Chapt. xiii, fols. XVIII^v-XIX^r. Another remark on the harmful effects of "fine letters" (Bonae literae) upon devotion: "Antes que las buenas letras viniesen, todos eramos buenos y obedientes a la yglesia y a nuestros perlados, *etiam discolis;* mas ya, aunque sean sanctos, los alegaremos que no esta asi en el griego," (Ibid., Chapt. XXX, fol. XXXII^v). See Fedèle de Ros, *Un Maitre de Sainte Therèse* (Paris: Beauchesne, 1936), p. 661.

[15]Dominicus Soto, *De natura et gratia* (Paris, 1549; facs. rpt. London: Gregg Press, 1965), fols. 2^v, 4^r.

[16]Melchioris Cani, *Opera,* ed. Hyacintho Serry (Bassani, 1746), fol. 331^v.

[17]Cano, *De locis theologicis,* III, capite postremo, p. 105.

[18]Cano, *De locis theologicis,* VIII, 1, p. 232. See also: "Cayó, cayó Babylonia, Babylonia, aquella confusión de vicios de sensualidad y apetitos desordenados sin rienda, que esto es lo que destruyó a Alemania y lo hizo venir a lo que es: y juntamente conzesso, aquel demasiado estudio de lenguas y procazidad en ellas para que muy de veras se pueda dezir Babylonia" (Fr. Felipe de Meneses, *Luz del alma cristiana* (Medina del Campo, 1582), fol. 37.

[19]See Antonio Márquez, *Los alumbrados* (Madrid: Taurus, 1972), pp. 119-35, Chapt. VII.

[20]Melchor Cano, "Censura latina autógrafa de Fr. Melchor Cano y Fr. Domingo de Cuevas sobre los *Comentarios del Catecismo Cristiano* de Fr. Bartolomé Carranza, ed. José Sanz, *Melchor Cano* (Madrid: Edit. Santa Rita, 1959), p. 530.